Joseph Cardinal Siri

Archbishop of Genoa

GETHSEMANE:

Reflections on the Contemporary Theological Movement

FRANCISCAN HERALD PRESS
CHICAGO, ILLINOIS   60609

In Cooperation with

Editions De La Fraternite De La Tres Sainte
Vierge Marie Via Caetana 13, 00178 Rome, Italy

Gethsemane: Reflections on the Contemporary Theological Movement by Joseph Cardinal Siri, Archbishop of Genoa was published first in Rome by Editions de La Fraternite de La Tres Sainte Virege Marie, Rome, Italy and in French by Librairie Pierre Tequi, Paris. Published with permission of the original publisher and copyright © 1981 by Franciscan Herald Press, 1434 West 51st St. Chicago, Illinois 60609.

Made in the United States of America

Library of Congress Cataloging in Publication Data

Siri, Giuseppe, 1906-
   Gethsemane: reflections on the contemporary theological movement.

   1. Theology, Doctrinal—History—20th century.
2. Theology, Catholic—History—20th century.   I. Title.
BT28.S5313   230   81-12569
ISBN 0-8199-0825-8   AACR2

Apart from me you can do nothing. Abide in my love. If you keep my commandments, you will abide in my love, just as I have kept my Father's commandments and abide in his love. These things have I spoken to you that my joy may be in you, and that your joy may be full. This is my commandment, that you love one another as I have loved you. Greater love has no man than this, that a man lay down his life for his friends.

SAINT JOHN, XV

Contents

FUNDAMENTAL CRITERIA

ALTERATION OF HISTORY
AND ETERNAL LIBERATION

GETHSEMANE

FUNDAMENTAL
CRITERIA

BASIC
CONSIDERATIONS

It is more than ever necessary to have a clear idea, global but precise and shaded at the same time, of what can be called the «contemporary theological movement». However an objective, concrete and accurate resume expressing profound reality, is a very difficult thing to achieve in spite of the great number of writings which for years now have been devoted to the subject.

On the other hand, hardly any analysis or any synthesis could claim pure objectivity, because there is often a general interior option of a spiritual, moral or socio-historic nature which colors all the judgements and the criteria themselves. To give an example, one of the latest papers of synthesis on contemporary theology can be referred to, "Evaluation of the 20th Century Theology" [1]; it is clear that a large part of this work follows the line of Karl Rahner. [2]

---

[1] *Bilan de la théologie du XXème siècle,* directed by R. VANDER GUCHT and H. VORGRIMLER; Ed. Casterman, Paris 1970.

[2] KARL RAHNER S.J., born in 1904, professor of dogmatic theology at the Universities of Munich and Münster, theologian at Vatican Council II, belonged to the International Theological Commission.

Neither does an objective synthesis depend on the extent of bibliographic information. That generally can be useful, but it doesn't always help minds to penetrate the reality of the movements of thought and life. Sometimes even the opposite happens: fascinated by the perpetual effort towards external information, the guiding inner thread is lost, in other words the major permanent references which must determine, more than any other thing, the criterion through which we must see and judge facts, ideas and things, are lost.

The whole problem of pure objectivity consists in perceiving the fundamental references which Revelation and sacred logic bring forth. If there is no fundamental, perceivable and definable reference brought into understanding and human experience by Revelation, and if there is not a logic which expresses in man an eternal order of the Creation, and which is thereby sacred, any problem of objectivity is annulled and all effort of knowledge is vain.

That is why beyond or even within the various notions of pluralism concerning knowledge, language or things, pluralism acceptable or rejected, there is a simple and absolute necessity not only to seek basic references, but to perceive in a true way the basic references imposed by Revelation. And to the degree that the will is free of every influence other than the unconditional love of truth, sacred and living logic rules in the intellect. It can easily be understood that these considerations can be part of an essential foundation of method.

SOURCES OF JUDGEMENT
AND VALUATION

Before anything else we must seek and clarify the sources of judgement and valuation. And to do that, we are obliged, in the midst of a limitless and unprecedented polyvalence of vocabulary, to clarify the notion of theology, a thing which allows us to establish a true theological criterion, and then we are able to understand what the theological movement is, to examine its roots thoroughly and evaluate its implications.(3)

In order to think and to speak in a just and adequate manner on what theology is, we must return to the basic notions, to the simple and pure concepts, to fundamental principles. These principles are known to all, but we must return to them, and even often in our pilgrim's life, in our daily apostolic mission, because at bottom of all that

---

(3) This difficulty is attested to by all those who study the intellectual and spiritual movements of our times: «It is not easy to orient oneself in the current vast theological production which has a value of differing implications, and of which the point of view at times corresponds to different cultural atmospheres which cannot be well understood through the translation of the texts alone». (ALFREDO MARRANZINI, *Correnti teologiche post-conciliari*, Città Nuova Ed. 1974, Introduction p. 11).

anxious and disorderly problematic, the fact is that momen-
tarily or in a permanent way we forget the origin, the
essence and ultimate finality of theology.

In general it is said that theology is the science of God
based on Revelation. It is an exact definition for an exact
comprehension of Revelation because its principles come
immediately from God.(4)

It is also said that theology is the science of faith. In so
far as faith is Revelation received, the definition is exact
because the content and essence of faith is Revelation.
Theology therefore, is the science of Revelation received
and we have no other revelation than Revelation received.

At times one speaks in a way which makes us think
that there is a difference between Revelation and the

---

(4) — «This science can draw upon the philosophical sciences, not as
though it stood in need of them, but only in order to make its
teaching clearer. For it accepts its principles, not from the other
sciences, but immediately from God, by revelation». (SAINT
THOMAS AQUINAS, *Summa Theologica* I, q. 1 a. 5).

— «Sacred theology rests on the written word of God, together
with sacred tradition, as its primary and perpetual foundation.
By scrutinizing in the light of faith all truth stored up in the
mystery of Christ, theology is most powerfully strengthened and
constantly rejuvenated by that word». (*Vatican Council II,
Constitution «Dei Verbum»*, n. 24).

(5) «The object itself of theology is placed and therefore exists in
fact, in an original and essential way, in the content of revelation
and faith». (H. FRIES, article *Teologia, Dizionario teologico*,
Vol. III, Queriniana Ed., Brescia, 2a ed. 1968, p. 473).

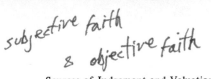
subjective faith & objective faith

content of faith.([5]) That can only have meaning when one speaks of individual faith in regard to the faith of the Church, which as universal and perpetual depositary, has received Revelation.

The Holy Father Paul VI, speaking of the faith said:

«Theology is nothing other than faith in the conceptual order: as Saint Augustine said, it is the 'scientia, qua fides saluberrima nutritur, defenditur, roboratur' (De Trin. XIV, 1)».

In the same discourse the Holy Father says:

«Theology is profoundly linked to the Magisterium of the Church because their common source is divine Revelation».([6])   *Revelation + Reason*

It is evident that the Holy Father is speaking of theology as the science of Revelation, which is the essence of the faith.

But sometimes we need a more expanded vision, more detailed and more explicative of the concept of theology; because generalizations and large scale synthetic formulae are very elevating and very useful for those who are in harmony with the univalent as well as nuanced and extensive inner meaning of the vocabulary. But we are far from that harmonious and universal accord. It is all the

---

(6) PAUL VI, *Discourse of May 13, 1973.*

more true as there is a search to «discover» or to coin
another vocabulary and even another language. _Rahner etc._

The notion of univalence must not be confused with
the meaning sometimes given to the notion of «univocality»; the latter is used by some authors in a completely
other sense than that of «univalence». The terms of the
language can have very shaded meanings which embrace and
synthesize many other terms. But the basic meaning always
remains the unique value which determines, puts in hierarchy and harmonizes all the nuances and all the secondary
meanings.

With the term «univocality» one can also mean univalence, that unique and fundamental value, unifier and
harmonizer of terms and nuances; but sometimes the term
univocality is used to define — in refuting or sustaining —
certain tendencies which concern the essential character of
human thought with regard to perception of truth, reasoning and judgement; that then affects the language in its
internal structure, and the term «univocality» is thus used
to express a different meaning from the positive meaning of
«univalence». (7)

---

(7) As an example of this particular sense of the term «univocality»,
    we quote a phrase from B. Mondin, «Dewart alone proposed the
    substitution of the doctrine of univocality for that of the
    doctrine of analogy: he asserts that the propositions of theo-
    logical language must be understood properly and literally». (B.
    MONDIN, *Il linguaggio della teologia radicale,* in *Il linguaggio
    teologico oggi,* Ed. Ancora, Milano 1970, p. 279.

The criteria of the profane sciences cannot be used nakedly for theology since theology deals with the supernatural element.

Sources of Judgement and Valuation

17

But the Pope speaking of the interpretation of the Word of God, states expressly:

«One can sustain that every human word is inadequate to express the unfathomable depths of the theological contents of a dogmatic formula...; and sustain the possibility of interpreting an identical dogmatic truth in the kerygmatic annunciation..., the legitimacy of the different theological and spiritual schools..., but we would not be faithful to the *univocality* of the Word of God, to the Magisterium of the Church which is derived from it, if we arrogate to ourselves the licence of a «free inquiry», of a subjective interpretation, of a subordination of the defined doctrine to the criteria of profane sciences, and still less to the fashion of public opinion, to the tastes and deviations... of the speculative and practical mentality of current literature».(8)

The Holy Father had already exposed the peril:

«... the peril of ambiguity, reticence or alteration of the integrity of the message in adapting the Word of God to our own mentality, our own culture, submitting it to this free inquiry which takes away... its *univocal meaning* and its objective authority and ends by depriving the community of believers of the adhesion to

in adapting the message, we cannot empty the content of the message.

---

(8) PAUL VI, *Insegnamenti*, VI, 1969; Tip. Pol. Vat., 1970, p. 957.

one truth and to a singular faith: the «una fides» (*Eph.*
4:5) disintegrates and with it the community itself,
which is called the sole and true Church».(9)

---

(9) PAUL VI, *Insegnamenti* VI, 1968; Tip. Pol. Vat., 1969, p.
1043-1044.

The Eternal Logic
of Infinite Charity

In any case we can say that theology is assertion, illuminated and demonstrated by the sources; an always more profound and more complete understanding of that which is asserted and basing itself on the sources; deduction always in the light of the basic principles and always controlled by the sources, by the data of Revelation. Thus theology, by the controlled and demonstrated affirmation from On High, always tends to form a stable and organized unity of knowledge in the light of the sources, that is, God. It is in this sense that one could say that theology tends to be «institutional».

This perpetual circle going from Revelation to the understanding of the thing revealed, from affirmation to demonstration and deduction, which leads to the understanding of the revealed thing, this marvellous movement issued from the infinite Goodness of God has often been badly understood, badly expressed and thereby deformed. Instead of seeing in this manifestation of eternal Logic a manifestation of the infinite Love of God and the participation of man in that love, which raises him towards an always higher understanding of God and the Creation, we have often wanted to see there a sort of drying-up naturalization of the mystery which brings man to knowledge of eternal truth and to union with God.

Theol. must stick to revelation.

With tranquil conscience we can assert that if theology escapes the control of sources and first principles of which we were speaking above, it is no longer continuously illumined by Revelation; it therefore no longer has as its object the essence of Revelation: God. Consequently this «theological» activity can no longer constitute a «stable and organized unity of knowledge» in the light of the sources.

It will always be able to speak of God and of the things of God. It will be able to have insights here and there and even penetrations into difficult problems; but all that will be sporadic, without order, the references will not always be those of Revelation which are immutable; there will not be the peace of truth and consequently there will not be the liberty which only eternal truth can give.

In the last analysis, if theology is not under the continuous control of the sources, if it isn't constantly in the light of Revelation which opens the way of knowledge, in love, towards the infinite and which annuls each time all artificial rigidity due to nature and experience of a purely human type, it cannot be truly institutional in a holy manner.

It has been said above that the perpetual circle from Revelation to the understanding of the revealed thing, from affirmation to demonstration and deduction, is a manifestation of the eternal Logic and infinite Love of God. Now manifold definitions may have been given for the term «logic»; there is, however, a general common understanding of the term, and this common understanding already constitutes a norm sufficient to speak with certitude and simplicity of human logic.

Man has an intellectual structure which is co-natural to his intelligence, that is, an intellectual structure which we can say is by its nature «logical». Logic orders, classifies and measures. Logic grasps the cause and grasps the effect and grasps the connection of cause to effect. Logic establishes the order of origin, the order of value and the order of sequence of beings and facts. Thus logic is a pure act of the order of intelligence which reflects in man the eternal order of creation. The logic of man, given him by God at the moment of his creation, allows in the life of charity the rediscovery of the order of eternal logic which manifests the truth and charity of God.

Now according to that same logic, we conceive that God revealing has «let down» heavenly things in the human forms of human thought. In this sense it is appropriate to say that God has assumed human thought. This means that the forms in which human thought is produced and manifested are directed to the objective real; they are forms assumed by God. If God has spoken to men, man's thought must correspond to the real. That is why man's logic and thought are co-natural with the intelligence which, in love, realizes the true knowledge of God.

At this point the doctrine of analogy appears with all its indefinable and at the same time incontestable mar-

vellous reality; it appears as a mysterious road of communication in the understanding, between the created world and
the divine eternal reality.

Certainly one must not think that every comparison
and every analogical expression of every man expresses a
truth; the doctrine of analogy puts in evidence a profound
law of the intellect and attests that human thought, in
reflecting divinely revealed things, is analogical. But that
doesn't mean that it is sufficient, in order to attain to the
truth, to simply refer to the analogical character of human
thought. That would correspond to another error: that
every man is automatically saved by the thought that Christ
offered himself for the salvation of all men. As salvation
depends on the free response to the unutterable love of
God, likewise the exact knowledge of the real depends on
the free love of eternal truth.

Divine realities are infinite and we can't attain to the
infinity of the divine real. It is by analogy that we
objectively have access to the divine truth, because God, as
we have said, has «let down» in human concepts, in forms
of human thought, His Revelation.

The basis of this assertion has an immense, far-reaching
effect with regard to everything and every object of our
thought. By analogy man can realize from whence he has
fallen, and also the kingdom to which he is called; we need
only protect ourselves by humility against the first temp-
tation: to want to know outside of God.

Analogy has very often been forgotten and even now sometimes is depreciated and rejected totally. Thus Father Battista Mondin ([10]) , speaking of radical theology, that is, of the trend called "Theology of the Death of God", makes the following remark:

«The radical theologians are in agreement to reject the traditional doctrine which recognized in theological language an analogical value.([11])

This oversight or rejection is a very characteristic symptom of several currents which all converge towards one sole tendency, an ontological monism, that is, towards *i.e.- naturalism* a vision which leads consciously or unconsciously, directly or indirectly to a concept of identity of two «parts» which can only be considered analogous.

This concept annihilates every distinction of order, essence and language. And a strange thing happens, only apparently strange, that is, that this rejection or omission of the analogy entails in an intrinsic manner the negation

---

(10) BATTISTA MONDIN, of the Missionaries of Saint Francis Xavier, born in 1926, dean of the Faculty of Philosophy of the Pontifical University Urbaniana at Rome.

(11) B. MONDIN, *Il linguaggio della teologia radicale*, in *Il linguaggio teologico oggi*, Ed. Ancora, Milan 1970, p. 279.
The principal representatives of this radical current are the Protestants Harvey Cox, Paul Van Buren, William Hamilton, Thomas Altizer, the Anglican John Robinson, and the Catholic Leslie Dewart, also called «theologians of secularization».

of every principle of objectivity and of every principle of eternal truth.

Now the analogy is an objective reality because beyond every other meaning of the term, it expresses in thought, in a functional way, the two orders of reality such as Revelation has unveiled them to us: the so-called «natural» order and the so-called «supernatural» order.

We can refer to the communion between the two orders which is realized in the state of prayer and in the state of ecstasy, states in which thought seems to be in passive receptivity and receiving the communications and the operations of God without the action itself of the soul. But there also, in the state of abandon and adoration, communion is realized within the mystery of charity, in the intimacy of the understanding, that is, in the intimacy of the intelligent soul by means of perceptions, notions or images of great subtlety, delicacy and transparence, but which do not lie outside of the fundamental character of the understanding which is analogical.

Human nature receives all that it can receive in its intelligent structure sometimes with a very great capacity for corresponding or adapting to the notion, thing or being perceived and received, and for all that, without the essence itself of that thinking creature being transmuted. There we have the principle of the limits of its order of creation, limits of order which the perfect purification and blessedness of vision of God do not annul.

And one can also refer to the promise and to the long-drawn nostalgia to see the essence of God. Now it is certain, according to several texts of the Scripture ([12]), that:

«Participation in the divinity is the blessedness of man and the goal of human life». ([13])

«For» says Saint Paul, «our knowledge is imperfect and our prophecy is imperfect; but when the perfect comes, the imperfect will pass away... Now we see in a mirror dimly, but then face to face». ([14])

All the words of the promise regarding the beatific vision concern the soul of the blessed after the earthly pilgrimage. We cannot conceive that the essence of God could be seen by a corporal vision or by an intellectual vision inasmuch as the soul is in this present life, on earth, in the life of mortal flesh. ([15])

Here we are touching on the essential point: that the human soul when it reaches beatitude will see the essence of God not by created images but by an intervention of God illuminating the intelligence of the blessed. The human soul cannot directly see the essence of God from this life.

---

(12) *John* 1 :12; 3:5; *I John* 3 :1.

(13) *Summa Theologica* III, q. 1 a. 2.

(14) *I Corinthians* 13 : 9, 12.

(15) *Summa Theologica,* Suppl. q. 92.

When Saint John says that «No one has ever seen God; the only Son, who is in the bosom of the Father, he has made him known» (16), he doesn't say, in speaking of Christ, that only he the Son has seen him; he says that the Son who is in the bosom of the Father has revealed him. He has revealed by His person the Father, His own person and the Holy Spirit. The Son-God has revealed the divinity of the most Holy Trinity. Now the question of the intelligence of Christ, of Christ Jesus' vision of the divinity, is a question still far beyond that of the vision of the essence of God by the blessed.

In no way can one find in the Scripture itself, in Tradition or in a thought in harmony with these sources, an indication that human thought — at least up until the grace of the beatific vision, that is, at least until the moment when the divine light puts the divine essence in our light — be transmuted, thus losing an essential character as that of the analogy.

If therefore this boundary of order of which we spoke earlier is transgressed, the basis of language is lost. All the words «God» and «Creation», «finite» and «infinite», «unity» and «multiplicity», «time» and «eternity», «image» and «sense» etc. can no longer have a meaning which corresponds to the real, nor a universal character, multiform but universal; the language no longer has any

---

(16) *John* 1:18.

reference and one sinks into an absolute subjectivism which at bottom corresponds to a sort of total nihilism.

For greater simplification we can say that the notion of analogy means that human thought reflecting divine things revealed, corresponds in part to the superior reality and expresses its truth, and corresponds in part to the natural «inferior» reality with respect to the first and expresses the truth of it; it is not a question really of two parts, it is a question of two correspondences of which the simultaneity in human thought brings a knowledge, and therein lies the mark of the distinction of orders.

Man, human thought, can rise indefinitely towards a more immediate, more direct perception of divine and eternal realities. But this perfecting can never attain by identity the infinite of God, of which we perceive the mystery; and we can live it more and more according to our acquired peace and our nostalgia for eternal peace and love.

That's how it is, as far as human thought is concerned; beyond, there is the immense mystery of the power, of the wisdom of God; the immense mystery of the Being who is uncreated light and infinite love. That is why Saint Thomas justly said:

«If anyone in seeing God conceives something in his mind, this is not God, but one of God's effects». (17)

---

(17) *Summa Theologica,* Suppl. q. 92 a. 1 ad 4.

* * *

It is upon these bases which concern the intellect, that the first theological criterion must be constituted. The criterion is certainly the means, the reference point through which judgement is made. The theological criterion concerns neither the method alone nor the essence alone; it concerns both method and essence. The theological criterion is an ever-present reference in the midst of every culture, every custom and every instinctive thrust, a reference given directly by the sources of Revelation, or, afterwards by the heirs confirmed by it and in complete harmony with it, that is, in harmony with the content of Revelation. And now, one could ask: what is the theological criterion according to which I can say that the Word was made man?

We should be able to give a simple answer to that question, and one which could satisfy every conscience and all upright reason, an answer which renders immediately present the source to which the spirit spontaneously refers, and finds the immutable truth revealed by God.

But we cannot shut our eyes to a phenomenon of capital importance for the life of Christians and consequently of all men: the words richest in meaning, the words consecrated by God, by the life and word of the Apostles,

by the life and the word of the saints, have for many
people ceased more or less to be reference points per se,
trustworthy and a guarantee of peace in thought and
conscience; they have ceased being living reference points
with all the unction of the mystery which they comprise
and signify.

Continual repetition of words expressing truths which
are stable, basic and controlled once and for all by
Revelation in faith, are listened to and treated by several
with distrust or indifference as if it were a question of
notions no longer valid, or at times even with scorn and
with a fierce desire to go beyond not only words but the
word itself, that is, the notions and meanings which it
«incarnates».

We often see that even very gifted people are drawn by
the vertigo of «perpetual research», feeling less and less the
need of stability, the need of immutable reference points
such as the words, phrases and formulae consecrated by
Revelation within the depths of the life of the Church.

If therefore someone asks, «What is the theological
criterion according to which it can be said that 'the Word
was made man'?», henceforth the simple answer to that
question does not come easily to the spirit of many, but
one must be able to tell him with the certainty and joy of
handing on an answer guaranteed by God, a word «engendered» by the Revelation from within the Church: you can
say that 'the Word was made man' because that is
consigned and formulated in the Symbol of the Faith: «et

incarnatus est de Spiritu Sancto». There it is, friend, the
essence of your theological criterion.

Very often however, that simple answer of profound
truth is considered as not corresponding to an exact
understanding of Revelation and the mystery of Salvation.
Even within the Church to refer to the Creed as a
fundamental criterion of truth is now considered naive and
foreign to the objective road of knowledge for man. In fact
the principle and the facts of Revelation have been
«tortured» by interminable prestidigitations of language.

This effort of distortion of the mystery of Revelation
has occurred several times in the Church from the outset,
but in each period with slightly different themes and
modified vocabularies. Today we are witnessing an unre-
strained effort to treat the most elevated subjects of
Revelation and Salvation with forced meanings and with a
language at times artificially abstract, which at base
detaches it from the word born of the eternal Word and
life of the Church.

But in spite of all the contestations and all the
prestidigitations of language, it is always sure in the heart
of the Church: first, that that which one can call
theological criterion is based on the sources, rooted in the
sources and issued from the sources of Revelation; second,
that we have two channels – also called sources – Scripture
and Tradition through which the unique Source of all truth
and all life has been revealed and its revelation comes unto
us.

At the beginning of the Second Vatican Council a very
sad event occurred: an attempt was made to deny one of
the sources of Revelation saying there was only one Source.
Now precisely because the Source of Revelation is unique,
if one of the channels is ignored, communion with that
unique source is altered or obstructed or ignored; if one of
the sources is closed that means that the pathway of the
unique source is obstructed. Therefore the Council has
stated:

«Hence there exists a close connection and communication between *sacred Tradition* and *Sacred
Scripture.* For both of them, flowing from *the same
divine wellspring,* in a certain way merge into a unity
and tend toward the same end. For Sacred Scripture is
the word of God inasmuch as it is consigned to writing
under the inspiration of the divine Spirit, while sacred
Tradition takes the word of God entrusted by Christ
the Lord and the Holy Spirit to the Apostles, and
hands it on to their successors in its full purity, so that
led by the light of the Spirit of truth, they may in
proclaiming it, preserve this word of God faithfully,
explain it, and make it more widely known. Consequently it is not from Sacred Scripture alone that the
Church draws her certainty about everything which has
been revealed. Therefore both sacred Tradition and
Sacred Scripture are to be accepted and venerated with
the same sense of loyalty and reverence». [18]

---

[18] Vatican Council II, Dogmatic Constitution on Divine Revelation
«Dei Verbum», no. 9.

In spite of the endless confusion of contradictory views and sophisticated observations and in spite of the multiform secular attack against the stability of our reference to Revelation, the profound meaning of the two sources will remain rooted in the conscience of the Church because it forms a part of the understanding that the Church had and has of Revelation. Moreover it is inconceivable to think that Tradition, the life of the Church, in the depths of its first years was deteriorating in its essence when the books of the New Testament had scarcely been written. If the life of the Church was no longer carrying within itself and henceforth no longer handing on the sure revealed truths, revealed through its living word and its life, the Scripture would be useless, because then it would be misunderstood. The «letter» would not have gone far without the spirit which understands it. And that spirit is the soul of the Church, in which the word of God has also been consigned from the very beginning.

But it is not only a matter of the understanding of Scripture. The question is deeper. He who denies Tradition its character as source, loses de facto the accurate reality of the Scripture. He who renders relative the one also relativizes the other; and there is at times a rendering relative of facts by the transcendent rationalistic criticism, which is worse than simple and frank negation. (19)

---

(19) As examples of the spirit of the relativization of Tradition one can quote:
  — «We find the original witness and message in the writings of the Old and New Testaments. All other witness of the

To maintain, for example, on the one hand that «Scripture is virtually the only material source of the faith», and on the other hand, that «tradition is not excluded» [20], is equivalent to denying Tradition its fundamental characteristic as original channel (source) of Revelation. And this minimization of Tradition is a great obstacle to perceiving in all its fullness and depth, what God has been gracious enough to reveal to us.

Certainly no one would contest that in order to arrive at the writings of the New Testament there has been a handing on, orally and in life, from the time of Christ and

---

ecclesiastical tradition, even the richest and most solemn, cannot at base do other than gravitate around this first testimony on the Word of God; cannot do other than interpret, comment, explain and apply this original document according to the always differing historical situation» (!). (H. KÜNG, *Chiesa,* Ed. Queriniana, Brescia 1972, p. 37).

— «In view of the experience of the faith and theology of our reformed brothers, it is our duty to take as seriously as possible the Protestant principle of Scripture alone, because that implies an authentic religious experience and in my opinion, an equally authentic theological tradition which goes back to Catholicism of the past» (K. RAHNER, *Sacra Scrittura e Tradizione,* in *Nuovi Saggi I,* Ed. Paoline, Rome 1968, p. 192).

[20] «For theology, Scripture is practically the only material source of the faith, to which it must refer as to the source clearly original, not derived and 'norma non normata'. With that, we are not excluding the tradition of theology». (K. RAHNER, *Sacra Scrittura e Teologia,* in *Nuovi Saggi I,* Ed. Paoline, Roma 1968, p. 168).

Pentecost until the Gospels and Epistles of the Apostles, but what is contested is that after the writings of the New Testament, Tradition kept its character and nature as the original wellspring of Revelation. Now Tradition and Holy Scripture are not two ways of handing on used indifferently by the Lord.

These two ways, the two sources by means of which Revelation is achieved and transmits itself until the end of time, correspond to the innermost reality of human nature. Man lives with his inner contribution in so far as a person and in so far as united and living with others; he lives in the midst of a universe where every being and every existence is at the same time both sign and language. From the very beginning he entered history by the word of God; he lives in a perpetual interdependance between his inner contribution and the sign of things. It is to this intrinsic reality of man that the necessity and the mystery of the two ways are due, by means of which God has revealed himself, and Revelation remains alive.

Man cannot have an understanding either of the language of nature, or of the word of man, or of the inspired word, unless it be correlated with the word which he has had within him from his origin and which transmits itself and grows richer. With Christ, this word of origin is the Revelation accomplished. The presence of Christ and the word of Christ is the Revelation received by the Apostles which fundamentally changed them. And the Apostles transmitted the Revelation, not as a lesson learned which could be forgotten, but as a living contribution; they handed it on in turn, as an inalterable presence and word which developed the Church. And it is that same truth which was consigned by divine inspiration in the Scripture; that same Holy Scripture would be mute letter without the contribution of truth which the man of the Church carries alive within him.

That is why each source has a particular intrinsic function directly linked with the other, and at the same time to the unique Source, which keeps the unique truth alive in man. Each way, therefore, has an intrinsic mission towards the other; and that mission cannot be substituted for the mission of the other. That is the reality, mysterious and obvious at the same time, of the two sources, the deep mystery of the life of the Church and of the eternal Wisdom of God. And in spite of the extent and abilities of the external human language, the truth that the Church has carried within her can never be permanently mutilated or stifled.

Now certainly in reading these lines many will be inclined to remain pensive before the fallibility of men, before so many inadequacies and errors, before persons who in all the history of the Church have had and have a great difference of opinion on basic questions, and who, in spite of that, by function and sacral link with Christ, constitute the Magisterium of the Church.

In a time in which all notions, all concepts have been put back into question, contested, reviewed, re-examined, it was inevitable that the notion and the principle of the

Magisterium be hit and seriously impaired in the consciousness of a large number. Here it is not yet the moment to examine this question in its full extent, a question so important from several points of view and particularly from the point of view of the theological criterion. But there is a truth which we must never forget if we want to penetrate that which is profoundly objective in the reality and the history of the Church.

Christ did not entrust the handing on of the sacred deposit to the relativity and instability of historic man. It is to liberate him from that relativity and instability that He was incarnated, that He underwent the Passion and founded the Church for the Redemption. Jesus Christ entrusted the handing on of the sacred deposit to his perpetual presence in «the work of the handing on», that is, in his Church inasmuch as it is a teaching Church. And that is why, through all the vicissitudes and fluctuations, personal ones and those of the entire body of the Church, and in spite of all confusion of ideas and concepts during long periods, the sacred deposit has always been handed on in its immutable truth, and will be until the end of time.

Shocks, be they more or less violent and deep, in the body of the successors of the Apostles, cannot prevail over that guarantee regarding truth, which Christ gave the Church.

The great trials and hard work which have accompanied the Church from the beginning are − in the mystery of iniquity − the accomplishment of its eschatological road and its salvific mission. The providential courses of the road escape human intelligence and on this providential, missionary and eschatological road, the successors of the Apostles, these fallible and uncertain men, constitute – by grace and through trials – the instrument of the true handing on of the deposit; they make up the institution of the teaching Church, the authentic Magisterium and inasmuch as authentic, infallible.

So when one says that the Holy Scripture «must bear witness to the whole faith of the Church» (21), one says truly; but that means that Holy Scripture bears witness to the contribution of holy Tradition just as Tradition bears witness to the origin and content of Holy Scripture. Tradition is not only «the testimony of the consciousness of the faith of the Church» (22); Tradition, we have said, transmits by word and life the truth of Christ received by his life, by his mouth, by the Holy Spirit; by the mouths of the Apostles, by their lives, by their prayer and acts; by

---

(21) «If it is true that Scripture cannot be its own witness, aside from that, however, in order to be what it is – Scripture inspired by God – it must bear witness to the whole faith of the Church». (K. RAHNER, *Sacra Scrittura e Tradizione,* in *Nuovi Saggi I,* Ed. Paoline Roma 1968, p. 195).

(22) «Tradition, if and in so far as it is the witness of the conscience of the faith of the Church and of the doctrine of the Magisterium, always remains, for every theologian, an authentic norm for the explanation of Scripture». (K. RAHNER, *Sacra Scrittura e Teologia,* in *Nuovi Saggi I,* Ed. Paoline, Roma 1968, p. 169).

the mouths, the prayer and the acts of the authentic successors of the Apostles; that is, by all that is covered and illuminated by the Holy Spirit in the life of the Church as a whole.

One cannot say «if and in so far as tradition is a testimony to the consciousness of the faith of the Church and of the doctrine of the Magisterium». What does «if and in so far as» mean? We cannot speak in the Church of a tradition which, according to a more or less great probability would be a testimony of the «consciousness» of the faith of the Church, because Tradition is an authentic norm for the doctrinal life and piety of the whole Church; and in that sense, it is also an authentic norm for the explanation of Scripture.

And when it is said that «the unity of the object of the faith renders inadmissible the hypothesis of two materially different handings on of the faith» (23), one formulates gratuitous norms. First of all, what things are materially different? Are the means of the two handings on diverse, or is the content different? And who ever maintained that Holy Scripture and Tradition hand on a diverse faith, in order to be able to say that «the unity of the object of the

---

(23) «Unity of the object of the faith... renders at the least hard to believe and inadmissible, from a religious point of view, the hypothesis of two sources of the faith, of two materially different transmissions of the faith, one called Scripture and the other tradition» (K. RAHNER, *Sacra Scrittura e Tradizione*, in *Nuovi Saggi I*, Ed. Paoline, Roma 1968, p. 197).

faith» is impaired by that material difference of the handing on? How is the unity of a flower damaged by the fact of being received in the intelligence, by sight, by smell and touch at the same time? To put forth such propositions is really to lose contact with the reality of Revelation and of the inner life of the Church.

At times, with an extreme sagacity of analysis, some believed they saw in the texts of Vatican II a will to show a «supremacy of Holy Scripture» (24) over Tradition. But that does not correspond at all to either the spirit or the letter of the texts of the Council, which are very clear and very explicit regarding Revelation. P. J. Alfaro (25), for example, maintains that the Council declared that only the Holy Scripture is word of God (locutio Dei), whereas tradition is a simple handing on of the word of God (26); and to uphold that acceptation he referred to excerpts such as the following from the Constitution of the Council on Revelation:

«This teaching office is not above the word of God, but serves it, teaching only what has been handed on,

---

(24) J. ALFARO, *Cristologia e Antropologia*, Cittadella Ed., Assisi 1973, p. 12 ff.

(25) JUAN ALFARO, S. J., Spanish theologian and professor at the Gregorian Pontifical University in Rome, member of the International Theological Commission.

(26) J. ALFARO, *Cristologia e Antropologia*, Cittadella Ed., Assisi 1973, p. 12 ff.

listening to it devoutly, guarding it scrupulously and explaining it faithfully in accord with a divine commission and with the help of the Holy Spirit». (27)

Now how can one conclude that «these words proclaim the supremacy of the word of God, of the Holy Scripture» over Tradition? From these words, even isolated, it is clearly evident that the Magisterium teaches the word of God, and that with the help of the Holy Spirit it keeps it in a holy manner and faithfully, having received it piously. With piety and in a holy manner we must listen and read, repeat the words listened to, and print written words. It suffices to examine the basic texts of the Council on Revelation in order to see clearly that all notions of supremacy of one or the other of the sources is excluded, and that on the contrary, the Council, moved by the Holy Spirit foresees every possible error on this subject:

— «Sacred Tradition and Sacred Scripture form one sacred deposit of the word of God, committed to the Church». (28)

— «The task of authentically interpreting the word of God, whether written or handed on, (scriptum vel traditum), has been entrusted exclusively to the living teaching office of the Church, whose authority is exercised in the name of Jesus Christ». (2 8)

---

(27) Vatican Council II, Dogmatic Constitution on Divine Revelation «Dei Verbum», no. 10.

(28) Const. «Dei Verbum», no. 10.

— «It is clear, therefore, that sacred Tradition, Sacred Scripture and the teaching authority of the Church, in accord with God's most wise design, are so linked and joined together that one cannot stand without the others, and that all together and each in its own way under the action of the one Holy Spirit contribute effectively to the salvation of souls». (28)

— «Therefore the Apostles, handing on what they themselves had received, warn the faithful to hold fast to the traditions which they have learned either by word of mouth or by letter». (29)

— «Sacred Tradition takes the word of God entrusted by Christ the Lord and the Holy Spirit to the Apostles and hands it on to their successors in its full purity». (30)

— «It is not from Sacred Scripture alone that the Church draws her certainty about everything which has been revealed. Therefore both sacred Tradition and Sacred Scripture are to be accepted and venerated with the same sense of loyalty and reverence». (30)

After such statements, there is no place for speculations which put in doubt the equality and unity of the two sources of Revelation.

---

(29) Const. «Dei Verbum», no. 8.

(30) Const. «Dei Verbum», no. 9.

If therefore we find in other texts of the Magisterium, as for example in the decree of Vatican II on priestly training, an insistence on the necessity of studying and using Scripture for theology and for spiritual formation, we must rejoice because the word of God is exalted, but we must always have the entire truth in our thought and in our heart, such as it was borne and lived in the Church, expressed numerous times in the long history of the Church and such as it is manifested in the ensemble of the texts of the Council concerning Revelation or theology:

> «Sacred theology rests on the written word of God, together with sacred Tradition, as its primary and perpetual foundation». (31)

If oral and lived Tradition, having come all the way to the written New Testament was no longer able to transmit with the same guarantee what it had handed on until then, by what means would it have grasped in the future the mystery that Scripture signifies? What constitutes a norm «normans» for being able to judge in the midst of the different and contradictory interpretations of Scripture which are encountered in the Christian world? Where would the Church be, what would the deposit of the faith have become, if a fundamental truth revealed and handed down from the beginning, by means of the life and the word of the Church, didn't keep alive, in the midst of all the contradictory interpretations and human controversies, this content of Revelation consigned to Holy Scripture?

---

(31) Const. «Dei Verbum», no. 24.

The question of two sources isn't a question of academic discussion. To refuse Tradition its character as perpetual source implies a profound alteration of the mode of reference to the essential truths, which damages more or less directly, the essential content of Revelation, and consequently the content of the handing on, by life and piety, of the Revelation itself of God about Himself and about Salvation.

But there is one consoling truth: even if someone denies a truth such as that of the two sources manifesting the revelation of the unique Source, that does not mean that this man is not affected positively or negatively by the truth carried all the way to him by the immutable unity of Tradition and Holy Scripture. It is like the man who would deny or hate God: he would none the less be living thanks to the Wisdom, Omnipotence and Goodness of God.

GENERAL CHARACTERISTICS
OF THE
THEOLOGICAL MOVEMENT

If our love of the truth leads us to the point of being free of all prejudice and in harmony with the principles and the fundamental teachings issued from the sources of Revelation, we can discern certain generic characteristics of the theological movement in our time. To grasp its reality, examination of all the printed material which defines itself — justly or unjustly — theological, does not suffice. Certainly the studies, the specialized works, the works of a general character and then the journals which are specialized or which welcome theological questions in the heart of their program, represent more or less, the movement called «theological». But that constitutes a representation which can be incoherent and chaotic if there is no criterion through which one can discern the value in itself of the writings, and their value from the point of view of influence over the people of the Church.

And then there is the handing on, the oral teaching; there is the interpretation of the texts and teachings, manifested by worship in its new forms, be they legitimate or foreign to the will and the spirit of the Church. It is in the midst of all this, and with all this, that we are urged to distinguish the data and the characteristics of the theological movement, which is extensive and full of contradictions.

In the movement two principal currents appear first: on the one hand, a multiple activity which tends to conserve more or less faithfully the doctrine professed by the Church; on the other hand, a very persevering activity which tends to go beyond every limit and obstacle established up until that point by the teaching and worship of the Church. On one hand resistance which is more or less strong, more or less intelligent, and also more or less just, to the new trends of radical transformation of the teaching and spiritual life in the Church: on the other hand, an effort to break free of every requirement of a supernatural order concerning the perception of truth and salvation.

In order to deepen our study of things and events, we must never forget that what is, came forth from what was. We can think, without erring, that the word of Christ regarding things «new and old» can be applied in a certain way as well for the good as for the bad, as well for the ascent as for the descent. Certainly when we want to examine what is new, what is recent, we cannot review each time the interminable series of facts, all the trends going back to the origin, in order to properly grasp the reality of these facts. It is impossible to go back through the whole course of history each time we want to study a contemporary manifestation, because we would constantly have to return to Adam. However this long course, with its highs and lows, must always be present in our consciousness and always illumined by this fundamental data of Revelation, in order to judge and understand every new reality.

For it is always in the light of the fundamental principles of Revelation that we can grasp the real reasons and the deep causes which connect the past to the new manifestations. Without that, outside of that light, we can never discern the true causes from the appearances.

Here one must confess very simply and clearly that a part of the works, large or small, works presented as theological, is devoid of the true theological criteria; and therefore the judgements, outlines, postulates are without consequence, without real logical connection, therefore without truth.

In any case, in the midst of the trend which tends towards total emancipation there appears simultaneously a pure and simple revival of Protestant rationalism of the last century, and a breaking of every barrier of theological and also philosophical order. And this break, this will of total emancipation, is taking place both among Protestant theologians and in the bosom of the Catholic Church.

What can be the causes of this singular tendency of the theological movement? If the causes are difficult to locate in their multiple origin and nature, it is possible nevertheless to locate the particular characteristic of each tendency.

Now prior to any other manifestation we see a mentality rising which expresses a return to the Pelagian heresy. Pelagius with his disciple Celestius sorely tried the Church about fifteen centuries ago. In the beginning, Pope Innocent I, called "The Great", hadn't recognized the danger. But the Oriental bishops understood the perilous heresy and joining together in Council, condemned it; and then it was recognized in Rome and Pelagius was again condemned. Then followed the different takings of position, especially in the two provincial Councils of Carthage — which from a certain point of view have the importance of general Councils — followed by the condemnation brought at the Council of Orange.

After fifteen centuries during which, here and there, one or another of the errors of Pelagius manifested themselves explicitly or implicitly in the doctrinal life of the Church, we are witnessing the appearance, both subtle and obvious at the same time, of the doctrine according to which there is no original sin, according to which man can live sinlessly by his own strength and without the help of grace. It is known that Pelagius and the Pelagians wanted at all cost to make man's salvation depend upon himself, and it is for the same reasons that they considered grace — that grace which they had been compelled to recognize — as dependant on man's merits; we know to what point the defense and worship of a false conception of human liberty led Pelagius and his disciples; into a capital error, into an obscurantism and a deformation of the writings of the Fathers.

Beside this heresy of the exaltation of man, an even older error reappears also, according to which the Son of God was a creature, an error which fundamentally affected the conception of the Holy Trinity and the reality of the Redeemer. Arius has had a large influence, but the truth has always been preserved and the error exposed; thus the Church proclaims during Holy Mass, in the Creed, the eternal truth of the Son of God.

A third characteristic of the tendency which in its ultimate outcome leads towards the total emancipation we have spoken of, is that of the whole of the thought which constitutes modernism, which Saint Pius X firmly condemned and wanted to extirpate from the life of the Church. But that was not fully realized. The modernist tendencies have survived more or less openly and in a latent state. Modernism, now as at the beginning of the century, with new designations and shades of meaning, first implicitly and then explicitly, damages the principle of Revelation which is replaced by the elaborations of a «religious sense» in the subconscious.

Today almost more than in its beginning, it pushes towards a quasi «transcendental» agnosticism and a «dogmatic evolutionism», in order to destroy every notion of objectivity in Revelation and in acquired knowledge.

This is how the Holy Father Paul VI views the rebirth of Modernism:

«Revelation is a fact, an event, and at the same time a mystery which was not born in the human spirit,

but it has come from divine initiative, which had many
progressive manifestations distributed over a long
history, the Old Testament, and which had its culminating point in Jesus Christ (cf. Heb. 1:1; I John 1:2,3;
Const. of Council, "Dei Verbum", no. 1). Thus the
Word of God is ultimately for us the Incarnate Word,
the historic Christ, and then living in the community
united to Him by the faith and the Holy Spirit, in the
Church, that is, his Mystical Body.

«It is thus beloved Sons; and in asserting that, our
doctrine detaches from errors which have circulated and
which still now appear in the culture of our times, and
which could totally ruin our Christian conception of
life and history. Modernism represents the characteristic expression of these errors and under other
designations it is still actual (cf. Decr. "Lamentabili" of
St. Pius X, 1907, and his Encycl. "Pascendi", Denz.
Schl. 3401, ff.).

«We can then understand why the Catholic Church,
yesterday and today gives so much importance to the
rigorous conservation of the authentic Revelation, and
that she considers it an inviolable treasure and that she
has such a strict consciousness of her fundamental duty
of defending and transmitting the doctrine of the faith
in non-equivocal terms». (32).

(32) PAUL VI, *Discourse of January 19, 1972.*

These three characteristic orientations, Arian, Pelagian and modernist, are combined more or less consciously with more or less subtlety and sometimes also guile, in a speculative amalgam, without precise outlines and without basic references, which serves as a basis for a rush towards integral humanization of all religion. This amalgam constitutes a kind of new «initiation» of Protestant origin which makes itself felt in all domains and in all milieus. The reaction of Protestant theologian Oscar Cullmann (33), a Lutheran observer at Vatican II, for example, is very significant:

«If it is permissible for me as a Protestant to make this statement, I will say that since then (Vatican II), certain Catholic milieus, far from allowing themselves to be inspired by the necessity of observing the limits of adaptation which should not be exceeded, are not content with changing the outer forms, but borrow the very *norms* of Christian thought and action, not from the Gospel, but from the modern world. More or less unconsciously they thus follow the Protestants, not, however, in the best they have, the faith of the Reformers, but in the bad example which a certain so-called modern Protestantism offers them. The great culprit is not the secularized world itself, but the false behavior of Christians with regard to this world, the

_____

(33)   OSCAR CULLMANN, born in 1902, professor at Basel, Switzerland, at the Sorbonne and at the Free Faculty of Protestant Theology in Paris.

eliminating of the 'scandal' of the faith. They are
'ashamed of the Gospel' (Rom. 1:16)». [34]

---

(34)   OSCAR CULLMANN, *Gravité de la crise actuelle et ses
       remèdes,* Message to the European Conference of Strasbourg
       1971, published in the collective work *Fidélité et Ouverture,*
       Ed. Mame, 1972, pp. 79-80.

ETERNAL PRINCIPLES
AND TEMPORAL REFERENCE POINTS
FOR THE UNDERSTANDING OF THE
PRESENT DAY THEOLOGICAL MOVEMENT

If one finds himself on a point of a circumference and wishes to travel completely around it, he could set out either to the right or to the left; because in any case it would be necessary to cover the same distance. But if one is in front of, or rather inside a huge ball of very tangled string of which the two ends are lost, one in a far-off past, experimentally inaccessible, and the other in a far-off unknown future, that is to say, at the beginning and at the end of history, it is useless to want to follow the whole length of the thread in order to know in depth the causes and the facts of a certain present. In any case, it is necessary to be able to establish a few points of reference. Now Revelation, with holy logic steeped in charity, always gives us valid principles for the whole of any course, in whatever epoch and regarding whatever group of phenomena and facts. These principles help us to establish — be it in the middle of the thick fog of ideologies, or in the midst of the general historic thread, infinitely tangled — some references of truth in order to know in truth and to raise ourselves towards eternal Truth.

These reference points can be men, isolated facts, or the inner forces and orientations of massive movements. We need such landmarks to discern and ascertain the basis of the manifestations of a given time and their true orientation. The multitude of points of view, of points of departure, investigations, speculations and systems, in the history of thought and facts, doesn't change anything of this truth: there are fundamental principles born of Revelation and founded on it, which always allow us to find, in the midst of all confusion and every disorder, the way of holy objectivity.

Relationship Between Natural Order and Supernatural Order

Three significant cases

1. FATHER HENRI DE LUBAC

If we go back about forty years, we see in the writings of certain theologians, a renewal of interest regarding the relationship of what was called up until then natural order and supernatural order. It is essential to understand that it is not an abstract issue, a «dilettante's» speculation which could not have long range consequences in the thought and life of the Church. In theology as well as in philosophy and in experimental science, there are few subjects, few cases absolutely neutral.

Father Henri de Lubac [35] had expressed about that time, new considerations, not absolutely new, but presented with a new language and special applications. In 1946 he published his book "Supernatural" which expresses all his thought of that time. [36] He asserted that the supernatural

---

[35] HENRI DE LUBAC S. J., born in 1896 professor at the Theological Faculty of Lyon-Fourvière and at the Catholic Institute of Paris, expert on Vatican Council II, member of the International Theological Commission.

[36] H. DE LUBAC, *Surnaturel, Etudes historiques,* Ed. du Seuil, Paris 1946.

order is necessarily implied in the natural order. As a consequence of this concept inevitably resulted that the gift of supernatural order is not gratuitous because it is indebted to nature. So if the gratuitousness is excluded from the supernatural order, nature, by the very fact that it exists, becomes identified with the supernatural. What was the reason set forth? The basic reasoning can be expressed like this: the intellectual act contains the possibility of referring to the notion of the infinite; that is why the supernatural is implied in human nature itself.

This vision of the intimate and essential reality of man was disseminated in the earlier writings of Father de Lubac. There are passages, as for example in his book "Catholicism" (37), the tenor of which cannot really be understood, nor the insistence with which certain biblical expressions are put in relief, if not in the spirit of the doctrine expressed later in "Supernatural".

One remains struck by the insistance with which the author wants to give a particular meaning to the words of Saint Paul «revealed his Son *in me*», which seems to go beyond the explanation accepted by all the exegetes who have read the word «ἐν ἐμοί» exactly as Father M.J. Lagrange. (38)

---

(37)   H. DE LUBAC, *Catholicisme, les aspects sociaux du dogme*, Ed. du Cerf, Paris 1938; 4th ed. 1947.

(38)   MARIE-JOSEPH LAGRANGE O.P. (1855-1938), professor of exegesis at the Catholic Institute of Toulouse and founder of the Biblical School of Jerusalem.

Father de Lubac writes:

«Paul spoke a word, one of the newest and richest in meaning that has ever come out of a man, the day when, constrained to present his own apology to his beloved Galatians, to bring them back to the right path, he dictated these words: 'When he who had set me apart before I was born, and had called me through his grace, was pleased *to reveal his Son in me...*' (Gal. 1:15,16). Not only – whatever may be the outward wonders, the account of which has been handed down to us by the Acts of the Apostles – to reveal his Son to me, to show him to me in some sort of vision or to make me understand him objectively, but, *to reveal him in me.* In taking possession of man, in seizing him and penetrating all the way to the depths of his being, he forces him to descend into himself also, in order to suddenly discover there heretofore unsuspected regions. By Christ, the Person is an adult, Man emerges definitively from the universe». (39)

Whereas for Father M. J. Lagrange, «in me (ἐν ἐμοί)» means:

«By an intimate communication which made Paul know the Son of God, treasure of his intelligence and his heart (Phil. 3:8). In giving to 'ἐν ἐμοί' its natural meaning, we have in verse 16 not a third blessing of

---

(39)   H. DE LUBAC, *Catholicisme*, op. cit. pp. 295-296.

God towards Paul, but the realization in his soul of the call of verse 15». [40]

Father de Lubac says that Christ, in revealing the Father and in being revealed by him, finishes revealing man to himself. What can be the meaning of that statement? Either Christ is only man, or man is divine. The conclusions may not be expressed so clearly, they nevertheless always determine that notion of the supernatural in so far as implied in human nature itself, and from there, without one's consciously desiring it, the way of basic anthropocentrism opens.

In general, speculative argumentation is conducted as if outside of principles, outside of notions accepted up until then as fundamental principles of the faith. How can one conclude with simplicity and non-sophisticated logic, that reference to the notion of the infinite, automatically means that the infinite is apprehended? But the argument was taken up again twenty years later in the book "The Mystery of the Supernatural" [41], which is much more shaded in meaning, more concerned about the consequences that such propositions can have for the minds of men, for it is very serious to state as a principle that the reference to the order of the infinite implies that the essence of the infinite is human nature.

---

[40] M. J. LAGRANGE, *The Letter to the Galatians,* Ed. Lecoffre, Paris 1918, p. 14.

[41] H. DE LUBAC, *Le Mystère du Surnaturel,* Aubier, Paris 1965.

No syllogism, as subtle and complicated as it may be, can fill up the difference between the notion of the infinite which man can have in himself and the infinite reality of God, positive, presumed, felt and at the same time inaccessible; the difference between the aspiration towards the infinite and that Infinite itself, such as man conceives it. One can certainly assert that man's aspiration towards eternity expresses the eternal finality of the created soul, man's possibility to participate in the grace of the countless lights of eternal Life; but one cannot say that this nostalgia means that man has existed from all eternity and that he can possess the eternal fullness of God. Likewise the notion of the infinite, the aspiration towards the infinite expresses the possibility of man's entering into continual contact with the infinity of God. But one cannot say that this aspiration towards the infinite means that man can participate by identity in the divine infinity. In that aspiration of man towards the infinite, the notion and the certainty of our limits are always present. Our journey may be interminable, but the essence itself of our journey towards the infinite manifests the difference between our notion, our participation and the Divine Infinite.

In 1950, four years after the publication of "Supernatural", the Encyclical of Pius XII, "Humani Generis", was given in the Church. It is regarding these conceptions that Pius XII said expressly in that encyclical:

«Others deform the true notion of the gratuitousness of the supernatural order when they claim that God cannot create beings gifted with intelligence without calling them and ordaining them to the beatific vision». (42)

Aside from the admiration or the criticisms raised by that encyclical, it is incontestable that Pius XII was the first to put his finger on the extremely delicate and dangerous point of that definition of man and of his relationship with God. If God, when he creates, imprints in man what we have conceived as supernatural, then the notion of this supernatural and the gratuitousness changes; and from there, in spite of all the efforts to profess the gratuitousness of the creative act of God, a multitude of considerations proceed regarding man, his freedom, grace, the relationship of man with God, the freedom of man and the freedom of God, etc... Considerations which can lead − as they often have − to the very reversal of the essential principles of Revelation. That non-gratuitousness of the supernatural order − for each case − easily leads to a sort of cosmic monism, an anthropocentric idealism.

* * *

---

(42) cf. Denz. 3891.

In his new book, "The Mystery of the Supernatural", Father de Lubac explains certain insufficiencies of expression of his first book "Supernatural", but he still maintains the same thesis and only wants to avoid new misunderstandings. [43]

He unfolds and interlaces syllogisms and speculations with an astonishing sagacity, thus endeavoring to bring together in balance the two concepts: on the one hand the supernatural implied in nature from the creation, and on the other hand the gratuitousness of the supernatural, of grace. He is careful to reject the accusation of "Humani Generis". Those who have read this book see clearly this desire of Father de Lubac, and certainly will ask themselves with him, the question that he asks towards the end of the book:

«Why do we vainly launch into so many discourses on this subject and uselessly multiply utterances and speak such a multiplicity of words? [44]

«That is perhaps», Father de Lubac continues, «what more than one reader may have said in skimming through this work. That is, in any case, what the author couldn't help asking himself very often, in the wake of a medieval disciple of Saint Augustine and Saint

---

(43) H. DE LUBAC, *Le Mystère du Surnaturel*, p. 77.

(44) «Ut quid in vanum hanc materiam in tot sermones prorumpimus, et frustra tot eloquia, multiplicamus et in tantam verborum multitudinem jacimus? ». (*Le Mystère du Surnaturel*, p. 290).

Thomas, who examined himself in that way one day precisely apropos of our subject». (45)

It is a humble query: but the answer to his question that Father de Lubac himself gives further down, leaves one perplexed, for he writes:

«The answer is inscribed in the nature of our intelligence, which cannot receive divine Revelation without a thousand questions immediately arising within and engendering one another. Our intelligence cannot do otherwise than to strive to answer them. But in its explanations, always groping, as far as it appears to go, it knows that it never advances far enough to meet unknown lands». (46)

This answer of Father de Lubac reveals his criteria regarding the ways of knowledge and thus his intellectual attitude towards the great questions of the relations of man and God. This explains the impossibility of finding by that route, the balance of which we have spoken, and a knowledge which, in harmony with Revelation, with the misery and the deep-seated aspiration of man, brings peace. Our criteria regarding the ways of knowledge are true and objective when they issue forth from the great eternal data of Revelation and when they are in stable, clear and immediate harmony with them.

---

(45) *Le Mystère du Surnaturel*, pp. 290-291, quotation of Gilles of Rome.

(46) *Le Mystère du Surnaturel*, p. 291.

In any case, Father de Lubac speaks of an «absolute natural desire» for the vision of God. This notion of an absolute natural desire rules out, in spite of all the speculative efforts displayed, the gratuitousness of the supernatural, that is, of the beatific vision. And in that, «the intelligence» to which Father de Lubac refers above cannot by itself be very useful. For the antinomy remains. It remains and it has had great consequences in the consciousness of man.

In order to understand the general orientation of Father de Lubac's thought and language and his role in the new and contemporary theology, and to understand also how that antinomy of which we have spoken remains, it suffices to refer to certain formulae and certain basic assertions of "The Mystery of the Supernatural":

— First type of assertion:

«The 'desire to see God' cannot be externally frustrated without there being an essential suffering». (47)

«The call of God is constitutive. My final end, of which this desire is the expression, is inscribed within my very being, as it is placed by God in this universe. And, by the will of God, I have no other true end today, that is to say truly assigned to my nature and

---

(47) *Le Mystère du Surnaturel,* p. 80.

offered to my free adherence, under whatever species, than to 'see God'». (48)

«In other words the true problem if there is one, presents itself for the being whose finality is 'already', if one can say that, all supernatural, since that is indeed our case. It presents itself for the creature whose 'vision of God' does not only mark a possible or futurable end — or even the end which fits best — but the end which, humanly judging seems to have to be since it is, by hypothesis, the end which God assigns to that creature. As soon as I exist in fact, all indetermination is lifted and whatever could have been in an existence otherwise realized, no finality seems henceforth possible for me except that which is now in fact inscribed in the depths of my nature; there exists only one end, for which consequently I carry in myself, consciously or not, the 'natural desire'». (49)

And in that regard, Father de Lubac asserts the correspondence of his thought with the doctrine of the «permanent, supernatural existential, preordained to grace» of Father Karl Rahner of whom we shall speak later on. (50)

---

(48) *Le Mystère du Surnaturel*, p. 81.

(49) *Le Mystère du Surnaturel*, p. 82.

(50) *Le Mystère du Surnaturel*, p. 82 note 4.

— Second type of assertion:

«Our God is... 'a God who surpasses every capacity of desire' (Ruysbroeck). He is a God of whom it would be blasphemous and crazy to suppose that he could ever be imposed on by any exigency of any order, whatever the hypothesis on which one took his stand in spirit, and whatever the concrete situation in which one imagined the creature to be». (51)

«God could have denied himself to his creature, just as he could and did want to give Himself. The gratuitousness of the supernatural order is particular and total. It is so in itself. It is so for each one of us. It is so with regard to what for us temporally or logically preceeds it. Furthermore — and that is what certain explanations which we have discussed have seemed to us not to allow to be seen enough — that gratuitousness is always intact. It abides in every hypothesis. It is always new. It abides in all the stages of the preparation of the Gift, in all the stages of the Gift itself. No 'disposition' in the creature will ever be able in any way to bind the Creator. Let us state here with joy, the substantial agreement not only of Saint Augustine, Saint Thomas and other ancients, but also of Saint Thomas and his commentators, beginning with Cajetan, as well as theologians who, even in our own century,

---

(51) *Le Mystère du Surnaturel*, p. 289.

diverge more or less in their attempts at explanations. As the supernatural Gift is never naturalizable in us, the supernatural beatitude can never become for us a 'necessary and exigible' expression, no matter what our actual or simply conceivable situation may be». (52)

These statements alone, cited as examples would suffice to show the antinomy and the impasse into which Father de Lubac brings the thought and heart with his effort to build his doctrine regarding the supernatural. A multitude of questions spring forth without the possibility of receiving an answer or a pacifying orientation of thought. How, for example, are we to understand «my true end» – that is to say «to see God» – is «assigned to my nature»? And at the same time it is offered to my adherence? When does that take place? At the instant of my creation or after, during the time of my earthly life? If it is at the moment of my creation how can I choose my adherence? If it takes place afterwards, during my life, how can I say that «the call of God is constitutive», that is, that my call to the vision of God is an integral part of the creature I am?

If «as soon as I exist all indetermination is lifted», how then could my adherence take place after the first moments of my existence? Because if everything is determined in an absolute way, as Father de Lubac insists upon saying, there is no adherence or non-adherence possible for me.

---

(52) *Le Mystère du Surnaturel,* pp. 289-290

If I carry within myself, even without being conscious of it — as Father de Lubac says — the «natural desire», how is that end offered for my adherence?

Father de Lubac repeats that God could have not created me. But he wanted to create me. So we can ask ourselves: once he created me, how can I say he is not committed from the moment of my creation to give me the joy of seeing him, since he himself, by his act of creation, put the absolute natural desire to see him in the center of my being?

If I grant that by his act of creation God committed himself and cannot refuse me my fulfillment, that is, the joy of seeing him, how could I say that the «gratuitousness of the supernatural order is particular and total; it is so in itself, it is so for each one of us»? One could also claim that the gratuitousness of the supernatural order is the gratuitousness of the creation, that is, admit the identity of the natural and the supernatural orders; but that, Father de Lubac does not want to admit. He accepts that there is the grace of the creation and that there is besides that, the grace of the supernatural call.

How can one say that «no disposition in the creature will ever be able in any way to bind the Creator», and at the same time say that «the call of God is constitutive»? For that «disposition» was imposed on the creature by the Creator. How could one then set forth that «the disposition that God would have put in man does not bind Him in any way? » What idea could we have then of the Creator and his sovereign liberty?

It is neither logically nor spiritually proper to present in every way — as is the case of the quote of Father de Lubac above — that God was not obliged to create us as he did create us, so as to declare the gratuitousness of the supernatural order; it is not proper, because it confuses the questions and the realities. Because to say that God could have refused to give himself to his creature, just as he could and wanted to give himself, is to speak of the beginning of man's creation, because the phrase means that God has already chosen to give himself. And when we speak of the gratuitousness of the supernatural order, we are speaking of all of God's graces and interventions during our terrestrial life, and that without any merit or possible exigency on our part.

Now, if «since the moment of my existence all indetermination is lifted», that is if everything is inscribed in man from the moment of his creation, and in the absolute manner of which Father de Lubac speaks, how could that creature not have an exigency for the appetites inscribed within him, and how can one conceive that the Creator of these appetites and desires is not «bound in any way»?

Such questions can be asked in great number and extended to all domains, and from several points of view, from the definition of the supernatural to the most evident and practical consequences in the life of the Church. But later, and in a more global perspective, we will be able to meditate more deeply on the entirety of this important issue. For the moment, it suffices not to forget this: if we can say that man, since his creation carries the possibility of hearing the call of God for the supernatural end for which He destined him, this does not mean that that possibility of hearing is already the call, and that the supernatural to which man is called is already present in him.

2. FATHER KARL RAHNER

The conception of the supernatural necessarily bound to human nature has been clearly propounded by Karl Rahner since the 30's. In his thesis «Geist in Welt» he clearly presents this conception of the non-gratuitous supernatural. Twenty years later, the propositions were developed more fully. At times one might think he rejects the theses of Father de Lubac, but one quickly realizes that actually Karl Rahner follows the same thought and even goes beyond it.

In several treatises similar ideas return. We must immediately note that in the writings of Karl Rahner, on the one hand the Hegelian dialectic principle is flagrant — as Hans Küng ([53]) himself, an undisputed disciple of Karl Rahner attests ([54]) — on the other hand the same process

---

([53]) HANS KÜNG, priest, born in 1928, expert on Vatican Council II, professor of the Faculty of Catholic Theology of the University of Tübingen (Germany) from 1960 until December 1979, and director of the Institute of Ecumenical Theology at the same university.

([54]) «In the most recent Catholic theology, Karl Rahner here as elsewhere, and with an exemplary intellectual courage and a vigorous strength of thought, has opened new horizons and has confronted classical Christology with modern thought. The remarkable spirit which hovers in the background of this thorough analysis — conducted with conceptual rigour — of classical Christology (chalcedonian-scholastic) down to its most profound conceptuality, is none other than Hegel (we find Heideggerian influences there also). The sporadic efforts to get

renders the basis of the thought very fluid and elusive, for we find ourselves before an antithesis that he tries to resolve in opting for one of the terms which at the same time annuls the dialectic process. This remark is made here solely to explain the contradictions that his position carries with regard to the thesis of Father de Lubac, and also to help grasp his basic accord with him.

In his writings on Nature and Grace, Karl Rahner writes:

«Is the fact that man is intimately ordained to grace so constitutive of his 'nature', that his nature could not be thought of without grace, that is, as pure nature? Would the concept of pure nature be unrealizable? It is the point where we must openly reject the conception which is considered the one adopted by the 'new theology'. "Humani Generis"... gives in connection with this an unequivocal teaching». (55)

«From the most deep-seated essence of grace follows rather the impossibility of a disposition to grace which belongs to the nature of man; or else it follows

---

away from Hegel — in secondary assertions — do nothing other than underline this fact. Rahner proposes to elucidate theologically, in pursuing his transcendental stand, the conditions of the possibility of an incarnation». (H. KÜNG, *Incarnazione di Dio*, Queriniana, Brescia 1972, pp. 643-644).

(55) K. RAHNER, *Rapporto tra Natura e Grazia*, in *Saggi di antropologia soprannaturale*, Ed. Paoline, Roma 1969, pp. 53-54.

that this disposition, in the case in which it would be necessary, belongs already to this same order of the supernatural. It does not follow, however, that that disposition as natural would allow the gratuitousness of grace to subsist». (56)

«One can accept with tranquillity the concept of 'potentia obœdientialis' refused by de Lubac. The spiritual nature must be such that it has an aperture towards that existential supernatural, without however, requiring it of itself unconditionally. This aperture will not be considered only as a non-contradiction, but as an inward determination, provided that it is not unconditional». (57)

Here Karl Rahner asserts: firstly, that the conception of the «new theology» according to which man's nature carries with it the determination to grace, must be rejected; secondly, that the essence of grace is incompatible with a disposition of human nature to grace, and that if such a disposition to grace should prove necessary, it would belong to the supernatural order, and in that case grace would not be gratuitous.

Later on, Rahner not only accepts that which he refutes here, but he proposes it with much stronger meanings. When for example he says that we can accept

---

(56) *Rapporto tra Natura e Grazia*, pp. 60-61.
(57) *Rapporto tra Natura e Grazia*, pp. 72-73.

with tranquillity the concept of «potentia obœdientialis» that de Lubac refutes, he gives the impression of wanting to present a more traditional concept.

Now in the same paragraph he has already said that the aperture of our nature to «the existential supernatural» is an «interior determination». And he adds that which again confuses the clarity of the thought, «provided that it is not unconditional». There is a basic contradiction in that declaration because if the aperture to that supernatural existential is an interior determination, that aperture is universal and constitutes a deep-seated condition of human nature, and it isn't enlightening to say that this aperture to the supernatural which is already an interior determination, is not unconditional.

But Rahner moves forward and by very precise formulae, proves that his thought is not only that of the «new theology», but that it goes beyond it. Referring to an article which exposes the principles of the «new theology», Karl Rahner says that to speak of an «unlimited dynamism» of nature which «objectively includes in its essence the supernatural as an intrinsic, necessary end» does not constitute a «direct threat to the supernaturality and gratuitousness of that end». [58] And more precisely he declares:

«The capacity for the God of personal love who gives himself is the central and permanent existential of

---

(58) *Rapporto tra Natura e Grazia*, p. 63.

man in his concrete reality». It is «the permanent supernatural existential, preliminarily ordained to grace». (59)

Now it may be asked: if nature includes objectively in its essence the supernatural as intrinsic, necessary end, if «the capacity for God» is the central and permanent existential of man, and if that permanent, supernatural existential is preordained to grace, if all that is so, how then can it have been stated previously that from the interior essence of grace follows the impossibility for man's nature to carry a disposition to grace, and even more, to state that if that disposition is necessary, it then belongs already to the supernatural order and furthermore that this disposition annihilates the concept of the gratuitousness of grace?

For Rahner the innermost core of man's nature is «the supernatural existential», that is, the capacity to receive grace. (60) Man, still in Rahner's opinion, cannot have true experience concerning himself except in so far as ordained interiorly and in an absolute manner to the supernatural:

---

(59) *Rapporto tra Natura e Grazia,* p. 68 and note.

(60) According to Rahner one can distinguish in the essence of man, «concrete and always indissoluble, what this real and not-owed capacity is of receiving grace, that we call existential supernatural, and what remains when the inner kernel of his concrete essence as a whole, his 'nature' is removed». *Rapporto tra Natura e Grazia,* pp. 69-70).

«Man cannot have experience concerning himself except in the loving supernatural will of God, he cannot present nature in a 'chemically pure state', separated from its supernatural existential. Nature in this sense remains a derived abstract concept. But this concept is necessary and objectively grounded if one wants to become aware, by way of reflex, of the gratuity of grace, though man is interiorly ordained to it and in an absolute manner». [61]

On the same subject he returns with a still more explicit vocabulary and with expressions which, if they were accepted as postulates, would lead to a reversal of all the foundations of theology:

«Man always lives consciously even if he doesn't 'know' it and doesn't believe it, that is, even if he cannot make it a particular object of his knowledge by introspective reflection, before the Triune God of eternal life. It is the ineffable but real objective of the dynamic power of all spiritual and moral life in the spiritual framework of existence, founded in reality by God, that is to say, supernaturally elevated». [62]

«Preaching is the explicitation and the awakening of that which is at the depths of the human being, not by

---

[61] *Rapporto tra Natura e Grazia*, p. 72.

[62] K. RAHNER, *Natura e Grazia*, in *Saggi di antropologia sopranaturale*, Ed. Paoline, Roma 1969, p. 109.

nature, but by grace. Grace which enfolds man, even
the sinner and the unbeliever, as the inevitable basis of
his existence». (63)

«Effective nature is never 'pure' nature, but rather
nature in the supernatural order from which man (even
the unbeliever and the sinner) cannot escape». (64)

It is certain, and no one could sincerely deny it − not
even Karl Rahner − that a large number of his texts, of his
expressions and definitions allow any orientation of
thought whatsoever. But in the midst of this polyvalence of
expressions and postulates, a basic anthropology is clearly
apparent, which not only agrees with Father de Lubac's
thought, but goes beyond it, so as to transform in the
consciousness of the followers of the new theology, articles
of the faith, such as for example those of the Incarnation
and the Immaculate Conception. Indeed, where can the
following affirmation lead theological thought or spiritual
meditation:

«In substance, the spirit of man is not possible
without that transcendence which is its absolute
accomplishment, that is to say, grace»? (65)

What meaning can there be in the fact of saying later
on that «that accomplishment remains gratuitous»? The

---

(63) *Natura e Grazia*, p. 110.
(64) *Natura e Grazia*, p. 112.
(65) *Natura e Grazia*, p. 118.

affirmation that the spirit of man doesn't exist without the grace of its absolute accomplishment is the basis of the teaching of this text.

And how are we to understand the proposition according to which:

«The attempt can even be made to see the hypostatic union in the line of this absolute perfectionment of what man is»? (66)

We cannot understand anything else than what it says, because to say that we must see the hypostatic union in the line of this perfectionment is to say that the hypostatic union is the perfectionment of man. The nuance of the expression «to see in the line of the perfectionment», is a linguistic softening of the bare affirmation that the perfectionment of man realizes the hypostatic union.

Rahner declares in every way that the essence in God and in us is the same:

«When the Logos becomes man... that man *in so far as man* is precisely the self-manifestation of God in his self-expression»; — «the essence, indeed, is the same in us and in him; we, we call it 'human nature'». (67)

---

(66) *Natura e Grazia*, p. 120.

(67) K. RAHNER, *Teologia dell'incarnazione*, in *Saggi di Cristologia e di Mariologia*, Ed. Paoline, 2nd ed., Roma 1967, p. 113.

It is therefore clear that God and man have the same essence, and we – says Karl Rahner – we do not call it otherwise than «human nature».

Certainly it is not given to man to perceive, to circumscribe and to go thoroughly into the mystery of the essence of God analytically and synthetically, nor even the mystery of human essence in itself and in relation to the essence of God. The question in its profound simplicity opens an endless road of meditation and at the same time of adoration of the Creator. But when one acts, when one thinks and when one expresses himself so as to lay down postulates such as the one of the identity of the essence of God and man, which reverse the doctrine issued from Revelation, one is not following a way of truth, but that of error.

The question of the rapport between the essence of man and the essence of God is the greatest problem that man can set forth with regard to God: it is the problem of otherness. Many servants of God, in their life-long instruction, have understood in the past and today, that before such things, such questions which loom up in the spirit and the heart, one must become small, very small. Except for the trinitarian mystery, of course, and all that accompanies it, the most difficult thing for us is to understand how, outside of God, there is us; that is the question of otherness. From there the question: how, beside the liberty of God, can one conceive of our liberty?

We can prove negatively that there is no contradiction between these two liberties. But in any case it is a mystery.

The assertion of Rahner on the identity of the essence of God and man, is probably the fruit of speculations on that immense mystery.

This is said here because the assertions of Rahner regarding the Incarnation and the Hypostatic Union leave no doubt that if one cannot accuse him of pantheism, one can, in any case define his thought and his doctrine as «pananthropist», and in that expression one can understand many things! For Karl Rahner, the humanity of Christ has to do with theology, not as a reality united to God, but as being itself the reality of the Logos: indeed, he says clearly, the humanity of Christ is not united to the Logos, but is the reality itself of the Logos. (68) And in his interminable linguistic acrobatics he voices the most improbable and contradictory definitions, but without ever clearly teaching the doctrine of the Church on the Incarnation or the Creation. Let us cite, for example, a few disturbing propositions:

> «We could define man as what appears when the self-expression of God, his Word, is uttered in love in the void of nothingness without God. If God wants to be not-God, man appears, truly himself and nothing else, we could say». (69)

---

(68) K. RAHNER, *Problèmes actuels de Christologie, Ecrits théologiques I,* Desclée de Brouwer 1959, p. 169.

(69) K. RAHNER, *Teologia dell'Incarnatione,* in *Saggi di Cristologia e di Mariologia,* op. cit. p. 114.

«Of God whom we profess in Christ, we must say that he is precisely there where we are, and it is only there that we can find him». (70)

And now, here is how Rahner, in more precise terms, speaks of the hypostatic union:

«The task of theology (task laid down with the definition of Chalcedon, without, for all that, being accomplished) is precisely that of explaining — which does not mean suppressing the mystery — why and how he who (71) is divested of self, not only remains what he was, but also definitively and perfectly confirmed in his state, becomes in the most radical sense (72) what he is: a human reality.

«But this is only possible if one shows how, in the essence of man, this tendency to annihilate himself (73) for the benefit of the absolute God (in the ontologic and not only moral sense) belongs to the most basic components of the human essence. Indeed, only the highest actuation (that which is perfect and which has been realized only once) of this obediential power

---

(70) *Teologia dell'incarnazione*, p. 115.

(71) The French translation states «that which» instead of «he who».

(72) The French translation states «truly» instead of «in the most radical sense».

(73) The French translation states «to divest himself of himself» instead of «to annihilate himself».

— which is not a purely negative determination, a simply formal non-repugnance — truly makes of the being who has annihilated himself, a man in the strictest sense and thus unites him with the Logos. The hypostatic union is going to carry out to perfection and render fully conscious this fact, that this divesting of self can be a datum of the self-consciousness of man; because it belongs to the consciousness of that man to have this disponibility to the annihilation of self, which is fully realized in the hypostatic union». (74)

This passage chosen among many others of the same tenor, refers clearly to the known text of the Epistle to the Philippians and to the doctrine of the Hypostatic Union, in order to speak of the mystery of the Person of the Redeemer.

According to Rahner, he who is divested of himself and who, confirmed, becomes in the most radical sense what he is, is a human reality, is a man. He also says that the tendency to annihilate oneself in order to abandon oneself to the absolute God, is a component of human essence. And he says moreover that in the supreme realization of such an annihilation, the being, man in the most radical sense, is united by this same way of annihilation to the Logos. And he states precisely that this disponibility to the

---

(74) K. RAHNER, *Problèmes actuels de Christologie, Ecrits théologiques I,* Desclée de Brouwer 1959, p. 143. Cf. also the Italian edition: *Saggi di Cristologia e di Mariologia,* Ed. Paoline, Second edition, Rome 1967, p. 41.

annihilation of self belongs to the human consciousness, and it is realized to a supreme degree in the hypostatic union.

We can give ourselves over to all kinds of meditations and make a lot of judicious speculations. But it is impossible for an upright conscience not to notice two basic points: on the one hand, one must know that this passage of the Epistle to the Philippians to which he refers, doesn't allow this type of juggling of vocabulary. He who is divested of self («ἑαυτόν ἐκένωσεν»), has divested himself, being in the form of God (in the condition of God) in order to add human nature to himself; he divested himself of the glory in order to take the form of a slave. Such is, in its simplicity, the meaning of the words of Saint Paul. Whether it is Saint Paul who composed them or whether it is a question of a hymn used by Saint Paul, that changes nothing at all of the meaning of the text. However in Karl Rahner's text cited above, it is man who divests himself in order to offer himself to God.

On the other hand, one should note that this divestment does not concern the essence in its own right of he who divests himself, as is stated in the above-mentioned text (to divest oneself of oneself). Saint Paul writes: to divest oneself, and he doesn't say: of oneself. What's more, this divestment is not a simple datum of conscience, and it is very important to know it, because it isn't in the human consciousness that the hypostatic union was accomplished. According to the author's text, the hypostatic union would be the result of the perfection in the inner life of a man. The reality is the opposite; it is the Incarnation and the Hypostatic Union which in Jesus Christ have given perfection to the human being; otherwise the hypostatic union would be an event which took place «in and by the human consciousness». Nevertheless, that is what Rahner asserts when he says a little further on:

«The immediate and effective vision of God is nothing other than the initial non-objective consciousness of being the Son of God; and this consciousness is given by the sole fact that it *is* the hypostatic union». [75]

There can be no doubt that Rahner here radically changes the thought and the faith of the Church with regard to the mystery of the Incarnation of the Word of God in Jesus Christ, such as it is related in the Gospel and by Tradition:

«If the essence of man in general is understood in this ontologico-existential sense as the open transcendence... to the absolute being of God, then the incarnation can appear as the absolutely sublime accomplishment (all the while being completely free, not

---

(75) K. RAHNER, *Considerazioni dogmatiche sulla scienza e autocoscienza di Cristo*, in *Saggi di Cristologia e di Mariologia*, op. cit. p. 224.

indebted, and unique) of that which 'man' means in general». (76)

This way of seeing and exposing Christianity has had very great consequences and repercussions in the formation of the present theological climate. It is quite possible that one doesn't realize how much this climate, how much the ideas and the comportment with regard to God and the Church, with regard to the principle of eternal truth, are linked to these speculations and to these ideas which have upset life and faith in the Church. Today it is not astonishing to hear taught that the incarnation of the Word realizes itself little by little during Christ's life and that no moment of his life realizes the fullness of his freedom, it is realized at the end of his life.

That is where the doctrines freely professed and taught lead to, which alter the objectivity of revealed teaching and which want to wrench the supreme secrets of God regarding the creation, grace and salvation, by the force of subjective intellection. And on this subject, here is a proposition of the same Karl Rahner, which illustrates the importance of this erroneous way of approaching the question of grace and the supernatural:

«If an adequate definition of grace is not to fall inevitably into empty verbalism, into mythology, into gratuitous assertions, it can only start from the subject,

---

(76) K. RAHNER, *Lexikon für Theologie und Kirche*, V, 956; Ital. trans. of Franca Janowski in *Incarnazione di Dio* by Hans Küng, Queriniana, Brescia 1972, p. 644.

from its transcendentalness and from its experience of a necessary orientation towards the reality of the absolute truth and love which has acquired an absolute validity». (77)

Once again Rahner concludes that grace is the accomplishment of our essence. Starting from a vision of things which, whether one wants it or not, rejects de facto the true gratuitousness of the supernatural order, he has reached the point of putting Christ and God in things:

«God and the grace of Christ are in everything as the secret essence of all reality». (78)

Consequently it suffices to refer to the accomplishment of the human essence in order to accept the Son of man, the Christ, because in him God took man upon himself:

«Therefore he who (still far from all revelation explicitly formulated in verbal form) accepts his existence, thus his humanity, he, even without knowing it, says yes to Christ. He who completely accepts his being-man... has accepted the Son of man, because in him God has accepted man». (79)

---

(77) K. RAHNER, *Teologia e antropologia*, in *Nuovi Saggi III*, Ed. Paoline, Roma, 1969, p. 58.

(78) K. RAHNER, *Teologia dell'incarnazione*, in *Saggi di Cristologia e di Mariologia*, op. cit., p. 119.

(79) *Teologia dell'incarnazione*, pp. 119-120.

Now we should be able to understand exactly the meaning of «to completely accept his being-man»; Rahner himself says that this acceptance is «indescribably difficult and remains obscure when we really make it». (80) But from all that follows — subtly perhaps, but clearly — the uselessness of the act of faith, and thus a fundamental datum is destroyed. The act of faith becomes useless because God is in my essence; because God performs all actions; the act of faith presupposes another relation between man and God, between the creature and the Creator. If I accept Christ by the simple fact «of accepting my essence», the act of faith is meaningless.

That is where one has gotten in starting from a concept concerning as great a mystery as the mystery of the supernatural, artificially presented as being part of the doctrine of the Church. All questions have been touched upon. Little by little all principles, all criteria, and all the foundations of the faith have been questioned and they crumble. Certainly it is not fair to say that it is Rahner himself who drew all these inferences. But it is fair to say that in following the vein which began from some erroneous concepts regarding the supernatural and the essence of man and God, this generalized alteration in the consciousness can have taken place. On the other hand, one cannot totally escape the consequences of an initial movement which one has set in motion oneself. It suffices,

---

(80) *Teologia dell'incarnazione*, pp. 119-120.

for example, to see how Karl Rahner considered the Immaculate Conception in the 1950's, and how he was led to speak of it later on.

In 1953 he cites the Definition of Pius IX, in confessing its infallibility. (81) Then he speaks at length of the role of Mary in salvation and of the common end of all of us and of the Blessed Virgin: blessedness. And he recognizes that the Blessed Virgin was preserved from original sin of which every man carries the stain in coming into the world. This acceptance certainly is enveloped in a multitude of considerations concerning the common destiny of man; and this with uncertain and sometimes very contradictory nuances, which attenuates the character of doctrinal certainty. But in any case he seems to admit in these texts, the doctrine of original sin and the preservation of the Blessed Virgin from the stain of original sin.

Now in his "Theological Meditations on Mary" (82) he writes:

«The dogma (of the immaculate conception) does not mean in any way that the birth of a being is accompanied by something contaminating, by a stain, and that in order to avoid it Mary must have had a

---

(81) K. RAHNER, *L'Immacolata Concezione*, and *Il dogma dell'immacolata e la nostra pietà*, in *Saggi di Cristologia e di Mariologia*, ed. Paoline, 2nd ed., Roma 1967, p. 413 and ff.

(82) K. RAHNER, *Maria, Meditazioni*, Herder-Morcelliana, Brescia 1970, 3rd ed., (1st edition 1968).

privilege. – The immaculate conception of the Blessed Virgin therefore consists simply in the possession, from the beginning of her existence, of the life of divine grace, which was given to her.– From the beginning of her existence Mary was enveloped in the redeeming and sanctifying love of God. Such is, in all its simplicity, the content of the doctrine that Pius IX solemnly defined as a truth of the Catholic faith, in the year 1854». [83]

However, the definition of the dogma in "Ineffabilis Deus" says clearly and repeatedly that the Most Holy Virgin was preserved from all stain of original sin. Here is the text of the Definition:

«We declare, pronounce and define that the doctrine is revealed by God and therefore to be believed firmly and constantly by all the faithful, which holds that the Blessed Virgin Mary in the first instant of her conception was, by an unique grace and privilege of Almighty God, in view of the merits of Jesus Christ the Saviour of the human race, *preserved exempt from all stain of original sin*».[84]

How, therefore, must we understand today, outside of the definition "Ineffabilis Deus", the notion of "original sin" of which the texts of Vatican II speak, as for example the Decree on the Apostolate of the Laity:

---

[83] *Maria, Meditazioni*, p. 50.

[84] cf. Denz. 1641.

«Affected by original sin, men have frequently fallen into many errors concerning the true God, the nature of man and the principles of the moral law»? (85)

And how are we to understand the more explicit texts of the same Council, calling the Mother of God «Entirely holy and free from all stain of sin, as though fashioned by the Holy Spirit and formed as a new creature», and declaring her «Immaculate Virgin, preserved free from all guilt of original sin»? (86)

For if man at his birth is not accompanied by a stain, as Rahner claims, of what stain does the Bull of Pius IX speak? How can one claim, as Rahner does, that there was not any stain to avoid and that Mary did not need a privilege?

It is not here that the luminous and profound reality of the Immaculate Conception must be spoken of. The sole intention was to illustrate simply by a subject concerning the entirety of salvation and eternal truth, the contradiction and the fundamental errors towards which one is led from this erroneous initial concept, and of an intellectual attitude towards the things of God which is far too rash.

---

(85) Vatican Council II, Decree «Apostolicam Actuositatem», no. 7.

(86) Vatican Council II, const. «Lumen Gentium», chap. 8, no. 56 and 59.

If through the fundamental data of Revelation, preserved by the Magisterium in spite of all the human
vicissitudes, one examines the current horizon of theology
patiently, with simplicity and moderation, it can be seen
how the initial vein leads to the doctrine of the «anonymous Christian», to the doctrine of the «death of God», of
«secularization», of «demythology», of «liberation», and so
many other currents beneath a multiplicity of often
ephemeral vocables.

3. JACQUES MARITAIN

A philosopher who in the same period of the 1930's has had a great influence on the formation of contemporary tendencies, philosophical as well as theological, is Jacques Maritain.[87] In his thought in general not only has he not sought to assimilate the natural order with the supernatural order, but on the contrary he has distinguished them so as to recognize in the creation and in human history, two distinct callings, linked by a principle of subordination certainly, but essentially autonomous, having their own ends and means: the earthly vocation and mission, and the supernatural vocation.

If someone wanted to understand, to immediately put his finger on, if one can say so, the characteristic of Maritain's thought regarding the autonomy of distinct vocations, it would suffice for him to read the last sentence of his book "Integral Humanism", published in 1936, and which was the fundamental reference for certain theological tendencies and also for the temporal and political action of many Christian spheres:

«The worlds which have risen in heroism retire in weariness, so that new heroisms and new sufferings come in their turn, which will make other worlds rise.

---

(87) JACQUES MARITAIN (1882-1973) converted to Catholicism in 1906, professor of philosophy in Paris, in Toronto (Canada) and at Princeton (U.S.A.).

Human history grows thus, for it isn't a process of repetition, but of expansion and progress, it grows as an expanding sphere, drawing near at the same time to its double consummation, − in the absolute below, where man is god without God, and in the absolute above where he is god in God». (88)

These two absolutes constitute a sort of intimate secret of all of Maritain's thought, and one could say of all his sensibility. They are at the base of all his writings; they are his leitmotiv and the fundamental prism through which he sees all things, the smallest up to the largest.

Already in 1927, in his book "Primacy of the Spiritual", he asserts in several ways that:

«Each one of us belongs to two cities; one terrestrial city having as its aim the common temporal good, and the universal city of the Church, having as its aim eternal life».

And taking up a formula of Etienne de Tournai, he specifies:

«In the same ambit and the same human multitude there are two peoples, and these two peoples give rise to two distinct lives, to two principates, to a double juridical order». (89)

---

(88) J. MARITAIN, *Humanisme Intégral,* Aubier, Paris 1968 (new edition), p. 294.

(89) J. MARITAIN, *Primauté du Spirituel,* Plon, Paris 1927, p. 17.

It is in "Integral Humanism" that Maritain most amply expressed his vision of the Creation and the reality of the spiritual world. And it is there that the doctrine of the distinction and the autonomous character of the temporal order and the spiritual order was exposed with a whole perspective of application in action, with a view to «a concrete historic ideal for a new Christianity», that is «a prospective image signifying the particular type, the specific type of civilization towards which a certain historic age tends».(90) And it is always through this principle of autonomy of orders, initial or acquired, that he envisages the course of the world:

«By virtue of a process of differentiation normal in itself (although corrupted by the falsest ideologies), the profane or temporal order in the course of modern times is constituted with regard to the spiritual or sacred order in an autonomous relationship such that it excludes, in effect, instrumentality. In other words, it has come of age. And this is moreover a historic gain which a new Christianity would have to maintain». (91)

Towards the end of his life, with his two books "The Peasant of the Garonne" (1966), and "About the Church of Christ" (1970), Maritain wanted to present the great doctrinal and moral crisis of the world and the Church. He

---

(90) J. MARITAIN, *Humanisme Intégral*, Aubier, Paris 1968 (new edition), p. 135.

(91) *Humanisme Intégral*, p. 182.

also wanted to denounce the «abuses» of certain concepts, of certain doctrines and formulae such as for example the expression «personalist and communitary» used by Emmanuel Mounier, the founder of the periodical "Esprit":

«Thanks especially to Emmanuel Mounier — he writes — the expression 'personalist and communitary' has become a commonplace for Catholic thought. I myself am not without some responsibility in that... It is from me, I think, that Mounier got it. It is true, but in seeing the use that is made of it now, I'm not very proud of it». (92)

In the basic desire for a deeper unity, Maritain remains always permeated all the same, with that general vision of distinction and autonomy. In order to see that, it suffices to note in the Preface of his last book, "About the Church of Christ", with what solicitude and perseverance he endeavors to defend the autonomy of philosophy compared with theology, showing the same concern that he had twenty years before, when he wrote:

«The philosopher will take into consideration the contributions of theological science — without ceasing for all that, to be a philosopher (if he really is a philosopher, he is more so then than ever), but while

---

(92) J. MARITAIN, *Le Paysan de la Garonne*, Desclée de Brouwer, Paris 1966, pp. 81-82.

asking the additional information he needs, from information sources worthy of faith». (93)

This is not the place to speak more deeply and in more detail of the implications of Maritain's work as a whole, and of all the influence he had on theology and the action of Christians of this century. This will be done later on, as it will for the others of whom we have just spoken. But it was necessary to recall first and foremost, with regard to the rapport between natural order and supernatural order, the principle of the distinction of the orders in the particular meaning it had with Jacques Maritain; because the repercussions of it were great in all directions, and often contrary to the orientation of his thought and to his inner aspirations.

By way of example, and before having to speak in detail of «liberation theology», we can here relate Gustavo Gutiérrez' (94) appraisal of Maritain, in his book "Theology of Liberation". Then we can understand the importance of this subject, of the distinction of orders, which can seem for some too abstract, anodyne or antiquated, and we can also understand the concern and sadnesses which Jacques Maritain, noble being that he was, had in the last period of his life.

---

(93) J. MARITAIN, *Neuf Leçons sur les notions premières de la philosophie morale*, Téqui, Paris 1964 (1st ed. 1951), p. 103.

(94) GUSTAVO GUTIÉRREZ, priest, born in 1928, professor of theology at the University of Lima (Peru) and at the Pastoral Institute of Medellin (Colombia).

Here then, for the moment, the words of Gutiérrez:

«The serious problems that the new historic situation poses for the Church, starting with the 16th century, and which became more acute with the French Revolution, are the point of departure of another pastoral perspective and another theological mentality, which, thanks to Maritain, will receive the name of 'new Christianity'. We find it expounded with all the desired clarity in his well-known work "Integral Humanism". This new Christianity will try to profit by the lessons resulting from the break between faith and social life, which were intimately linked to one epoch of Christianity, but with categories which will not succeed in freeing themselves completely — and we observe it better now — from the traditional mentality... Thomas Aquinas, maintaining that grace does not suppress nature, nor does it take its place, but perfects it, opens the way to a more autonomous and disinterested political action. On this basis, Maritain elaborates a political philosophy which even tries to make its own some modern elements. Maritain's thought had a great deal of influence on certain Christian sectors of Latin America». [95]

Here is a very significant text. Gutiérrez, by this judgement, permits us to clearly see the particular nature of the influence which Maritain's thought has exerted. At the

---

[95] G. GUTIÉRREZ, *Teologia della liberazione*, Queriniana, Brescia 1972, 2nd ed. 1973, p. 61 and note.

same time Gutiérrez criticizes Maritain as not being emancipated enough from the body of the Church. He even speaks ironically of his attachment to the ecclesial tradition. But all that only serves to illustrate even more the full doctrinal import of the fundamental principle of Maritain, regarding the distinction of the orders and the autonomy of the temporal.

At bottom, Maritain's philosophy is a «philosophy-theology» of history, which has had profound repercussions in the theoretic and social life of the Church.

« *The Impalpable* »

The preceeding pages are a sort of introduction to the study of all the theological reality in itself and with regard to the life of the Church. This study must be made with great and if it can be said, holy objectivity; and it must be made in spite of the great acuteness of problems and situations, in the immutable evangelical hope and in the peace of Christ.

Now it is useful to recall in regard to the rapport between the natural and the supernatural orders:

There is no question, however abstract it may be, which can be discussed or treated in the ambit of the Church, without its having direct or indirect repercussions on the formation of thought, morals and piety. And there are questions which always remain with a great halo of the impalpable, and which are nevertheless the foundation of holy, luminous and pacifying knowledge.

But when one wants to do violence to the mysteries of God and to succeed by force of will and intellection, in putting a heavy finger on that «impalpable», one seriously risks losing the vision of universal reality and true perception of eternal truth, inasmuch as man is permitted to have it; and this can cause great damage in the work of the Church with regard to salvation and with regard to truth.

That man is created in a state of grace, that he is destined for a supernatural end, that there is a natural disposition of the creature to the supernatural, makes up the fundamental teaching of the Church, ancient teaching founded on Revelation. But it doesn't follow that that supernatural end is that same disposition of nature to the supernatural, nor that that supernatural end be entirely present, either as conscious knowledge or as «absolute natural desire» of the beatific vision in the creature, from the moment of his creation.

All these notions of creation, grace, disposition, finality, nature, supernatural, are certainly notions with very rich and nuanced content, and they cannot be approached by reducing their meaning to the point of suffocation and petrification, nor by enlarging it beyond all norm and limit to the point of evaporation. All depends on the fidelity to certain norms of language, which themselves are directly issued from Revelation and confirmed by Revelation.

When, for example, Saint James says in his Epistle that God «brought us forth by the word of truth that we should be a kind of first fruits of his creatures» (96), when Saint Paul says that «neither circumcision counts for anything, nor uncircumcision, but a new creature» (97), and that «if any one is in Christ, he is a new creature; the old has passed away, behold, the new has come»; (98) when

---

(96) *James* 1 : 18.
(97) *Gal.* 6 : 15.
(98) *2 Cor.* 5 : 17.

Saint Peter says «we wait for new heavens and a new earth» (99) and in general when the Holy Scripture speaks of renewal and of new creation, it reveals to us a new event, not only moral but entailing ontological repercussions in man. If we want to remain faithful to the evangelical message, we cannot construct doctrines and postulates by forced intellections which, directly or indirectly suppress this new creature, this newness brought by the grace of Christ in present day historic man, in «just plain» man.

The fact that a spiritual creature is created for an end beyond the state of his creation doesn't mean that the fullness of that finality is put in the creature by God as a constitutive part at the moment of creation. All the revealed data and all man's experience affirm the contrary: it is the Creator who carries in himself the fullness of the finality. God, unfathomable Creator and freely manifested to man, Himself contains the mystery of the ultimate finality, unveils it and imprints it on the creature when he has already called him, and to the degree of his response; and man follows stage by stage, grace unto grace, the way of perfection and elevation of nature towards the supreme supernatural end.

The ensemble of the doctrinal considerations of all the Fathers and Doctors of the Church, Duns Scot included, regarding the finality of the creation and man, and

---

(99) *2 Peter* 3 : 13.

regarding the nature of grace in general and of the character of particular graces, do not allow the concept of the relation between natural and supernatural to be expressed as a postulate such as it comes forth from the doctrines of H. de Lubac and K. Rahner.

During these last years, Father de Lubac, a highly esteemed religious, has shown by his writings that he is very concerned with the defense of the faith, of the body and life of the Church in the world. But here we have spoken of the principles and doctrinal concepts which have contributed more or less strongly and more or less consciously to the formation of the contemporary theological movement.

And in this movement the evangelical message and the teaching of the Church on the new creation, on the renewal of man and of all things, have often been fundamentally affected. It is then the hope of the Church which has been affected. But it is certain that nothing can stop the accomplishment of the true work of Christ in His Church. David, in Psalm 103, had already sung the consoling announcement:

«When thou sendest forth thy Spirit, they are created; and thou renewest the face of the earth».

ALTERATION
OF HISTORY
AND
ETERNAL LIBERATION

THREE EXPRESSIONS
OF THE NEW CURRENT

The few reference points for the understanding of the present day theological movement — of which we have spoken — certainly have not suddenly emerged from the midst of «virgin soil» as if they were the first source of the movement which followed.

The reference point is fixed or placed according to a finality proposed or accepted, in order to meditate or bring a judgement to bear on an ensemble of events and concepts. This finality, which constitutes a criterion, can be more or less extended from the point of view of duration and of the sum of facts examined and from the point of view of a more profound and general view of things which the man who meditates arrives at; this finality-criterion can be more or less universal, more or less transcendental and eschatological, or on the contrary, relative and temporal.

Whether one wants it or not, there is always a criterion through which the reference points are recognized throughout the development of a series of facts in a lapse of time. And what has just been said here, that is, the inevitable necessity of having a criterion to be able to place reference points, is already part of the fundamental question upon which we are going to reflect now. Because, according to experience all through human history, without a reference point, thought and discourse manifest disorder and lack of balance.

In any case, the domain we are going to enter is more vast and already contains the more remote origin of these manifestations which are then the reference points of which we have spoken.

In the midst of the world of thought, the philosophic, scientific and political world, and more particularly in the midst of the Christian world, within and outside of the Catholic Church, a new event has been manifested, or rather a very old fact has manifested itself once again in a more acute manner, under a new form, a very old fact, which has always accompanied the adventure of man's thought and action: an ensemble of views, propositions, postulates and concepts has for a long time now created a polymorphic and at the same time uniform tendency, if one can say that, because its orientation is unique.

This tendency claims, under several forms of apparently diverse orientations, the moral and intellectual right to utterly renovate every notion and method of science, philosophy, theology, ethics and history. It concerns a powerful current which henceforth affects the notion and principle of life and the notion and principle of knowledge.

In this general current which embraces the whole field of intellectual, moral and practical activity, three facts best express the basis of this polymorphic and uniform phenomenon:

— First, the belief of having discovered a new dimension of man: the historic consciousness.

— Second, the belief of having discovered a «new» and unique road for the knowledge of truth: hermeneutics.

— Third, the belief of having discovered, a new fundamental perception of phenomena, a radically new way of perceiving Reality, universal life, the cosmos and the inner life of man, consequently a new transcendental reference regarding truth and knowledge which can be called: the existential reference.

These three facts summarize a great number of orientations often divergent but only apparently, because it is easy to realize that they are interdependent; they manifest themselves as if they were moved and brought about by one sole and unique factor. But the distinction of these three facts also corresponds to the reality of things, and that is why it helps us to go thoroughly into the general present reality and more particularly the contemporary theological movement.

Now in order to perceive, in so far as possible and permitted to man, the far-off origin as well as the general consequences of these three facts, that is, to be able to estimate, with the maximum objectivity possible, the meaning and consequences of the tendency which these three facts, these three generic phenomena express, one should be able to examine first of all and in depth the notion and also the reality of the notion «history», the notion and the reality of the word (speech, language and languages) and also the notion of the vocables «being» and «existence».

But there is a factor which must be taken into account from the beginning of every meditation, every inquiry, every study. For it is a factor which now is an intrinsic part of the three facts, the three phenomena of which we have just spoken. It is that in the multitude of the more or less scholarly, more or less doctrinal, more or less independant and revolutionary works, which directly or indirectly concern the question of the historic consciousness, the question of hermeneutics and the question of existential reference, the key-terms of the statements often seem ambiguous, contradictory and polyvalent, and that happens among authors of the same school, using the same terminology, and often within one work of the same author.

Thus one finds himself before a factor which more and more determines and transforms the word and sensibility of a great number of people in our century. Old terms and new terms which are at the base of theories, of fundamental propositions and which are repeated ceaselessly with a pathetic insistence and at times like an incantation, as if they alone contained within themselves the key to all arcana, often remain with a very uncertain content, without truly any liberatory nuance, and consequently lacking all strength to transmit a light of peace in the thought and heart.

Not rarely, one is witness to a sort of unimaginable prestidigitation of words: be, being, existence, interpretation, comprehension, hermeneutics, language, speech, word, substance, essence, subjectivity, objectivity, structure, identity, praxis, orthopraxy, liberation, acculturation, and many other old and new words, even of major importance change their resonance of signification in a way which recalls the chameleon in the sun and in the shade of the forest. From one school to another, from one chapter to another of the same book, the words flee, they continually slide, full of implications, implications with different resonances each time, in a way which does not allow any principle, notion or concept of fundamental, stable meaning to remain; in the name of a revalorization of the word, we are witness to a polyvalence and an anarchic dispersion of all essential order of the word.

This phenomenon, which now often accompanies the different manifestations of the three aforesaid facts — regarding the historic consciousness, regarding hermeneutics, regarding the existential reference — is a very significant and serious event. For it is not a matter of personal considerations and attitudes of dilettantes, but a whole philosophical and theological current and a transformation of the sensibility of language regarding the most important issues, such as those of truth, knowledge, man, God.

It is serious because it is a question of a «new consciousness» of man and of «new postulates» of deepening of the word and language. It is serious because it concerns the whole orientation of the thought and life of the Church and city. Thus one often sees an effort to create and define a language and to give a new meaning to the terms. One endeavors to create a language universally accepted, but at base without universal reference. It is a hopeless effort, for the terms of a language, as nuanced and subtle as one may wish them to be, must have an intrinsic, universal, real reference in order to be universal, true and efficacious.

But in the philosophic literature of diverse tendencies and theological literature of diverse Christian confessions, a more and more combative denial comes through against all reference to a simple and profound notion of being. One finds himself as if before a sort of ontologic allergy to every notion, word and feeling which evoke an eternal stability.

In order to realize this formidable differentiation of the sensibility of man regarding truth and also the blurred uncertainty of polyvalent language, it suffices, in spite of the great displeasure which this brings with it, before every patient inquiry and every study, to take examples at random, almost without choosing, from the different writings.

Now in order to illustrate this very important question of the confusion in the world of language, borne by the general tendency and manifested by the three facts of which we have spoken, we shall refer for the first time to the thought and language of Martin Heidegger ([100]), who has had a great influence in the philosophy as well as the theology of our century.

Heidegger speaking of language says at one point:

«An exhaustive definition of language could not moreover, be achieved, even if one were to put these various fragmentary definitions together in syncretistic fashion. The decisive point still remains the working out in advance, of the ontologico-existential whole of the structure of discourse on the basis of the analytic of Dasein».([101])

Certainly without a predominant and universal reference, no exhaustive definition can be made either of language or of any other manifestation in the life of thought and of the cosmos. But what one can conclude is that the «decisive point» which remains is that the expression «ontologico-existential» wants to suppress all notion of «being - ὄν», all reference of terms to stable meanings and realities.

In the Italian edition of Martin Heidegger's book "Sein und Zeit", "Being and Time", a glossary is added in order, certainly, to facilitate the understanding of the text. It

---

(100)   MARTIN HEIDEGGER (1889-1976), German philosopher, professor at the University of Marburg, the successor to Husserl's Chair at the University of Freiburg im Breisgau.

(101)   MARTIN HEIDEGGER, *Being and Time — Sein und Zeit*, Basil Blackwell, Oxford 1978, (1st English edition 1962), p. 206.

suffices to glance at the glossary in order to comprehend the impasse into which that tendency — which we can call here in order to be understood: historical, hermeneutical and existential — has caused and causes the thought of a large part of Christianity and the universities of the world to enter.

In this glossary we read:

— «Existence (Existenz): it is the being of the Being-there to which the Being-there always refers in the comprehension of the being which is proper to it. Therefore we must not confuse it with the *existentia* which tradition opposes to *essentia* and which in Heidegger corresponds rather to presence-at-hand (cf.)».([102])

And in following the reference, we go on to the term «presence-at-hand»:

— «Presence-at-hand (Vorhandenheit): it is a fundamental category, that is, it is a mode of being of the entities that the Being-there meets in the world. Before everything and above all (cf.) the Being-there meets the entity Being-in-the-world taking care (cf.) of it; in that case this entity is revealed under the categorical aspect of readiness-to-hand (cf.). When on the contrary the Being-there takes the cognoscitive

---

(102) MARTIN HEIDEGGER, *Essere e tempo*, Italian edition, (3rd edition), Longanesi & Co., Milano 1976, p. 544.

attitude, it goes beyond the immediate readiness-to-hand and tends to exhibit in the Being-in-the-world the presence-at-hand».(103)

And to better limit and show clearly what these examples point out, it is useful to see how Martin Heidegger himself defines the term «being»:

«There are so many things which we designate as 'being', and we do so in various senses. Everything we talk about, everything we have in mind, everything towards which we comport ourselves in one way or another is being: being is also what we are and how we are».(104)

And finally the glossary continues:

— «Being-there (Dasein): it is the term chosen by Heidegger to designate human reality. The being of the Being-there is existence».(105)

Now for every free man, psychologically and spiritually free, or even for a man of good faith who is agnostic, it is clear that of these three expressions «being», «Being-there» and «existence», at least one is superfluous, because if the being of Being-there is existence, and if the Being-there is the human reality in the temporal modulations and fluc-

---

(103) MARTIN HEIDEGGER, *Essere e tempo*, p. 548.

(104) MARTIN HEIDEGGER, *Being and Time*, p. 26.

(105) MARTIN HEIDEGGER, *Essere e tempo*, p. 544.

tuations of existence, the notion of being dissipates and disappears, fundamentally substituted by the notion of existence in time.

Heidegger's book "Being and Time" is one of the numerous examples typical of that baseless venture of the human language, manifesting the intellectual, spiritual and moral impasse of man in revolt against his natural and eternal references.

THE ALTERATION
OF HISTORY

The universal culture of our times, in all its intellectual and practical manifestations and repercussions, is in depth and on the surface dominated by an orientation of thought and sensibility which one endeavors to express by the word «history» and its derivatives. What one understands each time by this word «history», is a very changeable notion or reality or quality, which permits orientation of thought and discourse on the basis of this same moving vocable, in different directions, in such a way that things and vocabularies can no longer have either within man or in his discourse a universally understood and accepted meaning.

Nevertheless to speak of History or of the philosophy of history, of historical reason, of historical consciousness, of the meaning of history and other shaded derivatives of the word «history», presupposes at least, that some stable meaning of the notion «history» is accepted, a meaning which would constitute a general criterion, that is, a reference point.

For in order to give a definition or even a simple explanatory precision of an event or a series of events and facts, however uncertain or subtle they may be, there must be a central criterion, some reference point in and by language must be referred to; a reference point which is not only supposed or vaguely implied, but which is — with all the nuances one wants — made explicit and formulable. It is a basic necessity of the understanding, a necessity of elementary logic and coherence, intimately required in every man who is morally, if not intellectually free, and therefore in good faith.

That is true as much for philosophy as for science, metaphysics, theology; it remains valid for all the domains of thought and feeling.

Now in this phenomenon of polyvalence, more and more extensive in terms and vocabularies a more specific tendency has developed which could be called the height of the «linguistic frenzy»: it is an effort to find a new understanding of texts and facts, and even to present and resolve problems regarding life, history, the soul, faith, regarding the beginning and final end, basing itself on considerations of language, speech and vocabularies often sophisticated and super-subtle to the point of absurdity.

As will be seen when we deal with hermeneutics, this tendency has at times assumed the appearance of a new gnosis, an intellectual esoterism. But in spite of the character which this effort, this method assumes at times, the character of a wise and pious desire for objectivity, one cannot help but feel a profound malaise as when before a display of great disorder, great disarray and a depth of confusion. For we see clearly that in the effort to grasp and to explain the reality of the world, of man and of history by means of a more and more analyzed and twisted semantics, one ends up by losing sight of the true reference to the true interior word of man.

That is why this fact called by us «linguistic frenzy» which sooner or later leads to disintegration within every intellectual, spiritual and moral enterprise, must be taken into account.

In the ensemble of considerations regarding history, in the so-called modern times, the man of antiquity has often been seen as lacking intellectual or spiritual interest for the course of things of the earth, for the sequence of events and societies. And that, sometimes, for tendentious philosophical and sociological motives, and not in a pure research of the truth. In order to understand what is really new in the vast movement regarding history and also to avoid all the confusion which the «linguistic frenzy» has sometimes provoked, it is very useful to begin by referring to the meanings which the vocable «history» has had from the outset.

The word «history» (ἰστορία) is very ancient. Its origin is lost in the mysterious sacred source from which issue the human word and languages. In remote antiquity, we find it used with several nuances.

In principle it meant search - inquiry - information; and also the result of an inquiry; that is, according to the case, it meant learning or knowledge: Herodotus (106), Plato (107), Aristotle(108), Demosthenes(109). At the same time it was used with the signification of an oral or written report of what was known, of what was learned, of what had been found; that is, in the sense of an account: Herodotus(110), Aristotle(111), Plutarch(112).(113)

---

(106) HERODOTUS, *2, 118.*

(107) PLATO, *Phaedo 96 a.*

(108) ARISTOTLE, *On the Parts of Animals 3, 14.*

(109) DEMOSTHENES, *275, 27.*

(110) HERODOTUS, *1,1.*

(111) ARISTOTLE, *Rhetoric 1, 4, 13.*

(112) PLUTARCH, *Péricles 13.*

(113) There is the word «istoreo, ἱστορέω» which means to seek to know: HERODOTUS, *1,61*; SOPHOCLES, *Women of Trachis* v. 418. To look for someone — to examine or interrogate about someone: HERODOTUS, *2, 113*; EURIPIDES, *Ion v. 1547*; PLUTARCH, *Theseus 30*; POLYBIUS *3, 48, 12*. In a wider sense, it also means to know — to relate verbally or in writing that which one knows: ARISTOTLE, *On Plants 1, 3, 13*; THEOPHRASTUS, *History of Plants 4, 13, 1,*; PLUTARCH, *Morals 30 d*; LUCIAN, *Of the Manner of Writing History 7.*

— And there is the word «istor, ἴστωρ» from which, according to the opinion of Greek language specialists, are formed the words «istoreo» and the word «history, ἱστορία». It meant he who knows — he who is competent — he who knows something or someone.

— All these words, «istor, istoreo, istoria» are linked to the word «ido - ida, οἶδα,» which means to see with one's eyes: HOMER, *Iliad 1, 587*; EURIPIDES, *Orestes v. 1020*; PLATO,

From all these references, it is clearly seen that the term «history» was used with diverse nuances certainly, but which are all summarized by the words of Aristotle: «the inquiries of those who write about human actions». ("Rhétorique" I, 4, 1360a), and also the facts themselves related in their sequence.

In examining all this ancient information regarding the written handing down of accomplished facts and events, as well as the wide range of literature concerning the fate of peoples, interventions of the gods, destinies and repercussions in the future contracted by the acts of the past, one easily realizes some truths, in order to understand antiquity as well as modern times with regard to consciousness, history and notions of the sense of history and consciousness of history; notions which have penetrated and greatly influenced theological thought and the thinking and will in Christianity. Among these truths, which the examination of ancient information puts in evidence in any case, one must uphold the following:

a) If on the one hand, in any epoch whatsoever, the investigation of and the manner of investigating the past or the present have always depended and depend as much on

---

Republic 620 a. To observe — to examine: HOMER, *Illiad 2, 274 - 3, 364.* To picture in thought — to picture in mind: HOMER, *Iliad 21, 61*; PLATO, *Republic 510 e.*

To appear — to seem — to render oneself similar: HOMER, *Iliad 2, 791 - 20, 80*; HERODOTUS, *6, 69 - 7, 56.* To be informed of: HOMER, *Iliad 17, 219*; PLATO, *Socrates' Apology 21 d.*

the veracity as on the richness of the sources of information, it is also incontestable on the other hand, that this
investigation and this account depend on what can be
called the general personal point of view of the relator
regarding everything.

Before approaching the vast question of objective
knowledge and the notion of the real, one cannot but
admit that there is for each person a particular prism which
filters his whole experience, that general point of view
which chooses, links, colors and acts as the eye, which sees
all things with the natural possibilities always the same;
always the same except for basic differentiation in the
intimity of the consciousness and intellection of man and
except for a general alteration of the being. When we shall
speak here of the question of the objective knowledge of
the real, we shall be able to see why man should be full of
wonder before this harmony in the creation: harmony
between the ever personal ontologic prism of human beings
and the truly objective knowledge of the real.

b) There has always been a concern about being well
informed in order to report facts truly. The philologic
return to remote antiquity shows that the sense of
responsibility regarding truth to describe and transmit was
not inferior to that of modern times. The ingenuousnesses,
the inevitable gaps of good faith and the tendentious
descriptions and explanations without a true sense of
responsibility regarding truth, were no more numerous or
grave in antiquity than those which can be ascertained

among men from the beginning of «history» until our day; that is the least one can say.

c) In the accounts of the development of facts or ideas there have always been, for reasons intrinsic to human nature, implicit or explicit considerations which can be called eschatological.

It is necessary to always remember these three truths in order to avoid false references to the past when one speaks of the discovery of a new dimension of man. The only basically new thing which has occurred within the data and determinations of knowledge is Revelation.

The Historic Consciousness

Das historische Bewusstsein

The general notion of «historic consciousness» in philosophy as well as theology — from all evidence and according to the witness of everyone — was formulated and tirelessly presented by the German philosopher Wilhelm Dilthey(114) throughout his long life. He defines thus, what he called «the historic consciousness»(115):

«The constitution of historic science is a German initiative. It had its center here in Berlin. And I had the inestimable luck of living and studying here during that period. And if I ask myself what its points of departure were, they were the great realities engendered by the historic evolution, the teleologic systems (Zweckzusammenhänge) of the civilization of nations, and finally, humanity itself — their development following an interior law: then the way in which they act in the form of organized forces and from which history is born in

---

(114) WILHELM DILTHEY (1833-1911) German philosopher, Professor of Philosophy at Berlin.

(115) The French translator translated the expression «das historische Bewusstsein» by «the feeling of history». But the word «Bewusstsein» particularly designates the «historic consciousness», and not simply «the feeling».

the midst of rivalries between States. Infinite consequences are the result of it. I would willingly
summarize them in calling them the historic consciousness».(116)

That expression certainly does not mark the true
beginning of the orientation of thought towards historicist
criteria, but signals the theorization and doctrinalization of
the reference, for everything and as regards every reality, to
the generic and multiform notion of history. And that, we
must repeat, is not an elaboration which has remained
within the restrained ambiance of the philosophical milieu
of an epoch; it is an orientation of thought which
penetrated, or rather was embraced by Protestant and
Catholic theologians, so as to impress more and more in the
thought and general literature of the Christian world, that
kind of new «rationalistic mystique»: the meaning of
history — historic consciousness.

Martin Heidegger considers Dilthey as the founder-
theoretician of the new «historic philosophy»:

«The analysis of the problem of history which we
have just carried through has arisen in the process of
appropriating the labors of Dilthey».(117)

---

(116)   WILHELM DILTHEY, Discours du 70ème anniversaire, in Le
        monde de l'esprit, éd. Aubier, Paris 1947, t. I, p. 13.

(117)   MARTIN HEIDEGGER, Being and Time, Oxford 1978,
        p. 449.

There are an incalculable number of manifestations which prove that this new scale of criteria has penetrated deeply within the Christian world. These manifestations can sometimes be divergent and even contradictory among themselves and can eventually lead towards diverse philosophical or theological orientations, but they constitute an identical indication and proof: the proof of that in-depth penetration in the thought and even in the consciousness of Christians and also in the Catholic Church. It is always useful to take some examples to illustrate this reality:

One can refer to the "Course in Dogmatics" in eleven volumes under the generic title of "Mysterium Salutis".[118] To this dogmatic Summa written each time by a certain number of theologians (eighteen for the first volume) and under the general direction of two priest professors of theology[119], a twelfth volume is added at the end, under the title of "Lexicon of Theologians of the 20th Century" under the direction of Piersandro Vanzan S. J. and Hans Jürgen Schultz. The book begins with the work of Wilhelm Dilthey in the introduction as well as in the body of the text.

Father Piersandro Vanzan begins the introduction of the large "Lexicon" thus:

«Wanting to give a frame to the one hundred and eleven portraits which form the gallery of this *Lexicon,*

---

(118)   *Mysterium salutis,* Queriniana, Brescia 1967-1978.
(119)   R. P. JOHANNES FEINER and DOM MAGNUS LÖHRER.

we shall begin by framing the theology of the 20th century in the typical cultural turning-point of our epoch: the appearance of the historic consciousness, which Gadamer([120]) considers as 'the most important of the revolutions which we have undergone after the advent of the modern epoch'. And by historic consciousness is meant on one hand, the new understanding (aprioristic-transcendental) that man has of himself as 'Being-in-history' from which his concrete being is no longer understood in a static way nor universally given...) and, on the other hand the new understanding or discovery that in this determined aspect of his specific constitution, regrouping world and time, man draws from 'the history of his being'».

«The whole work of Dilthey, by which our *Lexicon* properly begins in order to make this cultural turning-point clear, consists in the effort to construct parallel to the Kantian critique of pure reason, a critique of historical reason with a view to redimensioning the pretention of the Hegelian philosophic consciousness, of being an 'absolute knowledge' and to draw out, on the contrary, a limited but sure comprehension of the sciences of the spirit».([121])

---

(120) HANS-GEORG GADAMER, born in 1900, Professor of Philosophy, Jaspers' successor at the University of Heidelberg in 1949.

(121) *Lessico dei Teologi del secolo XX: Mysterium salutis,* vol. 12, supplement, Queriniana, Brescia 1978, introduction p. XIII.

What also constitutes one of these manifestations of evidence is the position and importance which are given in a "Lexicon" devoted to the "Theologians of the Twentieth Century" to Wilhelm Dilthey who was not a theologian. Besides Dilthey, it is a demonstrated fact that this "Lexicon" includes people who can in no way be considered theologians: the philosopher Martin Heidegger, the professors of philosophy Karl Jaspers and Hans-Georg Gadamer, the psychiatrist Karl-Gustav Jung, the German marxist philosopher Ernst Bloch, the philosopher and playwright Gabriel Marcel, the French poet Charles Péguy, the French novelist Georges Bernanos, the physicist Carl Friedrich von Weizsäcker, the worker-priest Henri Perrin, the engineer Friedrich Dessauer.

On the other hand, one cannot help but see as a very indicative sign the fact that neither Father Garrigou-Lagrange nor Cardinal Charles Journet are included in the list of the one hundred and eleven representatives of the large Lexicon of the theologians of the twentieth century.

It is necessary to clarify here that that last remark in no way concerns the persons as such, who were cited in the dictionary. That is completely extraneous to the intentions and criteria of these pages. We are solely concerned with intellectual and spiritual manifestations, manifestations which fundamentally have to do with the intellectual and spiritual life of Christianity and the Church.

The writings of Karl Rahner are another proof of the extent and penetration of the historicist criterion and sensibility in the environment of Catholic theology. Here is one consideration among so many others which at base preaches the absolute historicity in knowledge:

«We live in history and it is only in its progression that we possess the eternal truth of God who is our salvation. In this history it (the truth) is always the same, while having had and still having a history. This univocality always exists but never allows us to separate it from its historical forms, thus to be able, at least in our knowledge of the truth, to come out of the continual movement and historic flux, so as to alight on the firm bank of eternity. In history we possess what this truth presents of the eternal, but precisely we only possess it if we put our trust in its continual progression».(122)

The Protestant theologian Rudolf Bultmann (123) is, with different nuances, a witness to the same general meaning of the notion of history and the historicist vision of reality. Here for example is one of his numerous considerations:

«The global result of development was an increasingly insistent appearing of the historicity of man, in the sense that man depends on history, is delivered

---

(122) KARL   RANNER,   *Sulla   storicità   della   teologia: Nuovi Saggi III*, Ed. Paoline, Roma 1969, pp. 109-110.

(123) RUDOLF BULTMANN (1884-1976), Professor of Exegesis of the New Testament at Marburg.

to it; and his Weltanschauung,(124) his judgements, his religion are conditioned by the historic circumstances in which they successively find themselves. This perspective is the leitmotiv of historiography, of what is called historical positivism; but it found its systematic elaboration on the philosophical plan in the philosophy of history of Wilhelm Dilthey. Reflection on history becomes here the 'understanding psychology'.(125)

In the same text Bultmann, speaking of the ideas of Gerhard Krüger says furthermore:

«It is evident that Krüger(126) must set history and tradition against one another, if history is continual change, on the contrary tradition is the constant element. This opposition between history and tradition seems to me impossible».(127)

«The answer to the question about what the constant element of man is, must therefore be: his historicity. Do we find ourselves in complete rela-

---

(124)   Weltanschauung: Vision of the world.

(125)   RUDOLF BULTMANN, *Riflessioni sul tema: Storia e tradizione*, extract from "Weltbewohner und Weimaraner", Zürich 1961, published in *Credere e comprendere*, Queriniana, Brescia 1977, p. 939.

(126)   GERHARD KRÜGER, born in 1902, Professor of Philosophy at Heidelberg.

(127)   RUDOLF BULTMANN, *Storia e tradizione*, in *Credere e comprendere*, Brescia 1977, p. 941.

tivism? Indeed, the analysis of historicity effected by Heidegger can be considered as the radicalizing of Dilthey's relativism».([128])

And in order to illustrate how much this mentality which we have named historicist determines and colors all the philosophic and theological thought of the universal Christian milieu, we relate here two considerations of the Protestant professor of theology Jürgen Moltmann:([129])

«The characteristic experience that modern man has of history is based on the ascertainment of the possibilities, infinitely new and oppressive, which one does not succeed in dominating by the means transmitted through tradition. These are new possibilities of good and evil, of progress and of definitive catastrophe».([130])

«The historic sense, the interest in history and the necessity of understanding, always spring forth in moments of crisis and anxiety, when new possibilities heretofore unknown and unsuspected begin to appear on the horizon».([131])

---

(128) RUDOLF BULTMANN, *Storia e tradizione*, in *Credere e comprendere*, Brescia 1977, p. 943.

(129) JÜRGEN MOLTMANN, born in 1926, Professor of Theology at Tübingen.

(130) JÜRGEN MOLTMANN, *Teologia della speranza*, Queriniana, Brescia 1971, 3rd edition, p. 237.

(131) JÜRGEN MOLTMANN, *Teologia della speranza*, p. 239.

These few illustrations and considerations certainly do not give a complete picture of the ensemble of the historicist phenomenon nor do they offer an explanation which can constitute a stable criterion of research and knowledge. Nevertheless they illustrate how much that reference to the notion of history, regarding all things, has become universal; universal in the sense that it touches all the domains of the thought and emotional life of man.

And that would not have a great meaning for the actual life of men and for the course of that same History of men, if it had not produced and did not continually produce, in the most intimate depths of the human understanding and will, an uprooting of the conscious and semi-conscious perennial references which are irreplaceable, confirmed, purified and universalized by Revelation.

The assiduous and collective work of more than a generation would be necessary in order to make a simple «anthology» of the writings and acts in all realms and of one epoch only, concerning the phenomenon of this uprooting and substitution of criteria. By the word «epoch» we can at the same time understand several centuries on the one hand, and few decades on the other. But even if such an «anthology», such an accumulation of texts and accounts of acts which would express this new mentality, this new direction of the thought and the will, were possible, it would be a useless and vain work and trouble.

And it would be useless and vain for two reasons: first, because for the man who has not lost the fundamental and essential references confirmed by Revelation, a rapid, all-encompassing glance would suffice to be informed and to have a picture of the extent and importance of the phenomenon of the historicist alteration of the criteria; second, because one who henceforth would have an altered general outlook, the accumulation of texts illustrating that transformation of mentality and sensibility in the face of the reality of the world and the Revelation, would only be confirmed in his altered point of view, by the simple fact of the quantity of examples.

Nevertheless one of symptoms of this era — let us call it historicist — is a desperate effort to constitute this chimeric «anthology»; at times one realizes the impossibility of such an artificious source of learning, that is, one realizes the impossibility of such a fullness of learning. And as one is taken by the current and tossed about henceforth on the limitless ocean by the ever new waves of fleeting knowledge, one has the nostalgia for terra firma, but one is searching for it in the non-existent islands, instead of raising oneself towards the origin of every reference.

The impasse is realized and confessed, without however declaring bankruptcy. And that confession is an involuntary witness perhaps, but all the same a witness of the vain wandering through a problematic knowledge, often sophisticated and always relative, a wandering to which the uprooting of stable criteria leads, which alters first of all the true notion of History, and in that way clouds the intimate consciousness of the rapport of man's identity, of man's call, with his mission, a mission both temporal and eternal.

This last consideration may seem exaggerated to some. For it is difficult to realize such a deterioration of the criteria. That is why, in all the realms of thought, it is necessary to constantly refer to the witness and proofs which dissipate doubts and illuminate the consciousness, and especially of the young, who, moved by some more or less profound desire for truth, and who are by nature generous, often remain disconcerted and doubtful at the first contact with certain words and certain realities.

Now there are texts which clearly indicate the tragic character of this intellectual adventure. Here for example, is how Karl Rahner expresses himself regarding the part played henceforth by the quantity of learning in the question of the knowledge of the real:

«What else can man do in his situation characterized by a 'gnosologic concupiscence' (which does not allow the enormous mass of learning to be elaborated or synthesized) but withdraw towards this original center; a center of this kind must exist».(132)

According to Rahner, this «gnosologic concupiscence», concupiscence regarding knowledge, has been from the

---

(132) KARL RAHNER, *Motivazione della fede oggi* in *Teologia dall'esperienza dello spirito, Nuovi Saggi VI*, ed. Paoline, Roma 1978, pp. 26-27.

beginning or has consequently become (the author does not specify), a permanent characteristic of man's state, at least of his present state. And the fact of this intellectual dilection does not allow the synthesis of the sum of learning. It does not allow, therefore, still according to Rahner, knowledge, because knowledge would signify a synthesis of the sum of learning in all realms. This would be an elaboration of man on that enormous sum of learning in the different realms.

But if that were true, man would have to cease hoping for anything whatsoever. For knowledge can never be considered as the result of a domination of learning nor of an analytic elaboration on the basis of that same learning.

And Rahner says that man, faced with this impossibility, can only withdraw to an original center. And he adds that such a center must exist. But if such a center exists, why withdraw to it after a failure to dominate learning, basing oneself upon one's own strength, that is, far from this center? Why not base oneself always on this center? Why follow the «intellectual concupiscence» which according to all evidence is anything but the joy of the knowledge of the spirit? But what is significant is that Rahner then says:

«Today it is no longer possible to arrive at a perfect synthesis between all the truths of the faith, on the one hand, and the present day learning and mentality on the other. That is why in our world the theologian also, who has worked during his whole life in his science, has the right to say for example that he himself in so far as he is not an exegete, is not in a position to explain how Matthew 16:18 and the office of Peter which exists and is accepted with faith in the present day Catholic Church, can positively be reconciled. For that end, indeed, he would have to possess such a quantity of learning that one mind alone is no longer in a position to contain. What basic theology said in times past regarding this question is no longer sufficient to give an objective reply».(133)

In these lines the impairment of the references and permanent criteria is expressed once again. Why is «that» no longer possible, if that had been possible at least at one time? Is it a matter of making a synthesis of all the truths of the faith with the learning and mentality of a given time? Is that what the expression «truths of the faith» assumes? Would learning with its increase really be allergic to the truths of the faith? Would it therefore be necessary to have a superhuman mind capable of containing an innumerable quantity of various learnings in order to be an exegete, so as to be able to understand that Saint Peter must have a successor, and that the Church of Christ couldn't be the figure of any other reality than that of the Kingdom, and that all the trials of her terrestrial days, all the alterations or human betrayals in her midst didn't remove either her character or the need of a legislator and supreme pastor?

---

(133)   KARL RAHNER, *Motivazione della fede oggi*, p. 27

But we see clearly that for Karl Rahner the office of Peter accepted with faith in the Church of today can no longer be received nor explained, because of the impossibility of dominating the vast extent of learning in order to be able to synthesize it with the faith and the current mentality. And thus Karl Rahner, in spite of his perseverant analysis of a «dilettante» as he himself says, often arrives in front of the wall which that same «gnosologic concupiscence» raised. And that is why, among so many other similar manifestations he exclaims:

— «It must be continuously inculcated upon the Christian today as obvious, that man even independently from faith and theology, must bear the given fact of gnosologic concupiscence. How many things exist in our world which we no longer succeed in guiding into a positive synthesis!».([134])

— «I am speaking of the rapport between papacy and episcopate and I perceive that I should also be precisely a philosopher of law and a specialist in constitutional law, which, on the contrary I am not and cannot become.

— «Today I am only able to write in the manner of a dilettante.

— «Leaving out of account some essays on the history of the dogma of penitence, all the rest of what

---

(134)   KARL RAHNER, *Motivazione della fede oggi*, pp. 30-31.

I've written isn't theological science at all and is all the less philosophical (of specialization). It smacks too much of the dilettante. On the other hand, in the modern situation which I have described, it is well justified and so I do not feel any shame about it.

— «I do not think that by this judgement I am depreciating what I have written. I absolutely maintain that today, when we speak to men who want to know something existential(135), we can neither speak nor write in any other way».(136)

Here is the significant confession: one cannot speak to men if they want to learn something about their own existence, except with a dilettante's language, and that, because it is not possible «that one mind alone contain all the learning of men», according to the actual words of Rahner. We must return to this subject in connection with language, objectivity and subjectivity. But this vision according to which man's speech, because of the amount of

---

(135)   Heidegger himself has specified the difference between «existential analysis» *(existentiell)* and «existential analysis» *(existentiale).* We can sum it up approximately thus: «Existentiell» corresponds, according to Jaspers' thought, to the question «what is it to be a man?» and «Existentiale» concerns the being in general, beyond the precise human being. *Essere e tempo* p. 29.

(136)   KARL RAHNER, *Semplice chiarimento al riguardo della propria opera* in *Teologia dall'esperienza dello spirito, Nuovi Saggi VI,* ed. Paoline, Roma 1978, pp. 738-739.

specialized learnings, can have neither architecture nor universality nor direct reference to a truth which transcends these diverse learnings, is a vision of infinite sadness.

For man, the possibility of formulating problems and proposing questions as expressions of an aspect of reality or of all reality, is infinite. For the human mind there is no limit to the modulation of concepts on the basis of endless combinations of data, be they of experience, speculation, be they for personal and gratuitous elaborations. Likewise there is no limit to the composition of melodic developments and harmonic ensembles through the combination of the seven tones and five half-tones conventionally accepted as the basis of musical language.

This possibility of engendering problems and questions is delimited and conditioned only when there is a consciously perceived and irremovable finality or permanent criteria and references in man.

Therefore it would be absurd to believe that we should be able to spread out before us all the possible combinations, at least all the combinations effected by men up to our time, in order to be able at last to penetrate the mystery of music, to recognize the laws therein and then to formulate statements of certain knowledge.

It would be absurd first of all, because such a possession and display are impossible. And secondly — what is most important — because even if such information proved possible thanks to some extraordinary technique, it could in no way promote our true knowledge of the mystery of music and of the musical universe. This also holds true for the total information imaginable in all domains.

Nevertheless, in the history of thought, we have often had the manifestation of such a tendency, and at times even such a disposition of mind, as Karl Rahner's declaration manifests, regarding the necessity of seeing and writing things as a dilettante.(137) Certainly on this earth we

---

(137)   «No matter how much indignation is aroused and how many prejudices one clashes with, it must be said, because it is the truth: *to be more, is first to know more*. Stronger than all the defeats and all reasonings, we carry within ourselves the instinct that in order to be faithful to existence, we must know, know always more, and so seek, seek always more, we do not know exactly what, but Something which, surely, one day or another, for those who have probed the Real right to the end, will appear». (PIERRE TEILHARD DE CHARDIN, *L'Avenir de l'Homme*, Ed. du Seuil, Paris 1959, p. 31 and 32.

— «Nature has not marked any end to the perfectioning of the human faculties; the perfectibility of man is really indefinite; the progress of that perfectibility, henceforth independant of any power which would want to stop it, has no other limit than the duration of the globe upon which nature has thrown us. Doubtlessly, this progress can follow a more or less rapid march; but it will never be retrograde — Everything tells us that we are touching on the epoch of one of the greatest revolutions of the human species... The actual state of illumination guarantees us that it will be happy». (ANTOINE DE CONDORCET, *Esquisse d'un tableau historique des progrès de l'esprit humain,* cited by JACQUES CHEVALIER, *Histoire de la pensée,* vol. 3, p. 469. Antoine de Condorcet poisoned himself during the Terror to escape the scaffold).

cannot go forward and think without some information. The fact of existing carries with it the necessity of information in so far as the immediate need of physical existence is concerned and in so far as disinterested thought, as well as worship, prayer and adoration are concerned.

Certainly we must never speak and feel as Auguste Comte who boasted of having worked out his philosophic system «in an irrevocable manner», as he himself said, without having read the known authors.(138) But that does not diminish the gravity of the fact that a large number among the studious or active youth, whether it be in the religious domain or the political and social realm, allow themselves to be led astray and at times with complacency, by the mirage of a «total information» and by the cult of «research», in the maze of interminable information with no real clew of Ariadne.

---

(138) AUGUSTE COMTE (1798-1857). It is very revealing and instructive to read these lines of one who is considered as the founder of positivism. He states in the Preface of his *"Course"* *(56th lesson)* that he has never read Vico, nor Kant, nor Herder, nor Hegel, which, he adds «contributed much to the purity and the harmony of my social philosophy. But that philosophy being finally irrevocably constituted, I soon intend to learn, in my own way, the German language, in order to better appreciate the necessary relations of my new mental unity with the systematic efforts of the principal Germanic schools». Cited by J. CHEVALIER, *Histoire de la pensée,* éd. Flammarion, Paris 1966, vol. IV, p. 308, no. 1.

In all realms the principal thing is the basic criterion which determines what we have called the general point of view. «Total information» has been in every epoch and will always remain a mirage which allows one to move without stopping, towards an end which is constantly changing position and moving away, without therefore, an inner commitment towards an absolute, irrefutable and transcendent Truth. For pleasure can be found in such a movement towards an unreal end; the mirage is not at the horizon's end, but in man. It is the absence of lived fundamental criteria, which can create either the mirage of «total information» or a «complacent agnosticism» conscious or unconscious, admitted or hidden.

Man's facility with words allows him to contest such a statement. But it does not prevent the active and enthusiastic movement towards the mirage of «total information» as well as «complacent agnosticism» from bringing to birth at each instant new criteria, and this creates a limitless pluralism of both criteria and goals. In these cases all new learning, all new information, all speculation and intuition enter the «ego» as in a cask of the Danaides. For — it must be said, hard though it may appear — it is because of lack of fundamental love that the ego cannot allow a criterion and reference which are objective and eternal. And in this case, information and new criteria can be accumulated ad infinitum; the cask of the Danaides remains bottomless. The intrinsic cult of the ego does not allow a Knowledge, a direct communion with the eternal real.

What Jacobi([139]) called «speculative egoism»([140]), to define Kant, is realized in effect. It is not a question here of a simple witticism apropos of psychology; it isn't even a question of ascertaining an occasional psychological manifestation; it concerns the ontological refusal which the ego, in its «self-cult» puts up against the objective eternal truth.

That is why, in meditating upon the nature and origin of the theological movement, it is not necessary — from a certain point of view it is even useless and at times inauspicious — to want to follow all the «analytic investigations» which have been and are always being attempted, which claim to state precisely the nature and the definition of philosophy, theology and science, their relations and the evolution of those relations such as for example, were developed by the penetration of Aristotle in the School ([141]), so as to be able to ascertain that in the time of Dilthey, the event whose importance we have pointed out, had become concrete in a special way; and for already

---

(139) F. H. JACOBI (1743-1819), German philosopher, opposed to illuminism.

(140) *Dizionario dei Filosofi*, ed. Sansoni, Firenze 1976, p. 623, col. 2.

(141) The penetration of Aristotle in the West is always considered as a fact that cannot be described historically with precision in all its details. Certainly to establish exactly who had the idea of the first translations, when, how and why they were made, and to establish with exactitude the whole succession of the translations and the influences within Christianity of the 12th and 13th centuries is not possible. Although since

a long time — but particularly one hundred years before, in the time of Kant (142), Hamann (143), Herder (144) and Jacobi — it had begun to change the orientation of thought and to transform the criteria in the Christian world: this event, the fact of referring to world history not only in so far as the simple phenomenon of the endless succession of events and relations between beings, and not only in so far as a chain of successive, interdependent facts through which or even by means of which the known or unknown

---

the 6th century Boethius had begun a translation of Aristotle's works, it is much later, in the 12th century that the translations of the principal works took place, which diffused the naturalist empiricism particular to Aristotle in Christian milieus. And it is thus by Abelard, and then by Saint Thomas Aquinas, that Aristotle and the scientific thought were utilized in the gnosologic argumentation of the theology of the School. One thing is certain: independently of Saint Thomas' utilization of the foundations of Aristotle's logic, the Western Christian world was greatly shaken — little by little, but shaken — by the naturalism particular to Aristotle. Refer to FERNAND VAN STEENBERGHEN, *La Filosofia nel XIII secolo*, Vita e Pensiero, Milano 1972, pp. 58 ff., and to MAURICE DE WULF, *Histoire de la philosophie médiévale*, Institut de philosophie, Louvain 1924, vol. I, p. 66 ff; and p. 147 ff.

(142)   EMMANUEL KANT (1724-1804), Professor of Philosophy at Königsberg throughout his life.

(143)   J. G. HAMANN (1730-1788), German philosopher, opposed to illuminism. Friend of Herder.

(144)   G. G. HERDER (1744-1803), German philosopher, considered by many as the founder of the philosophy of history, criticized illuminism.

destinies of man are accomplished; but referring to History as to the only source for philosophic speculation and «metaphysics», to obtain Knowledge and Truth, referring to History, to historical development as if it constituted in itself the essence and last ends of man.

This way of confronting and judging the reality of events and life, which crystallizes in criteria which we can term «criteria of historicist eschatology», has had in the course of time, unsuspected and incalculable consequences: it impaired the true sense of the mystery of History in the consciousness of men, and consequently the true reality of history.

Man's relations, original and constitutional relations, in so far as he is a being and a person, with his origin, with his mission and with his finalty, have certainly been impaired by initial sin, but have been intrinsically restored in the consciousness of men by the Revelation of the Redeemer. These relations have been reversed in a more or less radical way in people's minds, by the preponderance of the «historic consciousness»: the individual was led to look for his origin and his accomplishment, not only through and by means of the events which constitute history, but with a view to history and for history, «in view» of a future not extra-historic nor even intra-historic, but purely and totally historic.

Now, confronted with this image of our times, confronted with the writings and all the oral teachings which are diffused in the world in the name of theology, and particularly among young students, many often ask themselves this question: what are the cause and the fundamental laws of such a development of things from the time when Christ Jesus proclaimed that: «he who loses his life gains eternal life», since the time Saint Paul said in the name of Christ: «our city is in heaven», until the «historic consciousness» of Dilthey and the philosophical view of the historic consciousness of Gadamer, and the fundamental historicity of theological anthropology of Rahner [145]; and until the theology «always in situation» of Schille-beeckx [146] or the theology «from below» of Küng? [147]

---

[145] «A philosophy of today and thus also *theology* cannot and must not allow itself to remain behind in so far as the *anthropologico-transcendental revolution brought about by modern philosophy* since Descartes, Kant, through German idealism (included therein the opposing currents) right up to phenomenology, to existentialist philosophy and to the fundamental ontology of today. (KARL RAHNER, *Teologia e antropologia*, in *Nuovi Saggi III*, Ed. Paoline, Roma 1969, p. 61).

[146] EDWARD SCHILLEBEECKX, O.P., born in 1914, Master in Theology, Professor of Dogmatic Theology at the University of Nimegue, expert at Vatican Council II, director of the dogmatic section of the international review "Concilium", which he founded with Karl Rahner in 1963.

— «We have never had an expression 'totally' uniform and meta-historic of the faith. We have never had an expression which was not historic. Faith must always be rethought in modern circumstances...» (EDWARD SCHILLEBEECKX, in *La fede nel pluralismo della cultura*, Cittadella, Assisi 1979, p. 254.

In general all the philosophical theories and all the theological doctrines and historiography itself, in principle prepare a kind of answer. Because they claim to want to grasp, or to have grasped the fundamental causes and laws of the real, hence the basic laws regarding history, the evolution of the world, man's mission and his final ends.

Any doctrine and any system implicitly or explicitly involve a judgement on all that has happened up to their time. Since remote antiquity, through all the stages of the development of thought, there is always the presentation, by the thinker, the philosopher or the «theologian», of a grasp of the laws and norms of the real, as much with regard to the essences of beings as to existences, as much with regard to immutability as to movement.

Now this grasp of the laws and norms, real or illusory, implicitly involves an explanation (a proposal of an explanation) of the process of events and ideas which constitute

---

— «This contact in faith with the reality of salvation — God, Christ — is always 'situated' differently, according to the earthly circumstances. This is a central assertion in all of Schillebeeckx' theology, in order to justify his project of reinterpretation of the faith». (PAUL BOURGY in *Bilancio della Teologia del XX secolo*, Città Nuova; Roma 1972, vol. 4, p. 259.

(147)   «A future christology must examine the fundamental objections, which are only mentioned here — without dogmatic prejudice —. In short: why wouldn't a christology be possible, not speculatively or dogmatically evolved from the top, but historically from the bottom? » (HANS KÜNG, *Incarnazione di Dio*, Queriniana, Brescia 1972, pp. 560-561).

at least the exterior aspect of history. That is why it can be said that all the philosophical systems and the theological doctrines contain a principle regarding the evolution of things of the world, hence of history, and consequently, a principle by which to answer the question of how, from the word of Christ and Saint Paul, we have, in the Christian world, arrived at ideas and concepts, feelings and «views of things» which have given rise in the so-called modern times, to historicist concepts, and more particularly to the *philosophy of history.*

It is not therefore by «constructing» a sort of history of the «philosophy of history» that we could have an answer, an image corresponding to profound reality. And it is thus in principle and according to all human experience throughout the centuries. The aim and the intention are different here and they are simple and precise: to make evident, with as much patience as is necessary, certain data which are always present in the development of the doctrines and facts in life, and which can constitute a sort of constant in the succession of cities and systems. It has to do with these data of which the resultant has oriented and orients the thought and consciousness towards concepts and historicist conceptions of reality.

For it is within man's possibilities to see more or less clearly how great was and still is today, the influence of these intellectual and psychological data of this historicist tendency, in the formation and orientation of the ensemble of present day theological currents in Christianity in general and also in the Catholic Church.

And all labor done in order to grasp that influence would have no value if it were only a manifestation of culture, one more piece of baggage in the memory of man. For even the perception and penetration of the reality richest in arguments, illustrations and nuances, will in any case remain imperfect and without real value for man if they are not illuminated and interpreted through a reference, a permanent finality not conditioned by facts or by labor. And so it is towards this aim and in this light that perception and comprehension of the data of the historicist movement in general have an importance, so that man can emerge from that immensity of works, movements and tendencies of the centuries, and receive the light which harmonizes and explains the facts and doctrines and dissipates every useless thing: that is, obtain the true vision of history.

In the space of the 366 years which have passed from Luther's death (1546) (148) to Dilthey's death (1912), the world and more particularly the Christian world has known great upheavals of every kind, intellectual, spiritual and social. And during this time, numerous currents and tendencies manifested themselves which have deeply influenced the intellectual and spiritual life, consequently the doctrinal as well as the moral life in the Church and in the world.

---

(148)   MARTIN LUTHER (1483-1546) had a very great influence on German philosophy and he facilitated the sliding towards historicism in the Christian milieu.

If someone, a free spirit, free of all the misery of social ambition, of all intellectual vanity, free because he loves truth above all things, wishes to form an idea which corresponds more or less to the reality of this period, he will soon enough perceive that he is before an inextricable mass of concepts, classifications, designations, currents, ideas and persons. And he will remain stupefied before that immense energy of which a large part at least, has not succeeded in transmitting certitude, peace and joy of the love of truth, in the heart and mind of societies and the majority of men in Christianity in general.

That man, in so far as philosophy and theology are concerned, will have to labor a great deal in order to find, within the same theory or among several theories, some internal consequence in the utilization of the terms and classifications, of the trends and periods, regarding the thought, the action, and regarding the origin and final ends of history and life.

These words can be considered by someone as exaggerated or even clearly unjust, as not expressing objective reality. But they are neither exaggerated nor unjust, because as has already been said and will be seen later on, we are living even today in a blur of equivocal and contradictory terms and meanings.

Let's imagine a young man, baptized, sincere and of good faith, who wishes to study the theological and philosophical movement after Luther, in the thought of certain authors who are generally considered as «milestones» for the development of thought regarding history, philosophy and theology. Who could guarantee him the true understanding of the thought of those authors? Often, moreover, different authors or commentators endeavor, almost by prestidigitation, to present certain philosophical or theological systems or considerations with doctrinal aspects which nothing can justify, aspects which are not at all consequent with the foundations of the systems and considerations. These are efforts, one could call «deonto-logical», that is, efforts to hide lacks or errors by social conventions — interested or not — efforts therefore which have nothing to do with love of truth, but which thoroughly confuse the field of vision of young people and all people who are sincerely seeking to know the truth.

Hence it is very difficult, if not impossible for this young man to be able by his own strength, and without a reference which in his understanding and his sensibility, transcends all these commentaries, to make a breach in this vast pluralistic accumulation.

Milestones

For many, one of these «milestones» of the orientation of thought regarding history, philosophy and finally even theology, is the work and thought of Giambattista Vico.([149]) It seems that the expression «philosophy of history» is owed to Voltaire. But it is Vico who presented it to the world of philosophic and historic studies, with an ensemble of principles, ideas and considerations, as a «new science».

It is undeniable that the orientation of Vico's thought has with time exerted a very great, very varied and at the same time unilateral influence in all milieus. On the other hand, it is also undeniable according to the admission of everyone, his apologists as well as his critics, that his accounts are generally obscure or confused, and more particularly on crucial points of the development of the arguments. All of Vico's commentators, his critics or apologists, differ more or less as regards the interpretation of this obscure or confused character of his writings. They also differ as regards the real implication and meaning of certain formulae which can be called «key formulae» of Vico's conception, such as the formula: «ideal eternal history».

---

(149)   GIAMBATTISTA VICO (1668-1744), Italian philosopher considered as the precursor of the «Philosophy of History».

If we must go into the matter here, to a slight extent at least, of this obscurity of Vico's writings, it is certainly neither to judge the style nor the person. Only God knows what is really at bottom in souls. We must go into it because the contrasts themselves between the different interpretations allow us already to grasp the origin, nature and motive of this obscurity, of this intrinsic difficulty. And the grasp of this obscurity and of its origin directly concerns the argument of historicism, such as it is dealt with here, in so far as it is an important and significant and determinant factor in the development of philosophical and theological trends.

Some attribute this obscurity or confusion of Vico's, who was a Catholic, to a continual effort to protect himself against possible reactions of the Church, because of his philosophic and scientific orientation which was opposed to fundamental points of Catholic teaching and faith. Here is how Fausto Nicolini, one of the most sagacious specialists on Vico's work, explains the obscurities:

«...These hypotheses led directly to the negation of certain basic principles of the Catholic religion: negation which, in the country and at the time Vico was writing, it would not have been possible to arrive at openly without his exposing himself to all kinds of dangers. Whence the necessity of going beyond this dangerous obstacle, by a whole series of subtle expedients − thus it is explained why he set about intercalating continual professions of Catholic faith in his writings, particularly in the passages in which a clearly heterodox proposition was presented as an irrefutable proof of the truth of the Catholic religion. And what is most important is the fact that he forced himself to christianize as much as he could, that which gave forth a too anti-Christian sound, particularly in the doctrines of the Neapolitan «atheists».(150)

Certain others have claimed that this obscurity is due to the fact that he speaks of two histories in the course of development, an ordinary history of each nation or of several nations and an «ideal eternal history». And thus, according to them, the guiding thread in this «new science» becomes obscure and confused and that, at essential moments.

> «In Vico the two meanings are not always distinct nor always clearly recognized; and that is one of the reasons that harm the clarity of Vico's masterpiece so often accused of being obscure because of that». (151)

These interpretations have been sustained by several, with different important nuances. Benedetto Croce, the Neapolitan philosopher, one of the most fervent apologists and admirers of Vico and of the influence of his thought, after much study and much praise, admits that he is obliged to recognize among many other significant things, Nicolini's interpretation:

---

(150)   FAUSTO NICOLINI, Introduction to: GIAMBATTISTA VICO, *La Scienza Nuova,* Laterza, Bari 1967, p. XXI.

(151)   F. AMERIO in *Dizionario dei filosofi,* Sansoni, Firenze 1976, p. 1229, col. 2.

«The only ones who in the 18th century truly penetrated Vico's basic tendency, and who without wanting to, recognized his originality and greatness, were his Catholic adversaries who were then numerous: Romano, Lami, Rogadeo and especially Finetti. They saw that Vico, in spite of his firm intentions of religious orthodoxy, upheld an idea of Providence which was completely different from that of Christian theology; that he continually mentioned God in words but did not let Him intervene in effect as personal God in history». [152]

From all the interpretations one thing stands out unquestionably, that the exposé of the "New Science" entails intrinsic difficulties. On one hand these difficulties arise from the effort to make an impossible correspondence and conciliation: the correspondence or conciliation of a vocabulary now and then of eternity, with a vocabulary of desires and criteria enclosed in time; the desire to present fidelity to the aspiration of eternal liberation, with the desire of an autonomous science of the development of human events, infinitely prolonged in earthly time.

On the other hand, in spite of all the obscurities or incoherences easily evident in Vico's work, certain capital, fundamental and essential points of his general vision and reasonings are too clear to be able to take refuge in certain

---

[152]   BENEDETTO CROCE, *La filosofia di Giambattista Vico*, Laterza, 1973, p. 286.

obscurities, in order to be able by means of personal affinity or by some deontology, to remain in an uncertainty full of implications. For under the pretext of uncertainty, one avoids embracing fully or refuting clearly, that is clearly committing oneself before a difficult question. And as regards Vico, there have been and there still are several manifestations of such a deontologic judgement. Sometimes these manifestations are such that they offend both the author who is judged and the reader, common sense and all sense of inner sacred aesthetics. (153)

* * *

---

(153)   "La Scienza nuova", involved but imposing work by a man whom sickness, doubt which came from reading Lucretius, anguish and his natural pride kept apart from the schools — astonishing work which surprises, disconcerts but holds the attention by its genial disorder, by an incommensurate profundity accompanied by a lack of penetration, by that sort of incompletion and obscurity particular to the creator who is incapable of mastering and expressing ideas.» (JACQUES CHEVALIER, *Histoire de la pensée,* Flammarion, Paris 1961, t. III, p. 473).

— «Science is the creation of humanity registered again by humanity — One did not accept the golden twig that he (Vico) bore. Thus we can still hear in the "Scienza nuova" the cries of an indignant soul. Passion tries to raise the phrases too charged with thought to easily take their flight. — Vico, obstinate, repeats himself; impatient he goes too quickly, exposing the results when he is only at the first principles; he is intoxicated with the new, the audacious, the paradoxical, the true». (PAUL HAZARD, *La Crise de la conscience européenne,* Fayard, Paris 1961, pp. 387-388).

Vico expressed axioms which concern the question of knowledge and the objective reality of the world. These axioms are continually contradicted by other equally axiomatic assertions. This is attested in an explicit manner by even his most fervent defenders. The propositions are not only enriched by an extension always embracing more ground, with nuances which would remove the rigidity and habitually summary and perhaps too condensed character of the propositions. It is a question of proposition-axioms which cancel each other several times throughout the exposés, with no conciliation possible. And Vico's apologists ascertain that irreductibility and they are often led, sometimes in a pathetic manner, although disconcerting, to draw conclusions which are not justified.

Here is one of the key axioms of Vico's doctrine:

«In the midst of such a night of thick darkness, which envelops the first antiquity which is so distant from us, appears that eternal light without decline, of that truth which absolutely cannot be challenged: this civil world has certainly been made by men; therefore one can, because one must, rediscover the principles in the modifications of our human mind». (154)

It is clear that for Vico, man can find the principles from which history springs, because it is he who made it; and these principles can be found in the «modifications of the human mind». According to Vico, man cannot know

---

(154)   GIAMBATTISTA VICO, *La Scienza nuova*, no. 331.

nature. Only God can, because it is He who made it, whereas from history men can obtain knowledge, because it is they who made it:

> «To every man who reflects, it must cause aston-ishment, that all the philosophers endeavored seriously to obtain knowledge of the natural world of which only God — because it is He who made it — has knowledge; and one is astonished that the philosophers neglected to meditate upon this world of nations, or in other words, civil world, of which men, because it was they who made it, could obtain knowledge». (155)

The expression of this idea alone should reveal to all, the slipping of the thought, the will, the ensemble of the being, towards a gnosology without real or experimental or metaphysical content. But that is not the case.

And then following that, another axiom according to which the principles of all knowledge must be sought in things on which all men agree:

> «Now since this world of nations was made by men, let us see on which points all men unceasingly agreed and still do agree on, because these points can give us the universal and eternal principles as they must be in every science; upon these principles all the sciences have been built and are preserved in the nations». (156)

---

(155)   GIAMBATTISTA VICO, *La Scienza nuova*, no. 331.
(156)   GIAMBATTISTA VICO, *La Scienza nuova*, no. 332.

Therefore, according to Vico's words, it is in the agreement of all men on certain points that the universal principles of all science can be found. It is the accord of all men which determines the fundamental intrinsic reality of all science (!). Only a boundless deontology could allow such meanings to get by in peace and silence or only in silence in the philosophic and scientific world.

Vico has criticized Descartes certainly, and not only refuted his lack of reference to history, but in general his mechanistic rationalism. Yet that does not prevent him from seeing and judging, according to many of his apologists and critics, with the view of a rationalist and an idealist. Benedetto Croce characterizes him as the last great Italian idealist philosopher and as a rationalist, idealist philosopher. (157)

Vico, carried away by his desire to find the justification of all the reality in the movement of history, and by his desire to construct a scientific edifice on the basis of the observation of the phenomena of history in their collective and massive aspect, has rationalized, in a strangely arbitrary manner, all the elements in the name of which he criticized Descartes and all the philosophers; that is, in the name of all his references to poetry, imagination and everything

---

(157)   BENEDETTO CROCE, *La filosofia di Giambattista Vico*, p. 290.
         — BREHIER, *Histoire de la Philosophie*, Paris 1942, vol. II, p. 367.

which entails mystery, legendary reality and poetry, throughout the course of civilization right back to the highest antiquity of humanity.

Vico states that one can and one must find again the principles of the civil world in the modifications of our mind. What can this concept or principle mean? Can we proceed in simply saying: «it is obscure»? Certainly not, because first of all it is not so obscure. What is the real tenor and value of his principle thus stated:

«Verum ipsum factum» (158)

For Vico, only what man does is real. The notion of knowledge is identified with the notion of doing. And the young man of whom there was a question earlier, who was seeking to know the development of thought, can ask himself with melancholy: how can I have access to what my ancestors did, since it is not I who did it? How can this plural be understood: men have done, and consequently understand what I have not done? Since what I have done is minimal in history, what can I therefore know of all the history of humanity? How can I claim that I have participated in the construction of the Pyramids or that I took part in the battle of Marathon or that I wrote the "Dialogues" of Plato, in order to dare to claim that I have obtained some knowledge of these epochs and these civilizations?

---

(158) GIUSEPPE FLORES D'ARCAIS, Vico's *La Pedagogia*, La Scuola, Brescia 1962, Introduction p. XV.

These questions are not narrow sophisms. On the contrary, as fundamental a principle as this, cannot be pronounced regarding the knowledge of man, and afterwards want to cover its consequences with smoke, the smoke of words which contradict one another and contradict the axiom. For sometimes because of sentimental bonds or by indifference or by natural generosity, but lacking responsibility, or in order to justify an option taken without much reflection, one has the tendency to veil the intellectual and moral consequences of the stated axioms.

It is not by the nuances that one wishes to attribute to the words «science» and «consciousness» and to their rapport, that one can tone down the inevitable consequences of the principle stated by Vico: «Verum ipsum factum»: the True is what one does. In claiming that it is by an absolute reference to God that man can know little by little, or as Vico says, have «consciousness», one can neither cover nor minimize the basis of this principle according to which the condition for knowing something is to do it. And as God knows all things and made all things (it is insane to want to specify that God knows all things because He created all things), man cannot know, cannot have a real and perfect knowledge unless he is the independent creator of a thing.

Vico's fervent commentator and apologist, Giuseppe Flores d'Arcais, recognizes that man cannot arrive at a true scientific synthesis. According to him, man thinks in a limited manner, he describes, but always partially.

And Flores d'Arcais honestly draws the necessary conclusion:

«Nevertheless by means of one of these extensions which are not lacking in Vico's thought, the philosopher (Vico) applies to man the same criteria as to God: man also will be able to have knowledge of that of which he himself is the constructor. And in effect he is constructor: of mathematics, because it is he, man, who creates the point and the unit, and with the point, magnitude and with the unit, number — 'Mathematica demonstramus quia verum facimus' — How would it be possible, indeed, for our mind to recognize the absolute certitude of knowing if not because what is valid for the mind is this same principle of 'verum ipsum factum' which is valid for God? » [159]

Nevertheless, the simple man, deeply loving the truth, beyond all sentimental or interested deontology, can ask himself: How could man «construct» mathematics without having some knowledge and without that knowledge being due to something completely other than the fact of having «constructed» it? How can we refer to Plato to justify the «verum ipsum factum», when for Plato the very first movement is knowledge? How can it be accepted afterwards that man can have the science of history because he made it, and state at the same time that God is the creator

---

(159)   GIAMBATTISTA VICO, *La Pedagogia,* a cura di Giuseppe Flores d'Arcais, p. XVIII.

of all things and all reality? And how is it possible to make the other proposition of Vico himself agree:

> «In this fable the philosophers brought in their most sublime metaphysical meditations: the eternal idea in God is engendered by God himself, from whence created ideas are produced in us by God». [160]

Apart from any other observation that could be made apropos of all these diverse propositions, one truth is evident: first, a will to divinize man in his knowledge and his doing, outside of all reference to a notion of redemption; secondly, an inter-annulment of the principles. on one hand, «verum ipsum factum» and on the other hand, «created ideas are produced in man by God». This apologist, preoccupied by his intellectual and spiritual probity, is trying at all cost to emphasize Vico's reference to Plato, with some far-fetched applications, in order to retain certain principles regarding both man's knowledge and historic value, particularly for pedagogy.[161] Yet throughout his exposés, he feels himself obliged to emphasize certain incoherences:

> «This uncertainty between ideal moments and historic moments makes even the concept of human nature appear confused, which should be explained in its ideal moments, whereas it is often characterized only through the temporal moments of history.

---

(160)   GIAMBATTISTA VICO, *La Pedagogia*, p. XIX.

(161)   Cf. *Dizionario dei filosofi*, Sansoni, Firenze 1976, p. 396, col. 2.

«But this confusion between the ideal moments and the temporal moments, which is moreover the impossibility of establishing a perfect concordance between philosophy and history, is a constitutive flaw of Vico's mentality, and it derives from the fact that he wanted to apply to man in an absolute sense this same criterion of 'verum ipsum factum' which has its full meaning only for the Divinity. That is the deepseated defect of structure of the "New Science"». (162)

If the intelligentsia during these 250 years from Vico until our day had faced this «defect» with another sensibility with respect to the truth and with respect to Revelation, with less humanistic and naturalistic intoxication — which displaced the center of gravity of Christian hope —, Vico's inner intellectual and moral drama would not have become a fundamental doctrinal reference of historicism, because the notion of history would not be impaired, while being deepened each day by true hope in a true eternal liberation of man.

Now this «verum ipsum factum» is only an arbitrary slogan with neither experimental nor metaphysical basis. But it makes one think of an antithesis to the lofty witness of Saint John. That is, no longer «in the beginning was the Word», but «in the beginning was the deed»:

«'Tis writ, "In the beginning was *the Word*":
I pause, to wonder what is here inferred.

---

(162)   GIAMBATTISTA VICO, *La Pedagogia*, pp. XXII-XXIII.

The Word I cannot set supremely high:
A new translation I will try.
I read, if by the spirit I am taught,
This sense: "In the beginning was *the Thought*".
This opening I need to weigh again,
Or sense may suffer from a hasty pen.
Does Thought create, and work, and rule the hour?
'Twere best: "In the beginning was *the Power*".
Yet, while the pen is urged with willing fingers,
A sense of doubt and hesitancy lingers,
The spirit comes to guide me in my need,
I write, "In the beginning was *the Deed*"»! (163)

Another of Vico's principle-axioms is the one of «the ideal, eternal history». It is in this expression that the word «eternal», as we have said, is devoid of its inner Christian meaning. What can this «ideal history» be, which is at the same time «eternal»? According to what comes forth from the ensemble of clear, half-clear or contradictory propositions of the "New Science", it can only be:

— either the perpetual turning back on the same scheme of curves of the developments of peoples, perpetual endless developments and turnings back without any imaginable conclusion;

---

(163)   GOETHE, *Faust* I, vv. 1224, 1237, English edition, Penguin
Books, 1978, part one, p. 71.

– or a great city, a great civilization, towards which peoples advance, or should be advancing, through their advances and returns, a city which would be henceforth liberatory, but without return, a far-off city, losing itself in the depths of time to come, and which would be the inner secret of history;

– or a «joyance» (?) before this endless movement, before these flowings and turnings back of nations, by superior extra-historical minds; joyance before a spectacle of which the peoples, the men who are born and who die, would be the actors;

– or any other more complicated combination which could be imagined, in the interior of the massive movements of peoples in time.

What is essential that is brought out in the "New Science", is that man only finds justification for his existence in the extension of the flowings and turnings back of nations, according to one of the possible meanings we have just imagined. Any other commentary which would try to combine fragments of contradictory propositions scattered in the "New Science" in order to give to that expression of «ideal eternal history», a halo of justification according to the message of Christ, would be a mystification. For the notion of eternity in the "New Science" does not pierce the interminable house-top of history nor its always fleeting horizon:

«This Science describes an ideal eternal history, upon which all the histories of all the nations in their births, progress, conditions, decadence and ends, flow in time». (164)

The word «eternal» therefore takes on an immutable, implacable meaning. There is no little window towards the hope of a personal salvation of man, worked out in the midst of history and realized outside of the history of nations to come in time. In the "New Science", there is no personal salvation; there is no place for Christ incarnated and resurrected.

Nicola Abbagnano, in his "History of Philosophy", comments thus on the expression «ideal eternal history»:

«Ideal eternal history is the *structure* which sustains temporal history, the norm which permits that temporal history to be judged. In this sense, it is the *must be* of history in time, but it is a must be which does not annul the problematicity of that temporal history, which may also not correspond to eternal history and not rejoin the end that eternal history indicates». (165)

And Benedetto Croce, whom no one could class among the defenders of Christianity, recognized that in the history of humanity, according to the Christian doctrine, there has been a primitive revelation that Vico's «ideal history» ignores and rejects:

---

(164) GIAMBATTISTA VICO, *La Scienza nuova*, no. 349.
(165) NICOLA ABBAGNANO, *Storia della filosofia*, Utet, Torino 1969, vol. II, p. 316.

«Vico detached profane history from sacred history by such a sharp cut, that he arrived at an absolutely natural and human doctrine of the origins of civilization (thanks to the brutish state) and of the origins of religion (thanks to fear, to modesty([166]) and to the universal fantastic), there where the traditional Catholic doctrine admitted of a certain communication between sacred history and profane history, and in pagan religion and civilization where it recognized the leaven operating from a certain even vague knowledge of the primitive revealed truth». ([167])

That this is so, that the «ideal history» is an ideal «City» of an indeterminate future, an ideal reference but inaccessible, or accessible in an unknown time, the movingly faithful and at the same time honest Giuseppe Flores d'Arcais saw and attests:

«The ideal eternal history must be thus brought back to Plato's republic». ([168])

Vico, to conclude the "New Science", refers to Plato, and particularly to Plato's "Republic". He refers to it as if

---

(166)   From whatever point of view one wishes to understand or interpret Vico's assertions on the fear of thunder of the «primitive men» (dei bestioni) and on the sequestering of women in the grottos, one absolutely cannot speak of modesty. It suffices to refer to «La Scienza nuova», no. 1098 and no. 1099.

(167)   BENEDETTO CROCE, La filosofia di Giambattista Vico, p. 286.

(168)   GIAMBATTISTA VICO, La Pedagogia, p. LI.

that "Republic" were the ideal which in advance, as an immanent force, were pushing the human race towards that same republic. That is why he commences the last chapter of the "New Science", the conclusion of the work, thus:

«Let us therefore conclude this work with Plato, which makes a fourth kind of republic, in which good and honest men would be the supreme lords; it would be the true natural aristocracy. It is to that republic, such as Plato understood it, that providence has led the nations from their beginning». (169)

That «republic» of Plato's is therefore the ideal city of «ideal eternal history», towards which all the nations march, guided by a providence. This ideal city may be accessible or inaccessible, but it is the ideal goal of providence.

And Vico speaks of providence. But who exercises that providence? From whom does it emanate? He calls it «divine». But it is men who have made history, for it is because of this that they can know it. How can man know and speak with such assurance of a providence which he has not created, seeing that history is a creation of man, volontary and deliberate because «by choice»? The role that Vico gives to man in the creation of history is such that it is impossible to realize the harmony of the evangelic doctrine, that is the harmony between holy divine Providence, free will and predestination. Everyone has taken

(169) GIAMBATTISTA VICO, *La Scienza nuova*, no. 1097.

great pains to present «decently» the contradiction of certain terms such as that of providence in Vico' vocabulary.

It is superfluous, useless and above all overwhelming to put each of the very numerous propositions in front of its contradictory pendant. In any case, it is not the objective of these pages. Enough has been said so that every man of good faith can grasp not only the fact of that perpetual breaking away of every proposition towards others, but also the fundamental motive of such a whirlwind which has followed close behind the philosophy and theology of the last centuries.

In order to comprehend this central motive of Vico's continual contradiction, the imaginary narrative should suffice which wants to explain in «rational»(?) form, the beginning of humanity, the succession of civilizations, the passage from the bestial state to the state of imagination and then of reason; and more than everything else should suffice the crazy and trivial account regarding the institution of monogamous marriage in caves and the formation of social classes and the narrative regarding the growth of human beings in filth, to explain the formation of giants. (170)

One thing is certain; there is no place in Vico's historic vision, for a predisposition on the part of God both personal and creator within human histories, with the

---

(170)   GIAMBATTISTA VICO, *La Scienza nuova*, no. 1098.

mission of conserving the free access to the love of God and the eternal salvation of man considered in his separate personality and at the same time united to all the others.

That is why Emile Bréhier writes in his "History of Philosophy" that Vico admits a providence of God and he adds:

«He admits it, but for this same reason he deliberately leaves it (providence) out of his research, because he wants to determine the natural laws of history, which are independent of all miraculous intervention (thus depriving himself of all the documents which the Bible could give him)». (171)

All notion of justice is intra-historic, that is it manifests itself by the highs and lows of nations.(172) Nevertheless men, in undergoing catastrophes, illnesses and death, do not «undergo» history, because it is they who deliberately make it. Vico speaks thus:

«What made all this, was pure thought, because it is men who did it with intelligence; that was not fate,

---

(171) EMILE BREHIER, *Histoire de la Philosophie*, P.U.F., Paris 1942, vol. II, p. 367.

(172) Very significant is the fact that it is impossible to establish some criterion of evaluation regarding the history of nations; be it apropos of the rapport of primitive men, the «bestioni» with superior forces or rather the fear of superior forces, be it apropos of the formation and the evolution of the word and languages, the sense of the high and the low is polyvalent and arbitrary.

because men did it by choice; not by chance, because with perpetuity; always doing thus, they end up in the same things».(173)

In spite of the great multitude of propositions and contradictions of the "New Science", the conclusion is simple and can be fully expressed in few words:

— The will to find in the flux of history immutable natural laws which rule the succession of facts and cities.

— The will and the profound, sagacious desire to present humanity as autonomous in perpetual movement, outside of all notion of progress; and on the basis of a principle according to which all the «moments», the rational moments as well as the fanciful moments, are equal and according to which human action, even that which is unconscious, cannot entail elements of error and evil. (174)

— The will to present a general reference, however vague, far-off and contradictory it may be, to Christianity; and at the same time to detach man's gaze from all reference other than the endless becoming of nations, which for him is History.

This triple will explains the obscurity, confusion and contradiction of Vico's work, attested to in one way or another, by his critics and apologists. If Vico is not

---

(173) GIAMBATTISTA VICO, *La Scienza nuova*, no. 1108.
(174) GIAMBATTISTA VICO, *La Pedagogia*, p. XXIX.

considered by all historians of philosophy as a founder of a school or trend, that doesn't hinder him from being a «milestone»; milestone of the road towards historicist thought and sensibility in philosophy and theology.

It has been said that Vico detached profane history from sacred history.(175) The truth is that in spite of these two histories, the ordinary history of nations and the «ideal eternal history», at bottom he unified in one naturalistic vision, every notion and meaning of history. Vico's reference to «poetry», to the fanciful and to the imagination does not go beyond the epic image, massively heroic; no real vibration of the intimate poetry of man, of intimate nostalgia of the being preserving in him the imprints of his sacred origin, because created by God; no reading which is truly poetic and instructive about nature. No hope of each human person, hope of direct union with his Creator.

In Vico, ordinary history, in relation to «ideal eternal history» can be compared to the movement of the earth around the sun. There is no qualitative difference between the two realities: movement on one side and movement on the other. This will and vision of Vico's have closed the true outlet towards the essential and unique reference of eternity for every being in his relationship with his Creator, and have opened the way of the sliding towards the

---

(175) Cf. HANS URS VON BALTHASAR, *Il tutto nel framento — Per una teologia della Storia,* Jaca book, Milano 1972, p. 98.

simultaneously polymorphous and uniform historicism and massification which have deeply impaired the true vision and the true profound meaning of History.

And thus it is, that 150 years later, we see Dilthey, the founder of modern historicism, adopt Vico's arguments:

«The first condition for the possibility of a science of history lies in the fact that I myself am an historic being and that he who studies history and does research on history is also the one who makes history». (176)

And so it is that we see also in our time theologians of reknown, such as Karl Rahner, for example, adopt a vision of history which leads to the naturalization of grace and to the absorption of each man in the massive entity of historic society, which were the basis of Vico's philosophy of history:

— «With the advance of the history of grace, the world becomes ever more independent, mature, profane and must think of self-realization. That growing historic 'mundanity' of the world — in spite of the blame-worthy ambiguities and deformations which are always present — considering it carefully, is not a misfortune which obstinately opposes grace and the Church, but is on the contrary the way that grace is realized little by

---

(176)   Cited by PIERSANDRO VANZAN, in *Lessico dei Teologi del Secolo XX*, p. XIII.

little in the creation: as liberation and legitimation of the world in its specificity». (177)

   — «It is necessary to elaborate the principles of a 'political theology', that is, to develop theology as content in general and ecclesiology in particular in taking into account their socio-political importance which is creative of history. Only thus will the individualist reduction of revelation to the salvation of every man, be surpassed». (178)

Our young man, of whom we spoke earlier, without referring to any «theological place», or to any complicated discourse of the past or of our day, can, before these assertions of a theologian of this time, feel disconcerted and express his serious problem to the successors of the Apostles:

   — When one speaks of the «history of grace», it means that divine grace descends upon men, penetrates and transforms them, to the extent that it is received with good will by man, and thus a more or less large number of men succeed one another, and by that succession the grace of God spreads, penetrates and acts in the world. And that is what can be called «the history of grace». Now when

---

(177)   KARL RAHNER, *Teologia pratica e attività sociale della Chiesa*, in *Nuovi Saggi III*, p. 768.

(178)   KARL RAHNER, *Riflessioni teologiche sulla secolarizzazione*, in *Nuovi Saggi III*, pp. 744-745.

someone says that «in so far as the history of grace advances the world becomes increasingly independent and profane», what can be understood?

One cannot and must not understand something else, that is, no one has the right to claim that something else can be understood than that the profane world becomes more profane and that it breaks away increasingly from the «tutelage» of grace; and that this augmentation of its profane character and this independence in relation to divine grace is the work itself of grace; and that at base grace «is realized» little by little; and that this realization of grace is the emancipation of the world with respect to grace, and an autonomy in its specific character of world, which being already profane, has become even more profane by the advance of the history of grace.

In relation to whom could it become more independent? In relation to sin? In relation to evil? But then the word «profane» would mean the holy world, without sin. Why then would there be a need of grace, of the Incarnation and of the Passion of Christ? The word «profane» such as it is used by the Council in the Constitution "Gaudium et Spes" ([179]), is used to mean the whole of creation. Faith came to bring man out of ignorance, out of evil. That is why to say that by grace the world becomes more profane can only mean that the world loses the necessity of faith and must lose all dependency.

---

(179)   *Gaudium et Spes,* no. 36.

If, to the word «profane», one wants to attribute the meaning of a creation free of all the universal reality, even in that sense grace would not have as work, as mission and as result that of rendering the world more «creation», which would be an absurd proposition; neither to render it more independent, because it is the notion of sin which signifies the effort of independence of the will with regard to the order and the eternal will of the Creator.

Once again we are faced with the case of that unfortunate tendency of juggling with words and with the meanings of words. What meaning does the word «profane» have in Rahner's texts? For the comprehension of his whole formulation depends on that.

Often many people, in one way or another, refer to some of the texts of Vatican Council II in order to claim that the profane and the non-profane represent realities of equal value and equal ethical, spiritual and eschatological meaning. If that were possible, the statement of Karl Rahner could be in harmony with the Council. But it is not so. It is absolutely the contrary. And what is very serious is that this mystification recurs.

Now the word «profane» is used with a specific meaning by the Council in the Pastoral Constitution "Gaudium et Spes". In that Constitution is written:

«If methodical investigation within every branch of learning is carried out in a genuinely scientific manner and in accord with moral norms, it never truly conflicts with faith, for earthly (profane) matters and the concerns of faith derive from the same God». (179)

Here, by the word «earthly» (profane) the original creation is understood; and «the concerns of the faith» are those which were revealed to men after the original creation had entered the history of the disharmony between the law of God and the will of man. Now both realities have their origin in God. And so that no one can claim or want to insinuate some «autonomy» of the temporal, the Council, in the same paragraph specifies:

«But if the expression, 'the independence of temporal affairs', is taken to mean that created things do not depend on God, and that man can use them without any reference to their Creator, anyone who acknowledges God will see how false such a meaning is». (179)

How can one say that to the degree that grace advances the world becomes more independent and that it must «realize itself»? For then to become independent of grace means to become independent of God. And according to the phrase of the Council, «without the Creator the creature would disappear». (179)

Karl Rahner's text that was just cited above supposes a vision of the world and of history which is absolutely foreign to that which the Council expresses, when it speaks of the same origin of «earthly (profane) realities» and «concerns of the faith». In all the Constitutions and all the Decrees, even where all that can be of positive value in the world is stated, as in the Constitution "Gaudium et Spes", the fundamental vision of the Church regarding history remains immutable; it contains the prime duty of the perpetual spiritual combat to which man is called until the end of his life, and to which all men are called until the end of the world:

> «A monumental struggle against the powers of darkness pervades the whole history of man. The battle was joined from the very origins of the world and will continue until the last day, as the Lord has attested. Caught in this conflict, man is obliged to wrestle constantly if he is to cling to what is good, nor can he achieve his own integrity without great efforts and the help of God's grace». (180)

According to Rahner's second statement cited above, in order to correspond to the necessities of the world according to a «new understanding of reality and revelation, it would be necessary to create a theology and an ecclesiology, taking into account their importance which is socio-political and creative of history», because that would be the only means by which a universal theology could go beyond «the individualistic reduction of revelation to the salvation of every man».

And our young man, with the acuity and the depth of true innocence could ask himself: how can humanity be saved as a whole, as a universal entity, if each man is not

---

(180) *Gaudium et Spes,* no. 37.

saved as a unit? Man is a being each time unique, created in the order and for the order of harmony with all units but not destined to be absorbed and annihilated as such, in an immense limitless agglomerate.

Now a large quantity of writings rejects this notion of the being «each time unique», whose liberation consists in the direct union with the Creator, in the name of the so-called scientific exigencies of present day theology; it would be more exact to say: of the present day mentality.

This present day mentality is the same as that which is found in the writings of Vico and of a whole series of thinkers, philosophers and theologians who have followed him, such as Kant, Herder, Hamann, Jacobi, Hegel, Dilthey, Teilhard de Chardin, Heidegger, Bultmann, Blondel, Maritain, Rahner, Hans Küng, Schillebeeckx, Moltmann, Metz, Gutiérrez etc. It is not a question of an ideology; is not a question of an identity of specific «hope», or a particular aesthetic. It concerns a particular mentality, an option of the will which draws thought and even sensibility – if it does not dull it – towards a certain orientation, towards a certain view of the human being, of facts and the course of history. And what is remarkable – sadly remarkable certainly –, is that everywhere, with everyone, this historicist mentality in one way or another displaces the center of gravity of thought and of all speculation, and changes more or less radically, the content of Hope.

* * *

Johann-Gottfried Herder, much more airy, more orderly and in any case more of a poet than Vico, is considered the founder of the philosophy of history in Germany. By some he is classified as a theologian, as «the theologian among the classics of German literature».(181) Before anything else, it must immediately be seen that his view of history has really displaced, and clearly so, the center of gravity of the Reality and of the Message of Christ.

Certain Protestant exegetes and critics, as for example Hans-Joachim Kraus(182), attribute to his work a very great importance for the development of research regarding the Old Testament. And Hermann Gunkel(183) himself wrote that «he moved» in the traces of Herder and Well-hausen.(184) The same Kraus says that Herder, by his «Hebraic humanism» raised himself above orthodoxy and rationalism.(185) It is not our goal in this moment here to undertake a study of what Herder's «importance» was nor of the nature of his influence in the development, at once

---

(181) HANS-JOACHIM KRAUS, *L'Antico Testamento nella ricerca storico-critica dalla Riforma ad oggi,* Il Mulino, Bologna 1975, p. 183.

(182) HANS-JOACHIM KRAUS, born in 1918, Professor of Theology of the Reformation at Göttingen.

(183) HERMANN GUNKEL (1862-1932), Professor of Theology and Biblical Exegesis at Halle.

(184) JULIUS WELLHAUSEN (1844-1918), Professor of Exegesis and Semitic Languages at Marburg and Göttingen.

(185) HANS-JOACHIM KRAUS, *L'Antico Testamento nella ricerca storico-critica dalla Riforma ad oggi,* p. 195.

complicated and unilateral, of the historical critique and
exegesis in Germany and then also in the Christian world.
But it will be very useful to have a reliable image of the
spirit of Herder's historicism, in order to be able thus to
judge what that spirit really is which has had this
«importance» for which he is recognized.

Franco Venturi in his introduction to the Italian edition
of "Another Philosophy of History" says clearly that
Herder's view of the Holy Scripture was the result of the
struggle between two currents regarding Revelation and the
origin of the Holy Scripture, a struggle which went on for a
long time in his soul, as well as in the souls of many
writers of that epoch. And he insists on the fact that
Herder was influenced by the «deism of the 18th century»
and found himself in very distinct contrast with traditional
theology. According to Venturi's expression, it is true to
say that in Herder it is not theology which guided his
thought, but an «historical thought in formation»; theology
simply accompanied that thought. (186)

What is significant here is that Franco Venturi also
recognized a characteristic common to all the historicists:
That is, that Herder was permeated with the deism of the

---

(186) FRANCO VENTURI, Introduction to: *Ancora une filosofia
        della storia per l'educazione dell'umanità* of JOHANN-
        GOTTFRIED HERDER, Einaudi, Torino 1971, p. XVI and
        p. XXVI.

18th century and that his view of Providence disclosed the contradictions of his «nascent historicism». (187)

Herder, with an incontestable richness of imagination, saw history in immense frescos, full of agitation and movement of providence and of human will, a humanist «illuministically» anti-illuminist, he could not avoid being sucked in by the mirage «of the historicized justification» of History. The mystery of man «each time unique» is more and more superseded by the «agglomerate», and the humanist poet, fascinated by the movement of historic ensembles, often displays a dulled sensibility:

«In his own time no one is ever alone, he constructs on the past and he becomes basis for the future, he does not want to be anything else: so speaks the analogy of nature, the speaking image of God in all his works, and this is also the language of the human race. The Egyptians would not have been able to exist without the Orientals; the Greeks constructed upon them, the Romans established themselves on the shoulders of the whole world: real progress, development in continual process, *even if individuals gain nothing from it*» (188)

---

(187)   FRANCO VENTURI, Introduction to: *Ancora una filosofia della storia per l'educazione dell'umanità* of JOHANN-GOTTFRIED HERDER, p. XXVI.

(188)   JOHANN-GOTTFRIED HERDER, *Ancora una filosofia della storia per l'educazione dell'umanità*, p. 41.

One can and even must ask himself how Herder could reconcile that vision of historic progress, of progress in which everything is valorized by movements and transformations of large ensembles and where «the individual gains nothing», with the holy teaching of the Good Shepherd who left his ninety-nine sheep to seek one of them who had strayed and having found it, put it upon his shoulders and returned to his house to rejoice with his friends. (189)

In the perpetual contradiction, obvious or disguised, it is impossible − and we are within our rights to think that it was impossible for Herder himself − to find a consequence, a harmony of considerations, a harmony of hope. How can one conciliate this implacability of progress where‧ «the individuals gain nothing», and the following assertion in another chapter of the same work:

   − «The happiness of man is an individual good everywhere, and therefore everywhere is in relationship with his organic structure and the climate, it is the fruit of exercise, tradition and custom». (190)

   − «If it is possible to find happiness on earth, it is in every sentient being; much more, this happiness must

---

(189)   Matthew 18 : 12.

(190)   JOHANN-GOTTFRIED HERDER, *Idee per la filosofia della storia dell'umanità*. Zanichelli, Bologna 1971, p. 204.

be in him by means of nature, and even auxiliary art must become nature in him, if it is to give joy». (191)

There is no consequence nor harmony possible in Herder between the propositions, the allusions and the arbitrary pronouncement regarding the greatest events and the deepest mystery, which makes itself felt in all the manifestations, all the evolutions, all the ascents and descents of the linear process of history. One finds, with other formulae and other vocables, the same evading and the same incertitude and the same contradiction.

If we must observe from the Egyptians to the Orientals, from the Orientals to the Greeks and in all those and in the entire world, among the Romans, a «real progress», a development in continual progress, even if individuals do not gain anything, how is one to understand that «the happiness of man is everywhere an individual good dependent on his organic structure and the climate as well as on tradition and custom»?

But the whole position and the exposé of Herder's view bring to light the desire to justify the lives and all the sufferings of men, and to fasten hope upon the perpetuity of the evolutive movement of endless ensembles; and that, with allusions to other «superior ends» and other beings about which one must not think because it is not given to man by the nature of things to know them and to grasp them:

---

(191) JOHANN-GOTTFRIED HERDER, *Idee per la filosofia della storia dell'umanità*, p. 211.

«...because of the noble pride in which his destiny consists, the vision of the nobler beings has been taken away from him because probably we would despise ourselves if we knew them». (192)

And Herder adds this pronouncement-instruction which reveals as so many others, the character of his dream which can be called «occult illuminist»:

«Man therefore must not look towards his future state, but only believe in it». (192)

The use from time to time or even often of the name of God and the words «noble», «beauty», «goodness» and other similar ones cannot make up for the absence of a real reference of the thought and heart to God the Creator and Saviour; neither can one, in repeating from time to time the words «ἔσχατον» («eschaton»), «final ends» and «ultimate goal» make up for the rejection, at times impetuous and hostile, of the promise of resurrection and eternal life.

Herder himself doubtlessly felt at times the extent to which this method of information and formation of criteria and of research of the universal immutable laws was at base a utopian construction. In spite of the details and the numerous references to historic facts and realities, in spite of the wealth of images and arbitrary reconciling of facts,

---

(192)   JOHANN-GOTTFRIED HERDER, *Idee per la filosofia della storia dell'umanità*, p. 156.

at times Herder saw with great clarity the fragility and imperfection of the historic method of knowledge:

«No one in the world feels more than I the weakness of general characterizations. We proceed by depicting entire peoples, epochs and territories: and who has really been depicted thus? We include people and times which follow one another in an eternal succession as the waves of the sea: and who has really been depicted thus? To whom does our word, our description apply? We end up by enclosing them all in a nothingness, in a generic word which gives rise to diverse personal thoughts and feelings in each one». (193)

Nevertheless in spite of these flashes of discernment, all his work is full of frescos on often contradictory historic ensembles, interpreted on bases not always the same, very rich in imagination and diverse cultures; his descriptions and his collections of masses of facts alternate between perseverant efforts of classification and rational inter-pretation, or tolerant and pertinent admissions about the incompleteness of the method and the means of building a true knowledge of the mystery of History. And that is so much more evident as he finishes this first essay on the philosophy of history by quoting in Greek, the words of Saint Paul in the Epistle to the Corinthians:

---

(193)   JOHANN-GOTTFRIED HERDER, *Ancora una filosofia della storia per l'educazione dell'umanità*, p. 30.

«Now we see in a mirror dimly, but then face to face. Now I know in part; then I shall understand fully, even as I have been fully understood. Now faith, hope, love abide, these three; but the greatest of these is love». (194)

The young man will ask: when does the dim image in the mirror end for Herder? When and where does the face to face view begin? When must one see face to face? And when will I understand fully as I have been understood? What is the content of this word «now», when the Apostle says: «*now* faith, hope and charity remain»? Who really is He in whose name Saint Paul speaks? Neither Vico's historicism, nor Kant's, nor Herder's, nor Dilthey's nor that of many present day philosophers and theologians, no historicism can respond to the majestic depth, intimate as well as universal, and to the infinite love of the teaching of the Good Shepherd on the lost sheep that was found.

Now in order to understand the importance of the historicist mentality in the formation of the currents of present day theology, it is very useful to know the doctrinal and spiritual position of Herder, in so far as he is «the theologian among the classics of German literature», in regards to Christ, and also the Church and the notion of the Church in general.

---

(194)   JOHANN-GOTTFRIED HERDER, *Ancora una filosofia della storia per l'educazione dell'umanità,* p. 125: Saint Paul, I Cor. 13:12, 13.

The birth of Christianity is seen and described by Herder by means of the same criteria with which he wanted to embrace and explain all the civilizations. Jesus Christ the man who was a pure idealist, bearer of an interior civilization, died as Socrates through fidelity to his ideal.

Herder's feeling before the luminous mystery of Christ is clearly naturalistic and remains at the same time unclear; unclear, because it was so for all those of Christian or non-Christian origin, who have not wanted to totally reject the coming of Christ in the world; it is even the case for all the occultists and all the sects who accept Jesus as a great master or a great initiate. In all these persons there is a characteristic unclearness when they speak of Christ. According to Herder what Jesus Christ attested to in his life and confirmed with his death, is Humanity.

Concluding the introduction to his seventeenth book "Ideas for the Philosophy of History", Herder addresses himself directly to Christ and venerates his «noble figure»; he declares to him that never in history has one found a revolution «provoked so silently in a short time», revolution which spread «to the peoples under the name of Your religion». And then he says clearly that Christ transmitted in large part, besides his living plan for the good of man, a religion which believes in his person:

«... *a religion which believes in You,* an *ill-considered* adoration of Your person and Your cross. Your lucid spirit foresaw all of that and it would be a profanation of Your name if one dared name it in regards to every turbid stream which flows from Your source. Inasmuch as possible we want not to name it; in the face of all history which descends from You, may Your silent figure remain solitary». (195)

For Herder, Christ preached a Christianity which «must be a community deprived of leaders and masters».(196) The formation of the organized Church in the world, of religious families, consecrated souls, all was deviation or abuse or superstition or development of good wills under the protection of clever and adroit leaders. And thus Christianity spread combining with all the philosophic currents which ruled in each place. (197)

Herder speaks of a sect of pure and holy people, whose leader, whom he does not name, was in Bulgaria(198), and who was the sign of poverty and simplicity as opposed to the love of wealth and power of the leaders of the Catholic Church. The members of that sect dispersed throughout the world were supposed to have fought against all the abuses and magical superstitions of the institutional Church.

---

(195)   JOHANN-GOTTFRIED HERDER, *Idee per la filosofia della storia dell'umanità*, p. 389.

(196)   JOHANN-GOTTFRIED HERDER, *Idee per la filosofia della storia dell'umanità*, p. 390.

(197)   Cf. JOHANN-GOTTFRIED HERDER, *Idee per la filosofia della storia dell'umanità*, pp. 389-415.

(198)   It concerns pope Bogomile, founder of Bogomilism in Bulgaria in the 10th century. Bogomilism is a sect mixed with the origins of Catharism. (Cf. VACANT, *Dictionnaire de Théologie catholique*, article "Bogomiles").

Following those efforts of the heroes of the «true heritage of Christ» such as the Manichees, the sect of the Bulgarians, the Cathari, the Patarins, the sect of Henri and Pierre de Bruis and their adepts, the Vaudois, Wickliff, Huss, following the efforts of these heroes, still according to Herder, the Reformation was possible. (199)

And if one wanted to complete the image which comes forth clearly from Herder's attitude regarding Christ and the Church, it would suffice to glean some examples here and there among the very numerous statements concerning the notion of the Church and the sacramental life of the Church:

— «Christianity had only two sacraments but customs and rites of the most differing origins were swiftly superimposed upon them, and unfortunately that happened in a time of general decadence of taste». (200)

— «In particular that sect rejected the superstitious customs and beliefs, it negated their immoral magic power, and in their place recognized only a simple benediction with the imposition of hands, and a league of members under the official in charge, the prefect. The transformation of the bread, the cross, the mass,

---

(199) Cf. JOHANN-GOTTFRIED HERDER, *Idee per la filosofia della storia dell'umanità*, pp. 414-415.

(200) JOHANN-GOTTFRIED HERDER, *Idee per la filosofia della storia dell'umanità*, p. 390.

purgatory, the intercession of saints, the privileges particular to the Roman clergy were for them human institutions and fantasies». (201)

Such is Herder's view on everything which concerns the foundation of the Church and the work of Christ through her in the Creation. It suffices to read his assertions in other realms, such as that of «genetics in history», even his assertions regarding the correlation between natural facts and the data of the physiology of his time, to understand, first, the determination to confine all the causes of the creation and of the generation of the species and of the species of man particularly, strictly to the nature of observable phenomena, and second, the incoherence of these same observations and conclusions from one chapter to another, and third, the implicit and sometimes explicit avowal of the absence of any central and universal reference for his peregrinations through the history of facts, cultures and doctrines.

In so far as this explication of the foundation and extension of the Church is concerned, the least which even a confirmed atheist could say is that it is light, tendentious and passional. He is more serious when he speaks of the origins of polytheism and paganism, more serious and more friendly. All the sacrifices, the whole glorious message and the seeds of sweetness, of sacrificial love, of eternal hope,

---

(201)   JOHANN-GOTTFRIED HERDER, *Idee per la filosofia della storia dell'umanità*, p. 415.

which an endless succession of martyrs, Saints, servants and handmaids of God have poured into the nations, not to mention all that concerns the Revelation of the God-Man on behalf of knowledge per se, have been buried by Herder beneath the failings of the men who have peopled and people the Church of Christ.

But what is at the same time astonishing and revealing of the consequences of the historicist mentality and sensibility is that we rediscover today the same accent, the same arbitrariness and the same facility for crossing out the capital and essential facts of the advent of Christ and of the foundation of the Church, in the exposition and argumentation of the theologians of the 20th century; and that, in the name of a «purer», «more humane», «more apostolic», «more Christ-like» ecclesiology, as for example in the writings of Hans Küng regarding the Church and the person of Christ.(202) But we are again in the time of Gethsemane.

Herder says that every animate and inanimate being is subject to the laws of change. He clearly states that the rhythm is implacable, from the bad to the better and from the better to the worse; and «the cycle of every thing»(203) is like that. But what value for salvation and eternal

---

(202)   See below p. 289.

(203)   JOHANN-GOTTFRIED HERDER, *Fragmente 1, 152*, cited by VALERIO VERA, Introduction to: *Idee per la filosofia della storia dell'umanità*, p. 8.

liberation do Herder's «cycles» or Vico's flowings and turnings back have for each man in the endless procession which constitutes the shifting exterior aspect of history? What can be the relationship between these insensible and mechanical «cycles» with the deep aspiration towards accomplishment, of man «each time unique», and his liberation from death in historic time?

* * *

In any case, in the general image of the world, of Christ and of the Church which Herder gives, there is always a language which creates a first image of two realities, of two orders situating themselves as «inferior» or «superior», which meet and are always resolved within history and physical nature; it is more or less the perception of all the idealists and all the historicists. This image is contrary to another image, that of two orders one of which transcends the facts and the time of the other: the extra-historic eternal order which explains and orders history in the consciousness of man, because it transcends it.

All the subtleties of language and all the accumulation of erudition cannot make up for the lack of a real, little window towards eternity, to which every man enamoured of absolute truth and absolute love aspires. It is by this little window that man, each time unique, and each time united to all men each time unique, can be justified, redeemed and liberated.

If we insist upon this or that aspect of the thought of this or that writer who has made history the center of his information, speculation and meditation, it is because — it must be repeated several times — the historicist mentality and orientation in philosophy have overflowed into Christianity; thus they have transformed and deformed the criteria and aspirations of many among those who are active carriers of certain tendencies of disaggregation of the Church of Christ, in present day theology.

There are three references, mysteries, which confront man: God and the source of all things and thus of man; man between his birth and death and also his origin, thus God; eternal life, thus God and man. From the time we have had the testimony of human thought, a double movement has repeated itself indefinitely, through all history and particularly the history of thought. On the one hand an intimate personal effort and therefore also manifold and thus general, to penetrate the secret of the universe and history, of the world and the life of man, an effort which establishes more and more both man's knowledge and life upon an autonomous consciousness; and on the other hand, a conscious or semi-conscious effort to put oneself, in so far as possible, at the disposition of the Creator, to receive, with patience and humility, the truth which this Creator, ungraspable and always present and infinitely good, reveals to man «each time unique» whose fleeting life forms a link of history; and thus all knowledge and all personal life are established upon a consciousness directly dependent on the Creator regarding everything. In the first case, man moves away from freedom; he becomes increasingly the slave of the mirage of his autonomy. In the other case, man finds again the source of eternal freedom because he finds again loving dependency on the eternal truth of the Creator.

Now historicist thought and mentality cannot but orient more or less directly and more or less intensely but ineluctably towards the mirage of a justification and salvation by historic activity and the autonomy of man in history. And also ineluctable is that this orientation, admitted or not, is closed to both the essence and the real mystery of Revelation.

When one speaks of Revelation today regarding any precise argument, one often meets with a reticence, although sometimes hidden. It is one of the signs of the great differentiation that the historicist mentality and sensibility have brought about in many men concerning the data of the faith. Certainly from the beginning the true disciples of Christ have had and always have a double combat before them: either facing those who simply refute any notion of Revelation, or facing those who, very often unconsciously or semi-consciously alter the essence, the facts and the message of Revelation.

Regarding the alteration of Revelation, it is good to specify that it is not a question of disputes on matters not settled by the Church, nor of speculations perhaps too subtle, which take away from the thought the assurance and ease of being able to move within the limits of dogmatic formulae. It is not a question of too great a «stretching» or too strong an «aeration» of the concepts and propositions of the faith. As will be explicitly shown later on, it concerns an alteration due to a naturalistic sliding in the domain of the will, alteration of the central mystery, of the fundamental reality, upon which Christian theology was able to take root and grow as a manifestation of the love of God and of knowledge of the truth.

CHARACTERISTICS
OF THE
HISTORICIST MENTALITY

As we have already said — and it is good to repeat it — it is certainly not a question here of an effort to write a history of the philosophy of history, not even an outline; moreover, for many reasons, such an effort henceforth by anyone would be useless. Because that, in any case would not help anyone. But our young man could examine, with some profit perhaps, the work of this or that person more or less known in the world of philosophy and theology. For he would be able to find here and there a guiding thread of the mentality which we have named historicist, which, in spite of the differences of doctrinal formulae and also the differences of the characters of the people, would reveal common basic characteristics.

One of the most subtle and at the same time most revealing characteristics of this historicist mentality and its almost universal repercussion, is the attitude of thought before the reality of God: the effort by a large number of authors to get around the difficulty that the name and the intimate perception of God present for them. This effort, more or less subtle and insinuating, but always tenacious, characterizes the work of many known and even celebrated authors.

A whole vocabulary, a whole phraseology at times very fluid and too uncertain have been invented thus avoiding, unconsciously or not, a crystal clear declaration regarding the reality and the Person of God; an ungraspable reality but never vague or uncertain, because God is, he is not a conceptual, idealistic probability. Thus a whole language has been woven in order to speak of God, of faith and of hope, from a standpoint of false, neutral objectivity, without necessarily believing in God, or having faith or having hope.

One can see, for example in Herder's time and afterwards, a whole pleiad of authors who have influenced the development of the philosophical and theological currents, in whom this more or less conscious «game» which takes place in man's thinking intimity, is clearly manifest.

And there is a second characteristic of the same historicist mentality which is just as subtle and revealing. Regarding the values which the currents and the extent of the manifestations of the historicist mentality have imposed in the long run on public opinion, it becomes almost unseemly to expose the lack of consequence, the contradictions, the ambivalences of certain language-games which traverse the centuries.

One must have the carefreeness and innocence of children to face, not certainly, some universal «good sense», but universal taboos which are forged in the long run by the repetition of slogans which engender artificious reverence or artificious repulsions; as a consequence, often almost no one, on the one hand, dares point out the clearly anti-Christian thought and the baleful influence of certain authors regarding the perception of the Truth and real hope; and on the other hand, it happens that one dares not pronounce the names of certain authors, through fear of facing doctrinal slogans which are multiplying ceaselessly in humanity as a whole, drawn by the trend of the times.

These two characteristics we have just spoken of, constitute a phenomenon which is very serious and much more important than may be thought at first, because the spirit that this phenomenon expresses has infiltrated into all the milieus and has «permeated» the work of many authors and of many of these historians of philosophy and theology, who have molded and who mold the intelligentsia in Christianity. So it is very useful, through some examples, taken without a particular choice among a multitude of others, to try and illustrate this phenomenon, manifold and at the same time unique, that the two characteristics manifest.

The Idea of progress

Jacques Chevalier ([204]) is a professor of philosophy and an author who is clearly Christian. In his "History of Thought", a work now considered a classic, he writes of the time of illuminism, of the Encyclopedia, regarding the ideas «of progress, science and humanity» and of «their place in modern thought». ([205])

With all the esteem and respect due to the author of the "History of Thought"and in limpid charity, it must be admitted that in these pages, in a moving mass of intermingled formulae, Jacques Chevalier transmits, side by side with positive affirmations, a continuous uncertainty in his references and in his discernment regarding the historic factors and fundamental principles. Any reader faced with this relativization which preceeds and follows almost all the positive affirmations regarding God, nature, man and final ends, any reader of good faith cannot but be struck by this oscillation between the positive affirmation on one hand, and the justification of at least a part of the contrary on the other.

---

[204] JACQUES CHEVALIER (1882-1962), French philosopher, considered by many as Bergson's disciple.

[205] JACQUES CHEVALIER, *Histoire de la pensée*, Flammarion, Paris 1961, vol. III, pp. 448-470.

Jacques Chevalier, regarding the «ideas of progress, science and humanity and their place in modern thought», writes this:

«This idea, which was destined to remarkable success, is the idea of *progress:* a progress whose source, conclusion or end, is man, or if one wants, humanity; but man reduced to technique, and progress identified with material progress born of science.

«Men of today, according to the average mentality, tend to make an idol of it (of the idea of progress). What is new for them, is not the idea of an indefinite progress of man in his terrestrial destiny, but it is, beyond the limitless extension which they have given it, a certain conception which they have incorporated into it, or more precisely, which they have substituted for it, which they have then diffused in the mass under the name and figure of Humanity, but a humanity whose essence and progress stop precisely at its earthly destiny: so that the city of men replaces the City of God, and the Spirit of God yields to the Spirit of the Earth». (206)

The first quotation contains a critique of a certain idea of progress of which the «source» is not God but man, and the conclusion and the end are likewise man. «But» man reduced to technique, and progress a material progress. The

---

(206)   JACQUES CHEVALIER, *Histoire de la pensée,* vol. III, pp. 462-463.

whole formula implies that if man is not reduced to technique and if progress is not material, but intellectual or aesthetic, the idea of progress whose source and end is always man, is in harmony with the mystery of the Incarnation of Christ and the Redemption.

One can ask: is this harmony conceivable in spite of the fact that the source of progress is always man?

The second quotation brings out, with much good will on the part of the reader, that there is a progress by means of which humanity must one day go beyond the earthly destiny. From this quotation in the context of these pages in general, it stands out that this idea is the Christian idea as regards the essence of humanity and progress. The «novelty» brought therefore by the modern men of those days would be to «stop» the idea of progress at the earthly destiny.

After such propositions about the destiny of man, what light can be brought by the statement that «the city of men replaces the City of God — the Spirit of God yields to the Spirit of the Earth? » No light, because the texts which follow set forth, strange as it may seem on the part of a Christian author, that the fact that the Spirit of God yields to the Spirit of the Earth is not totally negative.

Regarding this idea, the text continues immediately thus:

«An idea which has its limits, but an idea which also has its greatness and answers to exigencies or new needs, which the Christian conception of human progress cannot but take into account». (207)

It is clear that according to Chevalier, the Christian conception of progress should grow richer with a new notion, with the notion: «the Spirit of God yields to the Spirit of the Earth», at least to a certain degree. And for that enrichment by the incorporation of that new idea, the idea — let us repeat it — of the Spirit of God yielding to the Spirit of the Earth, as a reference he leans on Teilhard de Chardin's (208) view expounded in his "Phenomenon of Man":

«At the end of the 18th century the course was clearly changed in the West. And since then, in spite of our obstinacy at times in claiming to be the same, we have entered a new world. —'We have just released the last moorings which still held us to the Neolithic'. A paradoxical formula, but luminous.— Our intelligence could no more escape the perspectives glimpsed of Space-Time, than our lips could forget, having once tasted it, the savour of a universal and durable Progress». (209)

---

(207) JACQUES CHEVALIER, *Histoire de la pensée*, vol. III, pp. 463-464.

(208) PIERRE TEILHARD DE CHARDIN, S.J. (1881-1955), priest, paleontologist, writer, inspirator and animator of a movement in the Church on the basis of a specific evolutionist vision.

(209) TEILHARD DE CHARDIN, *Le Phénomène humain*, éd. du Seuil, Paris 1955, pp. 236, 237, 257.

And Chevalier refers also to this text which constitutes the basis of the Charter of the personification of historicism, the mirage of generous declarations which lead towards total Death:

«Humanity. Such is the first figure under which, at the same instant he was awakening to the idea of Progress, modern man was compelled to seek to reconcile, with the perspectives of his inevitable individual death, the hopes of a limitless future which he could no longer do without. Humanity: entity at first vague, felt more than reasoned, where an obscure sense of permanent growth allied itself with a need of universal brotherhood. Humanity: object of an often naive faith, but whose magic, stronger than all vicissitudes and all criticisms, continues to act with the same strength of enticement both on the soul of present day masses as on the brains of the 'intelligentsia'. Whether one participates in its worship or one ridicules it, who can, even today escape the obsession or even the domination of the idea of Humanity? ». (210)

Chevalier, throughout his work, and more particularly regarding certain periods and certain trends, by assertions at times very true, at times very ambiguous, at times contrary to the first ones, and by references often «at variance» and contradictory, endeavors to connect his idea of Progress to the Christian tradition and to the doctrine of the Church.

---

(210)   TEILHARD DE CHARDIN, *Le Phénomène humain,* p. 272.

What at bottom, through the manifold formulations, is Chevalier's notion of progress? Now there is the idea of a sequence of the facts and ideas in history which evolves and accomplishes a terrestrial destiny of Humanity, «whose pole is the Infinite». The perspectives of Humanity in that pursuit must contain a «belief in the beyond». At the end of this human progress throughout the historic development, there is access to a destiny not only earthly.

And then there is this particular and very significant acceptation in so far as the essence, the laws and the orientation of this progress are concerned: «humanity is in motion towards justice and towards love»; and through its «peregrination in time» it waits — it is humanity who waits — for the «stability of the eternal abode». The end of this «imposing view of human history» is glory. And he attributes that acceptation to Saint Augustine and to all the Doctors and Christian authors and also to all the deistic and even atheistic humanists. He even cites specifically the authors of the Mysteries, all those who worked on theological summae, the scholars of the Middle Ages, Bossuet and Pascal; and he also cites Herder, Kant, Hegel, Cournot and even Condorcet and Auguste Comte. (211) And

---

(211)   JACQUES CHEVALIER, *Histoire de la pensée,* Flammarion, Paris 1956, vol. II, p. 115.
— ANTOINE COURNOT (1801-1877), mathematician, economist and French philosopher.
— ANTOINE DE CONDORCET (1743-1794), mathematician, philosopher of the group of the "Encyclopedists" and member of the Convention.

what gives us Ariadne's clew for this orientation, certainly not only Chevalier's but that of all those who were beguiled by this language and this view of a sovereign progress, is that he cites Giambattista Vico as the prophet of the true structure of history. (212)

Before continuing our meditation on the relationship which Chevalier wants to establish between Saint Augustine's "City of God" and «the Humanity» of Teilhard de Chardin, it is holily useful to bring out a fact seemingly very secondary, but which is from many points of view very revealing: Chevalier, among diverse assertions in favor of the supernatural and with many complaints because of the materialism of certain authors, to support his idea of progress and of the value for humanity of the continual development of science, refers to a text of Blaise Pascal (213); he refers to the "Preface on the Treaty of the Void". (214)

One remains very astonished to see a philosopher-historian present in support of his own idea of progress the text of a man, written in 1647, that is several years before

---

(212) JACQUES CHEVALIER, *Histoire de la pensée,* vol. III, pp. 471-472. See above pp. 150-180.

(213) BLAISE PASCAL (1623-1662), genial French mathematician and physician who, converted in the Catholic Church, radically changed his intellectual and spiritual orientation, totally captured by the Mystery of the Person and the mission of Christ.

(214) BLAISE PASCAL, *Préface sur le Traité du Vide,* in *Oeuvres complètes,* éd. du Seuil, Paris 1963, pp. 231-232.

his conversion which occurred in 1654. Chevalier knew well the work and thought of Pascal, because he edited his complete Works. Moreover Pascal himself never published this text which was edited after his death by his intimate friends, with a very meaningful preface for the real thought of the converted Pascal:

«For though he was as capable as one can be of penetrating into the secrets of nature, and had therein admirable apertures, he nevertheless had known for more than ten years before his death the vanity and nothingness of all these kinds of knowledge, and he conceived such a distaste for them that he could hardly endure that people of spirit should occupy themselves with, and speak of it seriously». (215)

That reference by Chevalier to Pascal is not at all justified, because Pascal's thought and his sensibility after his conversion are the opposite of both the notion and the vision of progress in history such as Chevalier presents them in his exposés.

Blaise Pascal independently of all thought that anyone could have apropos of the "Provinciales" and of his position regarding Port-Royal (216), manifested in several

---

(215)   BLAISE PASCAL, *Traité de l'équilibre des liqueurs et de la pesanteur de la masse de l'air,* in *Oeuvres complètes,* p. 233.

(216)   BLAISE PASCAL, *Les Provinciales* (Diverse letters regarding the Jansenist crisis which put the monastery of Port-Royal in opposition to the Hierarchy), *Oeuvres complètes,* p. 371.

ways his intimate conviction of the mission of Christ, of the value of human knowledge, of the way of salvation. Such a conviction does not allow reference in any manner whatever, to his person and his actual thought in order to sustain an idea of historic progress of eschatological value, according to the acceptation of Jacques Chevalier and Teilhard de Chardin. That is, one does not have the right to refer to Pascal in order to sustain the idea of a progress which would be realized by the development of learning, by the evolution of science, by the social organization in an «historic future».

Any of Pascal's texts after his conversion, leaves no doubt as to his true thought, his true convictions and his vision of the world, of the Church and of salvation, as regards the evolution of the world and of learning. Here are some excerpts gathered without specific effort:

«The year of grace 1654.
— God of Abraham, God of Isaac, God of Jacob, not of philosophers and scholars.
Certainty, certainty, heartfelt, joy, peace.
(God of Jesus Christ).
God of Jesus Christ.
Deum meum et deum vestrum.
Thy God shall be my God.
The world forgotten, and everything except God. He can only be found by the ways taught in the Gospels». (217)

---

(217)   BLAISE PASCAL, *Mémorial,* in *Oeuvres complètes,* p. 618.

«The world is a good judge of things, because it is in the state of natural ignorance where man really belongs. Knowledge has two extremes which meet; one is the pure natural ignorance of every man at birth, the other is the extreme reached by great minds who run through the whole range of human knowledge, only to find that they know nothing and come back to the same ignorance from which they set out». (218)

«To have no time for philosophy is to be a true philosopher. — We don't believe philosophy to be worth one hour of trouble». (219)

«Blessed are those who weep, not because they see all the perishable things flowing away, carried off by torrents, but because they remember their dear home-land, the heavenly Jerusalem, which they ceaselessly remember in the tedium of their exile! The rivers of Babylon flow, and fall, and carry away. O holy Sion, where everything stands firm and nothing falls!» (220)

«What does this avidity and powerlessness then cry unto us, if not that in the past there was a true happiness in man, of which only the mark and the totally empty trace now remain, and which in vain he

(218)   BLAISE PASCAL, *Pensées,* édition Brunschvicg, no. 327.

(219)   BLAISE PASCAL, *Pensées,* édition Brunschvicg, no. 4 and no. 79.

(220)   BLAISE PASCAL, *Pensées,* édition Brunschvicg, no. 458 and no. 459.

tries to fill with all that surrounds him, seeking in absent things the help which he does not obtain from things present, but which are all incapable of it, because the infinite gulf can only be filled by an infinite and immutable object, that is by God himself? » (221)

«For to speak to you candidly about geometry, I find it the highest exercise of the mind; but at the same time I know it as so useless that I make little distinction between a man who is only a geometer and a skilled artisan. − I wouldn't go two steps out of my way for geometry». (222)

«Jesus will be in agony until the end of the world. There must be no sleeping during that time». (223)

In order to understand the subtle but profound differentiation which Christian thought and hope undergo through the hidden or visible thrust of the historicist mentality, it would suffice to note with what lightness a man as hard working and cultured as Chevalier chooses as supporting reference for his concept of progress, phrases of the "Epistle to the Hebrews", regarding Jesus Christ; and he says expressly:

---

(221)   BLAISE PASCAL, *Pensées*, édition Brunschvicg, no. 425.

(222)   BLAISE PASCAL, *Lettre au grand mathématicien Fermat*, in *Oeuvres complètes*, p. 282.

(223)   BLAISE PASCAL, *Pensées*, édition Brunschvicg, no. 553.

«Most Christian thinkers, beginning with Saint Augustine, had forcefully proclaimed it, only making clear thereby the profound character of Christianity *which is not a timeless myth* situated in the cycle of a long year of periodic returns, but an event, an advent and a progress, *Jesus-Christus heri et hodie, ipse et in saecula»* (Jesus Christ is the same, yesterday, today and forever) (Heb. 13 : 8). (224)

With sadness it must be admitted that it is unexplainable that an assertion of the perenniality and immutability of Christ can be taken to illustrate a doctrine of progress according to the notion of Chevalier – Teilhard de Chardin. How can this be explained, seeing that even the context of that assertion is an exhortation by the holy writer to the faithful, to be courageous and faithful to the doctrine received by the word and the example of life of their master? «For – continues the sacred text – here we have no lasting city, but we seek the city which is to come» (Heb. 13: 14).

Is there a truly Christian conception of progress? Certainly there is one. Because there is for everything and every positive or negative term a true conception, both precise and nuanced, proceeding from the action and message of Christ in the world. But before all these considerations regarding historic Progress, our young man would surely ask himself: What light is there in all this?

---

(224)   JACQUES CHEVALIER, *Histoire de la pensée*, vol. III, p. 463.

Where is that City of God situated? And where is the city in which the Spirit of God must, by positive historic necessity, leave place to the Spirit of the Earth? Who are the citizens of that City of God? Are they all the saved dead, beyond the course of events in time, or may.be they are all the men of a far-off El Dorado, of an «eschaton» of the historic movement?

What is the fate of all the men who have lived, who will have lived and died up until the time of El Dorado? Where is the final accomplishment of progress situated? What is the meaning of the Resurrection of Christ, without which, as Saint Paul says, our faith is in vain (1 Cor. 15:17)? How can the so numerous texts of Saint Augustine's "The City of God", which show the citizens of that City, piercing in their time «the house-top of history», be harmonized with the notion of a Perfection which will be realized at the end of the historic movement?

What is the meaning of salvation in the midst of indefinite progress? When does man pass from History into the Kingdom? Where does «entire history» pass from time to eternity? Where does this differentiation of the citizen of the earthly city take place, in order that he become a citizen of the heavenly City?

Is there a real answer, an answer of light to all that, to all these questions and a multitude of others which our young man doubtlessly asks or could ask? Yes, there is one. But in order that there be an answer without ambiguity and with neither narrowness nor dryness, nor infernal heat and cold, but with eternal freshness and warmth, an answer with an unknown beneficence and holy certainty, a truly theological response of truth and hope, the whole historicist heritage must be overturned within itself.

The Kantian Mystification

The two characteristics about which we have just spoken (225), that is, on one hand the sophisticated reverence which constitutes almost a universal habitus of modern thought, and on the other hand the effort to avoid referring really and directly to the Being of God, have increasingly provoked a lack of true objectivity and intellectual and spiritual consequence. This form of thought has spread like a gigantic oil spot, thus provoking a subtle general relativism in a large number of works and movements.

Man has grown accustomed to living in this intellectual climate of the so-called modern times hardly realizing that often he contradicts himself. For sometimes, regarding works and authors, he puts forth considerations and judgements which, at base are contrary to his own fundamental convictions which themselves are often truthful and very noble.

That is why it is necessary to illustrate as much as possible the phenomenon, which is not only intellectual but also psychological and whose origin in the last analysis is the historicist mentality and sensibility.

---

(225)   See p. 197-199.

Everyone agrees in saying that Kant has exercised a very great influence in philosophical spheres and through that, theological, from his time until today; that influence was exerted in spite of the appearance of new systems and doctrines which did not refer at all to Kant's thought. That at first appears to be a mystery. But this is not the immediate subject of these pages. What is particularly strange is that many critics and historians of philosophy labor to cover with a christianizing veil the inner contradiction of the word, the radical rationalism, the «transcendental» agnosticism and the deep-seated anti-spiritualism of Kant.

This «christianizing veil» constitutes a much more important factor than one would suppose for the orientation of theological thought throughout the universities and the encyclopedias.

As example of an incontestable evidence of «christianization», the work of R.P. Sertillanges, a French Dominican and member of l'Institut of France, can be taken. In his book "Christianity and the Philosophies" (226), Sertillanges, regarding noumenal freedom and original sin in Kant writes:

«This freedom of the other world (non-applicable conceptual freedom) cannot be defined since it is outside of time and space by which all is defined. It is

---

(226) R.P. A.-D. SERTILLANGES, *Le Christianisme et les philosophies*, 2 vol., Aubier, Paris 1941.

ungraspable even to he who exercises it, since in reflecting on his acts, he can only find causes which are themselves involved in time and space. Instead of governing the facts of our life which are geared into the life of the universe, this extra-temporal freedom over-hangs our universe and leaves our human deeds under its hard and total grasp (grasp of the universe). It is really senseless and one can ask himself who would submit, not even Kant, to a freedom thus torn apart and as if absent from itself. Nevertheless, it is beautiful, so much the more beautiful morally and religiously the madder it is». (227)

— «One can never fail to foresee that a link is established between noumenal freedom according to Kant and the Christian doctrine of original sin». (228)

Independent of the unreality of this noumenal freedom, acknowledged by Kant himself and by all, independent of the obvious contradiction which the above quote from Sertillanges contains, one need only read one of Kant's numerous assertions in order to prove to the most ingenuous, how foreign the notion of original sin is to his thought and sensibility. In his book "Religion Within the Limits of Simple Reason", (the title is already a whole

---

(227)   R.P. A.-D. SERTILLANGES, *Le Christianisme et les philoso-phies*, vol. II, p. 192.

(228)   R.P. A.-D. SERTILLANGES, *Le Christianisme et les philoso-phies*, vol. II, p. 194.

doctrine), in the chapter "Of the Origin of Evil in Human Nature", Kant writes:

«Whatever the origin of moral evil in man may be, it is certain that among all the ways of presenting the diffusion of evil and its propagation in the midst of all the members of our race and of all generations, the most improper way is that of presenting evil as something which comes to us by heredity from our first parents.

— «We must not seek a temporal origin for a moral attitude which must be imputed to us; even if such a quest is inevitable. — The Holy Scripture may have presented the temporal origin of sin in that way in order to adapt to our weakness.

— «The original disposition of man (which no one outside of him could corrupt, if that corruption must be imputed to him) is a disposition to the good; therefore, there is no understandable basis for us here, whence for the first time moral evil could have entered into us». (229)

Putting aside the fatal contradiction, continuous in Kant's whole book on Religion, every man of good faith cannot but remain astonished before Sertillanges' assertions. The prestidigitations of words and formulae which

---

(229) EMMANUEL KANT, *La religione entro i limiti della sola ragione,* ed. Laterza, Roma 1980, pp. 41, 45 and 46.

interweave and inter-annul each other, cannot cancel the radical denial of the notion of original sin, in no matter what truly Christian acceptation. Even with the best of wills, Kant could never admit a truly Christian view of reality and the history of man, without deliberately leaving the enclosure where, as he himself determined it in a thousand ways, man has to deal with his own representations only and where all knowledge of things in themselves is forever impossible.

It is not only the notion of original sin that cannot be linked to some concept or postulate of Kant's. His conception of the world when it has been released from the «inextricable encumbrance» (Sertillanges' own term) (230) of the internal contradictions of his word, is such that it is not simply foreign to the mystery of Christ, but it is even hostile in essence.

How is it possible that such contradictions have entered the intellectual mores? Jacques Chevalier in his "History of Thought", amidst a crowd of contradictory considerations, writes that Kant's claim «to exclude the supernatural» and to deny to reason every other ideal than «an empty concept» leads to a deadly doctrine:

«This doctrine, from the beginning, removes from man all means of finding or refinding in things anything other than himself or that which he himself put, for

---

(230)   R.P. A.-D. SERTILLANGES, *Le Christianisme et les philosophies*, vol. II, p. 193.

which reason all that goes beyond our nature is absolutely foreign to him and remains forever closed to him». (231)

Then, further on, at the end of a whole discourse with no outcome, around the notion of God in Kant, Chevalier again concludes with ambiguous words:

«God can only be sought in us. It is in the idea of God that we live, that we act and that we are. That is what this man, this wise man discloses at the end of his earthly life». (232)

Having stated that it is wisdom to believe that it is in the idea of God that we must live — and not in God — Chevalier after much praise for Kant, adds:

«Nevertheless this God, according to Kant cannot be sought and cannot be found except in us. Such are in effect the *ultima verba* of the philosopher in search of a truth which he persists magnificently in seeking within himself, without succeeding in finding the source by reason». (233)

And the oscillation continues. However Kant's obstinacy is not magnificent, in spite of what Chevalier says.

---

(231) JACQUES CHEVALIER, *Histoire de la pensée,* vol. III, p. 632.

(232) JACQUES CHEVALIER, *Histoire de la pensée,* vol. III, p. 636.

(233) JACQUES CHEVALIER, *Histoire de la pensée,* vol. III, p. 637.

For he persists in an hallucinating manner to substitute the
idea of things and beings for the things and beings, the
concept of God for God. Kant did not find the truth,
either by reason or by any path. He found neither the
source of truth nor, consequently, the truth itself. And so
once again the impasse. Chevalier adds:

«For lack of having discerned this point (that God
is), Kant, in order to escape transcendental skepticism,
and in order to safeguard moral values, took refuge in
fideism. − But that belief, in the last resort is only built
upon the exigencies of a moral experience which bases
itself on nothing in reality». [234]

But in order to show still more clearly what Kant's
notion of God is, to which many authors try to attribute
some supernatural reality, be it only fideist, it suffices to
report the assertions of Kant himself in these posthumous
pages, in which he had, as he said, exposed the foundation
of his system and his doctrine:

«The concept of God − and of the personality of
the being represented by this concept − has some
reality. There is a God present in the practico-moral
reason, that is, in the idea of the relationship of man to
right and duty. But this existence of God is not that of a
being exterior to man». [235]

---

[234]   JACQUES CHEVALIER, *Histoire de la pensée*, vol. III,
        p. 639.

[235]   EMMANUEL KANT, *Opus postumum*, p. 60, cited by Joseph
        Maréchal, *Le point de départ de la métaphysique*, Ed.
        Universelle, Bruxelles 1947, vol. IV, p. 295.

Is it necessary to make comments on such assertions in order to show what is obvious? By what linguistic trickery is it possible to extract from this statement an image or even a concept which correspond to a notion of God, and more, of the God of the Gospel? This divinization of practico-moral reason is the negation of all supernatural reality and the «voluntary» closure of all opening towards the eternal God, to which the soul aspires.

A feeling of great desolation arises in every man when he begins to perceive the vast mystification which has been brought about by means of language-games torturing the reason and the heart, in the realm of philosophy and transmission of doctrine. There is no other word than that of «mystification» to express that entanglement of notions and vocabulary, in such a way as to upset the holy laws of eternal logic and to hide the horizon of the unique hope in Christ.

It is obvious now that the mentality which led to Dilthey's «historic consciousness» and to the «historic consciousness» intrinsic to a large part of the diverse specifications of present day theological trends, that historicist mentality is not the work of historians in general. It is not the result of the pure research of the realities of the past; it is the result of a penchant, conscious or unconscious, for the autonomy of man, for his emancipation from the true eternal kingdom; a penchant which has determined the philosophic speculation of many, and thereby the orientation of theological thought and consciousness.

Emmanuel Kant constitutes a stage in which the whole effort of that emancipation from all supernatural reality is synthesized. And philosophism, which characterized the evolution of theological currents, has made it so that Kant's thought is present in many of the works concerning theology. For – and this is said here in passing – Hegel's dialectic or that of historic materialism, the evolutionism of Bergson and Teilhard de Chardin, although they are considered as «dynamic» systems, apparently different from the illusory anti-historicism of Kant, are only differentiated expressions of the unyielding effort of emancipation, synthesized and doctrinalized by Kant.

There are assertions of Kant's which, in spite of all good will, do not allow one to speak of his «Christianity» or even of his fideism. What's more, they show how great the effort of that breaking away from divine order and the Being of God is, how tenacious and deprived of grace and love. Here are some assertions among many others which express the basis of the historicist mystification.

Assertion A

In which the person, the soul, in the sense in which the Gospel speaks, has no place, and in which the unique goal of nature is not realized in each man in so far as he is a distinct being each time unique, but in the abstract and anonymous notion of the species.

From the "Idea of a Universal History from a Cosmopolitical Point of View":

«Second Thesis. — In man, who is the only reasonable creature on earth, the natural dispositions ordained to the use of his reason, have their complete development only in the species, not in the individual.— If nature has established that life have a brief duration, an indefinite series of generations is necessary, which hand down one to another their lights in order to carry the innate seeds of our species to the degree of development which perfectly corresponds to its goal (of the species)». (236)

Assertion B

In which the possibility is excluded for man of the earth to hope, to realize, in so far as he is a man each time unique, his destination in his own life; and where Christ's promises for each righteous, good and meek soul in his "Sermon on the Mount" are suppressed.

«Perhaps among those (supposed inhabitants of other planets), each individual can fully realize his purpose in his own life. But for us (earthlings) things go differently: only the species can hope in that». (237)

---

(236)   EMMANUEL KANT, *Idea di una storia universale dal punto di vista cosmopolitico*, in *Scritti politici*, Ed. UTET, Torino 1965, p. 125.

(237)   EMMANUEL KANT, *Idea di una storia universale dal punto di vista cosmopolitico*, in *Scritti politici*, p. 130.

Assertion C

In which nature, needing to develop its dispositions (?) makes use of men's antagonism, an antagonism which is the cause of civil organization; and in which man is good and disposed to harmony, but nature, for the good of the species, compels him to insociability and struggle; in which vice, vanity and hardness are exalted; and in which all that is God's wise order, and not the result of a disorder contrary to the eternal order of the Creation.

«Fourth Thesis. — The means which nature uses to realize the development of all its dispositions is their antagonism (men's) in society, but in so far as such an antagonism is at base the cause of a civil organization of society itself. — Without the condition of insociability, in itself certainly not desirable, all the talents would remain forever enclosed in their seeds in an arcadian (238) pastoral life of perfect harmony, frugality, reciprocal love: men, good like the sheep they lead to pasture, would not give to their existence a greater value than that of their domestic animal; they would not fill the void of creation in regards to their end as reasonable beings. Thanks be then to nature for the intractable character which it engenders, for the envious emulation of vanity, for the cupidity which is never satisfied with goods or even domination!

---

(238)   Arcadia is a region of the Peloponesus whose inhabitants were shepherds and who represented, for the poets of antiquity, a place of felicity and innocence in the pastoral life.

«—Man wants concord; but nature knows better than he what is good for his species.— The natural impulses which push him to that, reveal the order of a wise Creator and not the hand of an evil spirit who through jealousy has damaged or ruined the magnificent work of the universe». (239)

Assertion D

In which human history only serves a hidden plan of nature, which consists in the creation of a world-wide political constitution, a cosmopolitical organization; in this political constitution, all the dispositions of the human species would come to develop themselves.

«Eighth Thesis. —One can consider the history of the human species in its ensemble as the realization of a hidden plan of nature in order to bring to birth a political constitution inwardly (and to this intent also outwardly) perfect — that is, a general, cosmopolitical organization which would be the matrix in which all the original dispositions of the human species reach development». (240)

---

(239) EMMANUEL KANT, *Idea di una storia universale dal punto di vista cosmopolitico*, in *Scritti politici*, pp. 127 and 128.

(240) EMMANUEL KANT, *Idea di una storia universale dal punto di vista cosmopolitico*, in *Scritti politici*, pp. 134 and 136.

Assertion E

In which Kant criticizes Herder specifically for the points which could be considered as supernatural references, and regarding the immortality of the soul.

From the "Recension of: J. G. Herder on 'Ideas on the Philosophy of the History of Humanity' ''':

«No member of all the human generations fully attains his final purpose but only the race does». (241)

Assertion F

In which the death of each man results from a monstrous desire of the «common body», because, by that death, the «common body» would be preserved.

From "Posthumous Manuscripts" (no. 1401):

«Every individual has a horror of death, but the common body which wants to preserve itself has good reasons for desiring the death of individuals».

Assertion G

In which eternal life according to the promise of Christ is only a beautiful ideal for an epoch of the world; man draws nearer to that epoch to the degree that he draws nearer to the greatest good possible on earth; in which

---

(241)   EMMANUEL KANT, *Recensione di: J.G. Herder, Idee sulla filosofia della storia dell'umanità, parte I e II*, in *Scritti politici*, p. 174.

consequently all evangelical teaching regarding the Resurrection of Christ and hope in the Resurrection, is rejected.

From "Religion Within the Limits of Simple Reason", the chapter on the «Historic Representation of the Progressive Founding of the Domination of the Good Principle on Earth». Regarding the eschatological view of the New Testament and the Kingdom of God, Kant concludes:

«This representation which gives an historic narrative of the future life, which in itself is not a history, is a beautiful ideal of an epoch of the world — towards which we only turn our gaze in our continual progress and our approaching of the greatest good possible on earth (in all that, there is nothing mystical, but all proceeds naturally in an ethical way)». (242)

Assertion H

In which the knowledge of God, the knowledge of the Father by the Son, the overcoming of the world by the love of God are excluded from the teaching of Christ regarding the Kingdom of God.

«The master of the Gospel had pointed out the kingdom of God on earth to his disciples only from the magnificent and edifying moral point of view». (243)

---

(242)   EMMANUEL KANT, *La religione entro i limiti della sola ragione*, pp. 149 and 150.

(243)   EMMANUEL KANT, *La religione entro i limiti della sola ragione*, p. 148.

Assertion I

In which rational psychology would be senseless because it could not make man know anything about himself; because there would be insuperable limits for reason, as a result of which the notion of the soul would be beyond these limits, thus only being an idea of reason; and in which it is considered madness to refer to the spirit in order to know oneself, for the spirit would have no basis in life.

«Rational psychology does not therefore exist as a doctrine adding something to the knowledge of ourselves. It exists only as a discipline setting in this field the insuperable limits to speculative reason; it prevents one, on the one hand, from throwing himself into a materialism without soul, and on the other hand, from foolishly losing himself in a spiritualism which for us has no basis in life». (244)

Assertion J

In which no act of worship can serve for salvation, it is only a religious superstition; and in which the desire of an intimity with God cannot serve for salvation and is only a useless pretention and religious fanaticism; and in which the whole liturgical mystery of the Church, which from the

---

(244) EMMANUEL KANT, *Critique de la raison pure,* éd. Flammarion, Paris 1929, vol. I, p. 345.

beginning has had an integral part in this teaching, is rejected; and in which all spiritual life which draws man interiorly towards God, is rejected.

«The illusion of accomplishing with religious acts relating to worship, something with a view to justification before God, is religious *superstition,* just as the illusion of wanting to obtain that end by an aspiration to a so-called intimity with God is religious *fanaticism».* (245)

Such is Kant's thought. Such is his agnostic absolutism, his certitude denying all spiritual reality. It is easy to draw up a list of assertions of a similar tenor as illuminating as it is overwhelming; a list which can be very long.

That is why one is left in amazement before so much labor spent to elaborate a theory of knowledge so unreal and so bleak, a method with no other point of departure than the «ideating» I; an a priori knowledge of the a priori and of the critique by a priori; so much work to demonstrate that one cannot know what is the only source of knowledge, life, liberty and true joy.

But what is surprising, is to observe that obstinacy in the past and still today, to want to find, all 'the same, in Kant's thought, thought so anti-eternal, a few seeds of Christianity, or at least a background of some sincere

---

(245)   EMMANUEL KANT, *La religione entro i limiti della sola ragione,* p. 193.

deism. And what's more, an obstinacy to want to find in that same theory of Kant's, a science of knowledge, and to want at any cost to make one believe that in that science even those who have received Christ can draw transcendent truths regarding the Real.

It is the spreading, in all milieus, of that mentality which inclines man always more towards ephemeral events, refuting all notion of the being in his eternal origin and finality; it is this spreading of the historicist mentality which alone can explain that there was and there always is such an effort to attribute to Kant a faith or belief or thought or feeling or general view of the universe which are connected in whatever way it may be, to a divine Being, to God and to the Person and to the Gospel of the God-Man, of Christ.

It would be lending oneself to the same vain game of intellectual dilection to want, by interminable and baseless cogitations, to specify if it is that mentality, which we have called historicist, which has provoked the deviation of the interior gaze towards the worship of false reason, or if it is a deviation of the inner gaze which has created that mentality leading to the worship of false reason. But incontestably there is a worship of false reason. One thing appears certain: in that mentality, men having faith in God have been driven to cling desperately to Kant's so-called Christian or deist image.

This effort, pathetic at times, to attach Kant's thought to the eternal reality of God and to the reality of God incarnate, of Jesus Christ, has led to great evils in Christian life and thought in general.

Some have thought that the influence of Kant's thought, and particularly his conception of religion stopped long ago, and that Hegel and Schleiermacher (246) diminished that influence and have prevented its projection into the future. (247) That opinion does not correspond to reality. It is the complete opposite.

On the other hand, the idea has spread that Kant was not interested in history, occupied as he was with his «anatomy» of the understanding. That does not correspond to reality either. For all the justification of life, all the human accomplishment of the individual, as of groups, are not conceivable for Kant except in the historic realization of the species. The fact for example, that Herder reproached Kant for his lack of interest in history, does not mean that Kant had another hope than the realization of a society that he himself called «cosmopolitical»; his

---

(246)   GEORG-WILHELM-FRIEDRICH HEGEL (1770-1831) taught philosophy at Iena, Heidelberg and Berlin.

— FRIEDRICH SCHLEIERMACHER (1768-1834), Protestant theologian and philosopher considered as principal representative of romanticism in Germany, denying all sacral reality to the Church; according to him, the consciousness that Christ had of his redemptive mission was the only testimony for his Divinity.

(247)   Cf. R.P. PIERRE CHARLES, S.J. professor at Louvain, *Dictionnaire de théologie catholique*, éd. Letouzey, Paris 1925, Article « Kant ».

concepts regarding knowledge and all his intellectual elaborations have had no other references, nor other foundations, nor other laws and finality in the future, than the unfolding of the events of the human species towards that «cosmopolitical» society which would be the major goal of history.

For Kant, the justification of existence and of all the shifting facts which make up history is progress. The fact that "The Critique" does not allow even that notion of progress to have the character of a transcendent ideal, does not change Kant's unilateral reference: the future cosmo-political society, to which the «dispositions of nature» and the particular dispositions of man contribute. Kant's cold and almost inhuman optimism was closed in the same changing enclosure as the enthusiastic and glowing optimism of Herder: History.

It is useful to repeat here that the historicist mentality means more than a particular theory. Several diverse theories, from many points of view, meet in a common characteristic: all the justification of the activity and thought, all notion of accomplishment of the species and the individual are realized in the frame of history and in the sense of an irreversible progress. The historicist mentality encloses the consciousness, thought and hope of man in a myth, in a future society on earth. Access could be had to that society by a linear or cyclical progress, foreseeable or unforeseeable, slow or rapid, but progress always through an incalculable number of generations which disappear forever.

It is this mentality which engendered or permitted the engendering of historicism in Christian theology. But for the moment, it must be said here that to class Kant as a non-historicist is to have failed to perceive his essential references, the historicist conditioning of his a priori. For in Kant there is no little window, for any accomplishment whatever, which would open towards some reality outside of the simple fact of the succession of the generations on earth. Progress, as relativized as it is by Kant, remains irreversible. That fundamental notion, which cannot but be the criterion and filter of all his speculations, reveals the historicist mentality of the origin, work and legacy of Kant.

In order to put one's finger on the reality of all that we have said regarding the two characteristics of the historicist mentality, that is, regarding the sophisticated reverence and the effort to get around the difficulty which the holy Reality of God presents for many, and to put one's finger on the consequences of that mentality in theological thought right up to our days, it would suffice for our young man to stop a little before Father Maréchal's (248) prodigious effort to «go beyond» Kant's criticism. Certainly the young man, in order to discern the essential truth within an enormous work of brilliant intellect, should be able to liberate himself from the sophisticated criteria which are created and imposed by that same socially and intellectually historicist mentality.

---

(248)   JOSEPH MARECHAL (1878-1944), S.J. Professor of History of Philosophy at Louvain.

The chapter «Existence of God» in Maréchal's extensive work "The Point of Departure of Metaphysics" begins with a few lines, which alone could serve as a typical illustration of the loss of criterion and of the will to «recuperate» at any cost, systems, ideas and even intentions:

> «After a rapid course through the Opus Postumum, the existence of God must seem to many readers, the most disconcerting of the themes sketched in this collection of fragments. The assertion borders on the negation; the *sic* and *non* alternately try to occupy the ground; but other passages intermingled with the first, are full of innuendoes which invite the spirit to keep away from extreme positions». (249)

After these words one wonders first what these «extreme positions» can be: either Kant believed in a personal God, a Being existing outside of man, or Kant did not believe in a personal God, Being existing outside of man. There is no other position that Maréchal could intend by the words «extreme positions».

And then it is necessary, according to Maréchal, to beware of attributing to Kant one of these extreme positions; that would clearly mean that Maréchal believes that in the voluminous writings of Kant, there are no elements which permit the saying of yes or no; and what is more, it is necessary, still according to Maréchal, to beware

---

of taking one of these extreme positions, for the reason that in Kant's construction there are «innuendoes». Nevertheless these «innuendoes» can only be found beside many more-than-explicit assertions which deny the existence of God in so far as a Being outside of man; assertions which affirm that:

«This existence of God is not that of a being existing exterior to man – as would be a substance distinct from man and acting as counterpart to the world... The reality of the one and the other ideal, (God and the world), is of the order of the idea». (250)

And Maréchal also brings in this other assertion of Kant's:

«That no precept, no defense, have in actual fact been intimated to men by a holy and all-powerful Being; that even in the hypothesis of a message from on high, the men to whom it would have been destined, would have remained incapable either of perceiving it, or of convincing themselves of its reality: this admits of no doubt». (251)

Now the young man inevitably will wonder:

---

(250) EMMANUEL KANT, *Opus postumum,* cited by Joseph Maréchal, *Le point de départ de la métaphysique,* vol. IV, pp. 295, 296 and 197.

(251) EMMANUEL KANT, *Opus postumum,* cited by Joseph Maréchal, *Le point de départ de la métaphysique,* vol. IV, p. 299.

— Is it possible to believe that Kant wanted to annul such assertions by the «innuendoes» in other passages of his writings?

— Is it possible to understand that Maréchal, after his short introduction to the chapter on «The Existence of God», where he states that «the assertion borders on the negation and that the *sic* and *non* alternately try to occupy the ground», seeks to find some sincere innuendoes; and then, that on the basis of these innuendoes he endeavors to demonstrate the presence in Kant of a belief in God eternal?

— Is it possible to understand that an enormous work and gifts are dedicated in order to prove at any cost that in a thought which is contradictory in itself, transcendentally anti-transcendent, dogmatically anti-dogmatic, aprioristically categorical and at the same time in flight, there is a perception and a faith in God eternal; and to find thus a correspondence of that thought with the most profound and transcendent thought and assertions of all the great Confessors and Doctors of the Church of Christ?

These questions can be asked by our young man and also by many other people who resist the mirage of the «games of intellection and vocabulary», the kaleidoscope mirage which was spoken of at the beginning of this book. The mirage is constituted by man's possibility, during his earthly pilgrimage, of indefinitely combining schemes of concepts without their corresponding to a reality; that is, schemes of concepts which prove themselves to be without correlation to eternal Truth or an eternal mission of each man beyond his own death. Such is the mirage of the «intellectual kaleidiscope».

Any person who has received the Truth of the eternal Word in the intimity of his intelligent and loving being, is inclined to ask such questions of which we have just spoken, and an infinity of others; and that, always in charity and in harmonious correlation with the deep knowledge, ontological and highly objective, which communicates faith to man.

The Historicism
of Hegel and Dilthey

In a great forest the foliage of the large trees, shrubs
and bushes, apart from some exceptions, are green in color,
more or less dark, more or less light, but always green.
Therefore it is a meaningless enterprise to try to prove for
each branch of each tree that its foliage is green. One
recognizes the color at a glance, whether outside or inside
the forest. It is the same for the dominant characteristics of
innumerable representatives, more or less conscious, of the
intellectual trends, which cover long periods.

And such is the case with historicism. For a long time,
much before Kant, right up until today, the work of a
great number of authors, philosophers, men of letters and
also theologians, is tinged with this historicist color. And in
this atmosphere Christian thought and meditation have
been led, with an almost implacable rhythm, through Hegel
and Dilthey also, towards the «historic consciousness» of
present day theology.

Therefore it is henceforth useless, for true knowledge
about that which concerns God, eternity, man, the world,
history, it is useless and even harmful often, for the mind
and charity to dedicate long, hard work in order to

determine by interminable analyses, the intellectual relationship between authors; in order, for example, to determine to what degree Hegel is a continuator of Kant and to what degree he refuted him. It is certainly useful to follow the great veins of the development of the intellectual climates; but one finds himself always in the same basic data.

Discussions often filled with a priori deductions not always devoid of sophisms, so as to ascribe or deny such a system or such an assemblage of thought or belief the title of metaphysics, or the accumulation of exhaustive inventories of authors, of discussions and of subtleties, inventories, recensions and historical reports claiming objective «neutrality», have not been able to lead to any light. Often they have only served to fill the intellectual and spiritual horizon of all humanity and Christendom with still more bleak historicist mirages.

If the young man, in the radiance of his innocence and integrity wanted to try to understand and elaborate Hegel's essential thought and the intimate origin of that thought, — driven by a great innate love of the Truth in order to conform his life to it — he would remain astonished before two things: first, before the absence of all real life in the artificial edifice created by the games of words and concepts, games which bring no learning and no peace of true knowledge regarding man, regarding God and regarding the secret of history; secondly, he would be astonished before the inconceivably large number of commentaries, apologies, partial critiques of Hegel's works.

He would have read for example, apropos of the fundamental notion of the being:

«General division of the being: the being is above all determined in general against *other*.

«In the second place, it is determined within itself.

«In the third place, inasmuch as that anticipated division is rejected, the being is the abstract indetermination and immediacy, in which it must constitute the beginning». (252)

So he could ask himself:

— How, after having read that definition of the being, can one in the course of the book and the works of that author, continue to look for some truth, either about man, or about God, or about things?

— How is it possible that so many commentators did not feel shocked in the deepest intimity of their being and also of their whole existence?

— How can one ,reconcile this perception, so unique and so basic of the being, as determined above all by a «COUNTER», reconcile it with the being and the teaching of Christ?

— How can one reconcile the incessant self-negation and recuperation in the succession of infinitesimal abstract

---

(252)   G.W.F. HEGEL, *Scienza della logica*, ed. Laterza, Roma 1974, vol. I, p. 81.

moments, with the intimate ancestral experience of men and with the foundations of logic amidst every experience regarding movement?

— What can be the contribution of such an edifice, which finally offers no learning, no transcendent understanding, no knowledge of peace and grace? For even if that edifice were — at least inwardly — coherent with the basic principles of logic, it would offer no useful learning, no knowledge which could quench those who thirst for eternal Truth.

— How is it conceivable that one use the basic principles of the internal logic of the word in order to annul it and to construct, by combinations of words, a system set up like a huge «Erector Set»? How is that possible, given that even if this edifice were inwardly coherent and solidly set up, it remains inert and useless? Children, once the «Erector Set» is assembled, no longer know what to do.

And later on our young man could have read in Hegel's books, texts which constitute typical examples of the annihilation of the eternal principles of the internal logic of the word, and their replacement by artifices of words which do not leave in the consciousness any sign of order of the creation, any beneficient harmony of true knowledge, any savour of charity and hope.

There are texts which are pronouncements. They cannot be annulled indirectly by other texts even clearly contrary, because the presence of the opposing texts, as expression of the thought of the same author, constitute in themselves one more inadequacy. Among the very large number of such witness-texts of Hegel's thought and spirit in general, the young man might stop at the following text of his "Science of Logic".

«The law is also *the other of the phenomenon as such,* and its negative reflection as in its other. The content of the phenomenon, which is different from the content of the law, is the existent, which has as its basis its negativity, that is, it is reflected in its non-being. But this *other,* which is also an *existent,* is likewise a similar reflection in its non-being. It is therefore *the same,* and the one which appears is not there in fact reflected in an other, but it is *reflected in itself,* it is exactly that reflection in itself of the set being which is the law. But as such as it appears, it is essentially *reflected in its non-being,* that is, its identity is itself at the same time its negativity and its other. The reflection in itself of the phenomenon, the law, is therefore also not only its identical basis, but the phenomenon has its opposite in the law, and the law is its negative unity». (253)

Hegel's biographers report that one of his disciples is said to have asked him the meaning of a passage of one of his writings. It seems that Hegel answered in saying: «When I wrote it, there were two of us who understood it, God and I, now I fear that there is only God». (254)

---

(253)   G.W.F. HEGEL, *Scienza della logica,* vol. II, p. 163.

(254)   Cited by Jacques Chevalier, *Histoire de la pensée,* vol. IV, p. 17.

However if one succeeds in following a thread through all these inter-reflections among contraries and these inter-annulments, within this apparent effort of grasping, by means of the opposites, the always ungraspable reality of the being, then one witnesses the real effort of all these works which is hallucinating: the effort to annihilate all notion of the being and all possibility of man's situating himself as a creature endowed with an eternal permanence. Hegel alone would remain as a stable reference for the whole universe and for all spiritual reality outside of man's own ego; Hegel the perfect accomplishment who, moreover, had declared himself to be the perfect accomplishment of the Idea of philosophy.

How does man come to believe that by such internal dissociations he can attain the intimity of the real? It is not easily explainable because it is not the result of erroneous reasonings. It is rather these erroneous reasonings which result from a general inner disposition which concerns, above all, the will. The historicist mentality is due above all to a twisting of the will and thereby, of the thought before the phenomenon of the world.

For Hegel as for Kant and Vico, men are instruments for the realization of the plans, the dispositions of Nature or Reason. The providential character of these linear or cyclical accomplishments always remains indefinable, because it clashes with these authors' and so many others' inner inclination to avert a direct reference to a supreme Intelligence outside of man, who acts eternally in an inconceivable but ever present harmony of providence and liberty. The differences between the diverse theories and systems regarding the nature and the role of peoples and the particular laws of their evolution do not take away the common characteristic: the personification of the massive movement in time, a movement which in itself constitutes the being-made, its achievement and its justification; justification before whom? before itself, History.

The differences which can be established in the frame of the philosophy of history between the diverse notions of the «historic sense» are not of real help. An infinity of differences between twins can always be established, without thereby suppressing their common origin, their resemblance and their inner attraction. The dialectic movement of Hegel as expression, as process of argumentation, as projected image of the universal movement, certainly differs from various conceptions and expressions of the historic fact and sense, such as they can be seen in the works previous to him; different surely, up to a certain point.

But nothing can be constructed on these differences because these different theories of several epochs already greatly resemble each other, sometimes as twins, in their common refusal of the Being of God and in their effort to evade, by subtleties of expressions, the difficulty which this refusal presents.

There are more or less profound differences between theories, doctrines, ideas and methods which are offered under the same vocable and at times under the same formulae. But these differences, if they are not radical, are not sufficient to annul the fundamental identity or homogeneity of origin, process and finality. And there are differences which, in spite of certain intrinsic similarities, manifest the difference of the authors' point of departure and intention; they manifest the difference of intention and of hope.

Thus there are some more or less distinct and perceptible differences between the diverse ideas and theories which have been set forth under the name of phenomenology. Indeed there is a great difference at times for example, between the notion of phenomenology in «the phenomenology of the spirit» of Hegel, and the phenomenology of Husserl. (255) There is the difference between two beings, two intentions, two wills, two sensibilities.

Nevertheless Husserl's intellectual development only confirms the principle which is directly or indirectly in question in all the pages which have just been written: it is not possible to escape the agnostic and materialistic enclosure of idealism without making one's way towards the Being, towards the supreme Intelligence, creator, organizer, conserver of the being and of everything and every reality.

Husserl seeks an apodictic evidence which would be the absolute proof of the truth, but of the «scientific truth». He searches the essences of things, which make things be

---

(255) EDMUND HUSSERL (1859-1938), German philosopher, founder of the phenomenologic school.

such continually. It is difficult to see in this tendency a phenomenology which is purely descriptive and not at the same time explicative and therefore making appeal to speculations. In other words, it is impossible to claim an absolute proof of the truth by the simple description of the phenomena in the inner life of man.

When Husserl published his book "Logical Researches" (256), many believed that his rejection of Kant's critical idealism brought him closer philosophically to the thought of Saint Thomas. His book was considered as Neo-Scholastic. Later on, when several years after, he had published the "Ideas Regarding a Pure Phenomenology and a Phenomenologic Philosophy" (257), several of his disciples left him because they believed that he was returning to idealism. His student and assistant, one of the most beautiful souls of our century, Edith Stein, the future Sister Theresa-Benedict of the Cross (258), who for long years followed him and worked with him, attested to this fact by these words:

«It was (the book "Logical Researches") considered as Neo-Scholastic because it did not start with the

---

(256) *Logische Untersuchungen,* 2 vol. Halle 1900-1901.

(257) *Ideen zu einer reinen Phänomenologie und phänomenologischen Philosophie,* Halle, 1913.

(258) EDITH STEIN, (1891-1942) born at Breslau, of Jewish origin, Husserl's assistant, converted in the Catholic Church; arrested with her sister, also a convert, died with her in the gas chamber at Auschwitz.

subject to go then towards things: to know, was once again a process of reception of which the laws were given by the things, and it was not — as in critical idealism — the imposition of laws upon things. All the young phenomenologists were convinced realists. Nevertheless the "Ideas Regarding a Pure Phenomenology and a Phenomenologic Philosophy" contained certain passages which made one strongly think that 'the Master' was turning towards idealism. And his explanations in the discussions did not take away this doubt». (259)

Husserl recognized a value of truth in the propositions of evidence. It is according to this criterion that he judges the events of the past and classes them. But this desire of absolute «scientification» in knowledge makes him leave these notions of evidence in the background.

Absolute science, absolute objectivity, exterior real world, unexplained phenomena, evidence and many other terms, are notions with which one can play with a serious and good intention, in the effort to penetrate and possess the real, outside of the supreme Reality ordering all the real.

A painful march, as Husserl's, full of hard work on idealist and rationalist bases, under the name of a simultaneously objectivist and existentialist phenomenology,

---

(259) EDITH STEIN, cited by Sr. Theresia de Spiritu Sancto in *Edith Stein*, London 1952, p. 34.

leads us once again before an image of distressing efforts, truly desperate this time: efforts to avoid engaging upon — in the name of a mirage of absolute science — the unique way of the real as regards the individual, and history, and the universe.

Husserl was conscious of the impasse and of the idealist-agnostic-materialist enclosure of which we spoke earlier: Two years before his death, in a conversation he had with Edith Stein, among many other significant and enlightening declarations and avowals, he said:

«Man's life is nothing other than a way towards God. I tried to reach the goal without the help of theology, its proofs and methods; in other words, I wanted to reach God without God». (260)

After the long obstinacy of «scientizing» outside of any revelation, the contribution of the phenomenon of the interior life, many other of Husserl's writings, words and testimonies present him in a melancholy light, as having slowly become conscious of the impasse: to know outside of God.

The Absolute, a mysterious term, imprecise and at the same time limpid and concise, often serves in philosophy to substitute the Name and the Being of God. In the effort both multiform and unique, to by-pass the obstacle which

(260)   *Conversation with Edith Stein — December 1935,* cited in *Edith Stein,* éd. du Seuil, Paris 1954, p. 113.

is presented for many by the eternal Reality of the supreme Intelligence, in so far as a distinct and immutable Being, the term «Absolute» is a luminous subterfuge, lofty but often deprived of reality; whether as concept, being or objective fact in the creation.

There is an infinity of meanings of the term and the notion Absolute, in so far as it is a catalytic word for every difference and every variation. And it happens that in the name of some Absolute, the notion of absolute Truth and absolute Being is refuted or subtly altered.

That is why the young man, instead of tiring himself out to pursue the alternance in Hegel between the Absolute in itself and the Absolute which is being made, so as to grasp a major criterion in order to understand Hegel's spirit in the face of history, that is, in order to understand the meaning of his philosophy on history, could meditate on some indubitable signs.

When in 1806 Napoleon entered Iena, Hegel poured out his feeling and his judgement in view of this fact in a letter, which expresses a criterion of philosophy of history:

«I saw the emperor − that Soul of the world − ride across the city in reconnaissance; it is truly a marvellous feeling to see such an individual who, concentrated here in one point, upright on a horse, conquers the whole world and dominates it». (261)

---

(261) G.W.F. HEGEL, cited by Karl Löwith, *Da Hegel a Nietzche*, ed. Einaudi, Torino 1949, p. 324.

Our young man will certainly remain stupefied by such an authentic witness of the intimate feeling and view of the «sense of history» of a man who considered himself the perfect accomplishment of the Idea of philosophy in history. But he would hesitate to believe another witness-text written ten years later after the fall of Napoleon, in a letter to Friedrich Emmanuel Niethammer. That letter is all the more enlightening as the historicist giantism of Hegel only sees the gigantic strength of «the spirit of History» which advances relentlessly. And that image fills him with enthusiasm:

«I myself consider that the spirit of the world gave to the times the countersign to advance; such a command is obeyed; that being advances irresistibly as an armoured phalynx in tight order and with the imperceptible movement of sunlight through every obstacle; innumerable light troops moving about in every direction and the majority of them not even knowing what it is about, and only taking the blows which come as from an invisible hand. All the boasting in order to try and gain time are useless; all that, one can say, only reaches the shoe-laces of this colossus and serves only to shine those shoes or throw a little mud on them, but certainly is not in a position to unlace them, and even less to take off the divine shoes fitted with rubber soles, or the 'sevenleague boots', if it pleases the giant to wear them. The surest side to take *(interiorly and exteriorly)* is to watch this giant who moves forward». (262)

After that reading the young man would certainly understand why Hegel considered himself as the dialectic accomplishment of philosophy and that thus, in a certain sense the development was «closed» and the Absolute was reached in him.

He would be flooded with a profound sadness at the thought that the mentality which is manifested by this apersonal, cold and inhuman view could penetrate so deeply and be accepted by the world of study, science and also in Christianity.

Later on, the young man would realize also that the intrinsic historicism of Kant's thought is explicited in Dilthey's doctrinal historicism. For Dilthey, Kant is not only the light of the philosophic world, but he was also «a profound interpreter of Christianity». (263)

How could Dilthey have thought that of Kant? In this case it is not a question of sophisticated reverence. It is an identical intellectual attitude before the mystery of life. Dilthey's whole work, all his historicism is an effort to construct a uniquely experimental psychology based on the two great norms of Kant: the impossibility of knowing beyond the historic phenomenon on the one hand, and on the other, the postulate that the experimental inquiry can only be transcendental in the Kantian sense (that is, non-transcendent).

---

(262)   G.W.F. HEGEL, cited by Karl Löwith, *Da Hegel a Nietzsche,* p. 325.

(263)   WILHELM DILTHEY, *Le monde de l'esprit,* vol. II, p. 295.

Thus, in Dilthey everything proceeds by classifications, parallelisms, abstractions, always a priori and by a priori categories. Just as Kant, Dilthey, even when he speaks of spirit, cannot and does not want to leave the flow and drawing along of phenomena. We have already said how great Dilthey's influence was in philosophy and theology up until today.

For Dilthey philosophy is linked at its outset to the religious life. But with its development, with the development of the sciences, the desire to «found the solution of the universal enigma on solid bases» grows, and it is then that the methodic struggle of philosophy, literature, science begins, that is, the struggle of all which constitutes «normal life» according to Dilthey, the struggle against religion. Their maturity demands their autonomy. Philosophy implies the negation of the religious mentality, of «dogmatic faith and heavy authority of powerful clergies». And Dilthey specifies:

«This negation has the intelligence for its weapon, which decomposes the irrationality and transcendence of faith. It takes the defense of the joy of living, legitimizes the goal of life in profane work — struggles against the completely inadequate means of appeasement which are the sacrifices, ceremonies and sacraments». (264)

---

(264) WILHELM DILTHEY, *Le monde de l'esprit*, vol. II, pp. 291-292.

All that Dilthey wrote regarding religion and particularly under the title "The Problem of Religion" is of this tenor. In spite of his desire to appear as a samurai of thought and historic inquiry, he leaves no doubt regarding his anti-religious convictions and feelings. He ends these pages thus:

«Religion is a psychic ensemble, which, as philosophy, science and art, constitutes an element of some individualities and objectivizes itself in the most diverse ways in its products. — Each of these religions has a history, and it is possible to submit all these creations of historic order to the comparative method, in order to grasp the elements of religion which are common to them. But then one falls into a vicious circle...» (265)

The manuscript, written in 1911, the very year of his death, is interrupted at that spot.

What profound sadness before that useless and empty perseverance, right to the end, to close the inner gaze and hearing to the call of Revelation and to the true language of nature.

And when the young man has closed that book, he will continue to wonder, without certainly, having an immediate answer: what has happened in the minds and hearts, that such a word, so dissolvent of every fundamental essence of

---

(265)   WILHELM DILTHEY, *Le monde de l'esprit*, vol. II, p. 306.

ARC OF THE THEOLOGICAL CURRENTS ISSUED FROM THE HISTORICIST MENTALITY

In the midst of that huge river of events, doctrines and controversies of philosophic order, the mentality that we have called historicist has in all realms given rise to a spirit of criticism and of anthropocentric autonomy; and that has with time conditioned and oriented the study of Holy Scripture, historic study and research, and the formulations of the propositions and concepts as much in positive theology as speculative theology.

Some attribute the development of German philosophy to Protestant theology. [266]

Others believe that German philosophy influenced many theologians and exegetes in the Catholic Church. [267] Others go back to Luther to find the source of historicism

---

[266]   Cf. KARL LÖWITH, *Da Hegel a Nietzche*, p. 482.

[267]   Cf. ERNEST RENAN (1823-1892, writer and French exegete, having refuted the divinity of Christ): «I especially who owe to Germany what I hold most dear, my philosophy, I would say almost my religion». (*Pages françaises*, 5e éd., Paris 1921, p. 101).
    − Cf. CLAUDE TRESMONTANT, *La crise moderniste*, éd. du Seuil, Paris 1979, pp. 268-269.

and philosophic criticism in the world of Protestant as well
as Catholic theology.([268]) Others stop at Kant with a great
«hinterland» of thinkers and authors before him and of his
time ([269]): Others stop at Schleiermacher as at the father of
Hermeneutics ([270]); and at Hegel as at the father of the

([268]) Cf. LUDWIG FEUERBACH (1804-1872, German philosopher
product of Hegelianism): «The mission of the modern epoch
was that of realizing and humanizing God, that of transforming and resolving theology in anthropology. The practical
or religious form of that humanization has been Protestantism». (*Principi della filosofia dell'avvenire*, 1-2, Einaudi,
Torino 1946, p. 71).
  − Cf. KARL BARTH (1886-1968, Protestant theologian,
professor at Basel) who signaled to the theologians of Vatican
Council II «the danger that one could easily slip into by the
blameworthy repetition of the errors committed by modern
Protestantism». (*Ad limina Apostolorum*, 1967, p. 23, cited in
Bilancio della Teologia del XX secolo, ed. Città nuova, Rome
1972 vol. 4, p. 34).
  − Cf. H. ZAHRNT (born in 1915, Protestant theologian,
professor of practical theology at Hamburg): «Luther, whether
he wanted to or not, pushed the door which opened onto the
modern epoch». (*Aux prises avec Dieu,* éd. du Cerf, Paris
1969, p. 195).

([269]) Cf. DANIEL ROPS (1901-1965, French Catholic writer,
academician): «Emmanuel Kant, who, with his defiance of
reason is something of a lay Luther, nevertheless also had
'reduced religion to the limits of simple reason'». (*Storia della
Chiesa del Cristo,* ed. Marietti, Torino-Roma 1969, vol. VI-3,
p. 246).

([270]) Cf. HANS-JOACHIM KRAUS: *L'Antico Testamento nella
ricerca storico-critica dalla Riforma ad oggi,* p. 268.
  − Cf. A. RIZZI: «The moment the hermeneutic question
from a technical problem becomes a philosophic problem, is
represented by the work of *Schleiermacher*». (*I libri di Dio,*
ed. Marietti, Roma 1975, p. 275).

method and even the sensibility most adequate to «reality»: to the infinite dialectic movement. (271)

Each of these considerations can find supporting points in facts and writings, for each one expresses an aspect of the phenomenon. From the midst of this long amalgam a truth comes forth: the historicist mentality has profoundly altered the notion and the sacred vision of history and has little by little implanted in modern theology and the reading of Holy Scripture, the common character of the notions of historic consciousness, of new hermeneutics and of philosophic existentialism. And these notions, assimilated by many people, are the cause – and are at the same time the result – of a movement which took place and takes place in the innermost depths of the will, and thereby, in the consciousness: *the displacement of the center of gravity of Christian hope.*

This displacement, we have just said, is result and at the same time cause of three generic forms by which historicism has penetrated the modern mentality and thought, and has oriented, in great part, modern theology.

Now outside of all explanation and critique, the free man clearly sees that the historicist differentiation of hope is an enormous event; it is a great venture and trial for

---

(271)   Cf. KARL LÖWITH: «Hegel's work not only contains a philosophy of history and a history of philosophy; but its whole system is in addition, a thought fundamentally in an historic perspective as no other previous philosophy». (*Da Hegel a Nietzche,* p. 61).

Christian thought and consciousness. From the time of
illuminism, from Kant and Herder a headlong fall began,
because a greater and greater number of souls let themselves be drawn astray. In our century and particularly in
our time, the movement has become more rapid and
wide-spread, manifesting itself under a thousand forms, by
doctrinal formulae and postulates each time unforeseeable,
and yet almost fatal and at base of an identical essence.

Nevertheless in the deeper waters of the Church, the
movement forward persevered for the accomplishment of
her history which concerns the eternal salvation of each
man each time unique; an advance signaled in modern times
by the two dogmas of the 19th and 20th centuries on the
Blessed Virgin: the Immaculate Conception and the
Assumption. At the same time, a Christian historicist
liberalism permeated the peoples, transmitting an effervescence of emancipation; emancipation of man from every
hierarchic view in the universe, emancipation of the
Christian from the notion of the sacraments of the Church,
and from Revelation in so far as an eternal norm of
knowledge.

Regarding Hermeneutics

The word of man is issued from an order of supreme harmony. This is a fundamental immutable knowledge. The word of man is issued from the order of the eternal Intelligence of the Creator. No recourse to images of man and human society in the most distant past, no analysis of data of speech and languages, no speculation about the data of so-called experimental psychology no research in any realm whatever can alter that great and profound truth which is and must always be at the base of all meditation and all speculation regarding the truth, God, man and his eternal destinies. The word of man has its origin in the Word of God.

We have been witness for quite some time now, to a persistent effort to renew the fundamental notion of the word and the relationship of man with his own word and the word of others. That leads, whether one wants it or not, first to the negation or forgetting of the origin and the nature of the word of man, and then ineluctably to the destruction in man of the fundamental ontological bases of the human word.

This alteration is accomplished within hermeneutics, radically altering every norm of eternal logic of Interpretation. In all directions and in all intellectual activities one easily notices an effervescence of research of a new language, pathetic research of a new reading of texts, and not only of the Holy Scripture, a new conception of the fact of «understanding»; new norms, always in flight, for the interpretation of the texts, the signs and also the facts. That research leads, by the force of things, to an effort of analysis of the relationship between text and author, between text and reader, between author and reader, between interlocutors, between work and historic ambient; endless analyses, because it is not possible to establish some stable point of reference; because all notions and all contacts between the works and men are caught in the dance of an «impalpable existential».

This effort of analysis makes the ontologic bases of the word of man disappear from consciousness. And man feels himself thus caught in an interminable flux and reflux between subject and object, between reality in flight and the perception of that reality in flight. Man thus has no point of support, in his natural impulse to know; he loses all possibility of a stable reference to his own being, he no longer has an immutable, interior norm for the human word. The texts, learning, recollections, grammar, the sense of self and the sense of the other, are so recalled into question that they become as it were diluted, losing all consistency. At every instant the world vacillates; in the desire to grasp, not one thing or one idea, but the quintessence of a «moment of understanding», the words lose their intrinsic relation to the original order of the word; the words lose all possibility of stabilizing a meaning.

Then, along with the basic meaning, all the possible nuances of the words and meanings disappear. Man thus becomes incapable of receiving a certainty. Such is the major trial of the word of man, in the frame of the hermeneutics of our time.

In the centuries which are marked by the development of the historicist mentality, an ever new reading of the texts of the Old and New Testament has come forth and has developed. It is thus that all the particular forms of the new criticism of the Holy Scripture have come forth and have developed.

This new reading, and always newer, this criticism emerged and has developed under a double historicist criterion: on one hand, to recontrol all the facts and all the witnesses brought by that same Holy Scripture, through criteria and information sources of the general history; on the other hand, to receive the message of the Scripture as a message of intra-historic eschatology.

At the same time, this same control and this same analysis of the texts of Holy Scripture are carried out on literary, philologic, archeologic, ethnologic bases, and also according to the always renovated data of the experimental sciences, such as physics and astronomy.

As all things on this earth, parallel to this historic criticism, which has evolved in the sense of the historicist mentality, a critical study has continued, a deepening of the Holy Scripture, transmitting right up to our day, in a more or less imperfect manner, but always faithful to the revealed Truth, the real sense of the deepest mystery of the Old and New Testament and the facts of Holy History, of the Incarnation of the Word of God and the Resurrection of Jesus Christ.

This parallel advance is rarely made in the life of the world similarly to the extension of the two rails of a railroad track. There is an interpenetration in which one or the other tendency dominates, sometimes in the same person or the same period.

The historic criticism, literary and philological, has not restricted itself only to the frame of Holy Scripture; it extends to all the apostolic, patristic texts, the Acts of the Councils and the whole Magisterium of the Church.

And thus was born a tendency of reinterpretation of scriptural texts, theological texts of the Fathers, dogmatic texts of the Church; a tendency which ended in «reinterpreting» every writing and every fact and teaching brought down to us by Tradition; totally «reinterpreting» the advent and the message of Christ.

It is evident that this whole vast event of the new criticism has influenced in many, in a fundamental manner, the notion of the faith of the Church, and consequently the orientation of the so-called Biblical theology and theology in general, because the dogmatic basis of the Church has been put in question by successive «reinterpretations».

An encompassing and deepening view of all these hermeneutic phenomena brings forth something even more important and significant: that this thrust which could be called almost instinctive, for a reinterpretation of everything, has taken on the character of a general theory of knowledge. And this is where philosophic hermeneutics has been spoken of. It is not therefore a question only of the interpretation of a text or an account which reached us by oral transmission. It has to do with a theory which concerns the nature of understanding, of comprehension in itself.

This «research» has been the theoretical justification, justification in the hesitant conscience, of the general emancipation of man; emancipation with regard to a knowledge of revealed truth and with regard to a perception and a «reading» of the natural universe and of human history according to norms inscribed in man as ontologic bases of the word.

This emancipation, this more or less conscious, more or less intense effort towards emancipation, has taken the form of a revolution which has touched the whole realm of thought and charity of the Christian life. This emancipation is beyond the divergencies of ideas and doctrines, divergencies which take place on the same bases of the human word. For by this emancipation Love and Knowledge have been put to a great test in Christendom, because the word, the notion of the word, has been shaken in its human bases of ontologic and eternal order.

Our young man will certainly perceive all that effervescence of the hermeneutical evolution; but it will be very
difficult for him to master his experience and organize his
information. What's more, he will feel himself almost in the
impossibility of finding a means of communicating with the
others because the relativism of the word having now
become the doctrinal basis of the new hermeneutics, takes
away all points of reference. Within this perpetual calling
into question of every perception and transmission of every
notion regarding the word, understanding and knowledge,
the young man will be thus inclined to refer more than
ever, and apropos of everything and every one of his and
others' words, to the basis of all human life and all true
knowledge; to that universal basis of the interior word. For
the interior word is part of the essence of man, in so far as
being, and in so far as existence.

The young man, in following during long periods of
time, the historic exposés on the different stages of exegesis
of the criticisms of the texts, the diverse restatements of
the Magisterium, the endless, divergent, philologic commentaries and analyses of the texts and doctrines, will also
become aware of two things:

First, that the diverse itineraries of hermeneutics, as
different as they are, lead in any case to the conclusion,
that the divergencies within historicism, only serve to
confirm the historicist identity of all its ramifications in
theology and exegesis.

Second, that henceforth it is not very illuminating, in
so far as the essential reality of the present day theology is

concerned, to continue examining all the analyses of texts and all the divergent arguments, and all the commentaries and all the interpretations which have filled and every day fill the world of study and also the world of prayer.

For he will have already seen that the three general characteristics, the historic consciousness, the new hermeneutics and the existential reference make up the same intellectual agglomerate in the present day theological movement; and this, in such a manner that one can only with difficulty discern them separately in whatever exegetic and theological proposition.

And that certitude will be confirmed to him by the examination of every manifestation of the theological currents born of the historicist mentality. He will see spread out before him the arc of all the theological currents which express the great ordeal of the Church, of the whole of Christendom and of the world.

Global   Reinterpretation
of Christianity

The most noble and beautiful events of the history of the earth, the extraordinary sacrifices of pure love, the manifestations of tenderness and fidelity, of a grandeur and depth which cannot be found in any profane literature, the meditations and intellectual speculations around the mystery of God, man and knowledge, which, even by their cathedralic architecture alone, cause respect in every person of good faith and wholesome sensibility, the legislations and mores, which in any case have tempered the revolt and blindness of peoples; works of music and architecture, which have unveiled secrets of universal harmony of the creation, the works of the human word, which engender and transmit the peace of eternal love and the love of eternal peace, all the living everlastingness of Christ, who, by his Church, through all the material and intellectual human vicissitudes, has maintained the luminous content of the Faith, all that must, according to the «historicist theology», be reinterpreted and fecundated by a «profane self-interpretation» which man possesses at a certain epoch.

And by what way must this content of the Faith, which has kept great men of science in profound piety and filled the souls of many children of God with superior knowledge, let itself by fecundated?

Historicist theology of our time thus proposes: authentic theology must assimilate the profane conception that man has of himself and «allow itself to be fecundated» by that profane conception, in so far as language is concerned; but much more, theology in order to be authentic must allow itself to be fecundated by that profane conception that man has at a certain epoch — not only in what concerns his language — but especially in what concerns its content. (272)

But the result of this fecundation, that is, that which would come forth as doctrine and theology, must once again assimilate the profane conception that man would have of himself at that new epoch, that is, assimilate the world. And after theology has assimilated the profane conception that man would have of himself at that new period, it would have to let itself once again be fecundated by that profane assimilated conception; that is, theology

---

(272)   «Theology is authentic and preachable only in so far as it succeeds in entering into contact with all the profane self-interpretation that man possesses in a determined point of time, in entering into dialogue with it, in assimilating it and in letting himself be fecundated by it regarding language, but still more regarding the thing itself». (KARL RAHNER, *Corso fondamentale sulla fede*, ed. Paoline, Alba 1977, p. 25).

would have once again to let itself be fecundated by the world. Thus there would be a continual assimilation by theology of the profane opinion of man and continual fecundation of theology by the assimilated profane opinion.

Such is the generic view to which the historicist mystification leads. Christ came to save the world, to fecundate the world by the message and hope of eternal life. He did not come to be fecundated by the world.

The young man, struck by that view and language, surely wonders:

— How is it possible to give the name of Christian theology to all that? What would remain of what is called authentic theology, after such a multiple fecundation of itself by all that it would have assimilated in the way of profane world?

In this will to reinterpret Christianity, which is explicitly manifest in a large number of works of diverse writers and theologians, the young man will recognize the presence of the agglomerate of which we have spoken: the historic consciousness which deems that all must be considered and understood as perpetual variation in time; hermeneutics which wants to impose a new interpretation of all Scripture, of the whole mystery of the Church: a

---

(273)   Cf. P. MARC EL NEUSCH: «Today hermeneutics takes new flight, linked to the taking into account of the collective dimension of humanity. With Moltmann and the political theologies, a third generation of hermeneutics makes its

general reinterpretation of Christianity; the existential reference, which is at the base of the judgements of the
historic consciousness and of the comprehension and
interpretation of hermeneutics. (273)

---

appearance, which displaces the accent from orthodoxy to
orthopraxy from Christianity as 'doctrine' to Christianity as
'praxis'. – Hermeneutics gives itself the task of liberating the
Word of God in order to restore to it its efficacity in
History.– These foragings in the field of hermeneutics leave
the feeling that the term takes an uncontrollable extension.
We see at least that the problems are displaced: historic truth,
existential signification, social authenticity». (*Au pays de la
théologie,* éd. du Centurion, Paris 1979, pp. 133-134).

Absolute Existential Relativism

All the words of Christ, his message, his warning addressed to the Apostles: «that your word be yes, yes and no, no», all the words of the Apostles regarding their witness and the truth to transmit, every word of the Holy Scripture concerning the truth to know and transmit [274], all that must be reinterpreted according to the «new theories» of language. Thus theology would have to change its reference points and deliberately and consciously enter the era of «transcendent relativism».

The Church could never formulate sure propositions in order to define her faith, because «she will have to reckon with the problematicity inherent in all the propositions in general», and no truth can ever be conceived and expressed with certitude.

According to that new philosophy of language [275], «the propositions of faith are never the direct word of

---

[274]   Matthew 5:37.
        Mark 13:31: «Heaven and earth will pass away, but my words will not pass away».
        Titus 1:1: «To further the faith of God's elect and their knowledge of the truth».

[275]   Küng, regarding the new philosophy of language, refers to M. Heidegger, H.G. Gadamer, H. Lipps, B. Liebrucks, K. Jaspers, M. Merleau-Ponty, L. Wittgenstein, G. Frege, Ch. W. Morris; H. Lefèbvre, N. Chomsky. (HANS KÜNG, *L'infallibilità*, ed. Mondadori, Milano 1977, p. 114).

God», and that is why this mediate word is «perceptible and transmissible in so far as it is a human proposition. As such, the propositions of faith enter into the general problematicity of human propositions». For: «the propositions do not correspond to reality»; «the propositions are equivocal»; «the propositions are only relatively translatable»; «the propositions are in motion»; «the propositions can be ideologically exploited, and the proposition 'God exists' can be ideologically exploited». It is thus that Hans Küng expounds in five points his creed on the impossibility of ever having a sure creed. (276)

Such predicates cannot be veiled by other texts of the same authors, voluminous texts perhaps, but always in the same direction and very often fleeting. For these predicates manifest an absolute relativism, establishing within the Church an absolute relativism; they transmit a doctrine of language such that no one can ever feel himself in the truth, either acquired by dint of speculation and research, or revealed by God.

Relativism is far from corresponding to the natural desire for objectivity and to an objective perception of the continuous relations between beings and things. It is a predicate as far from the truth as conceptual monolithism despoiled of nuances and eternal reference; for conceptual monolithism wants each time to impose concepts despoiled of any real relationship of charity with the Principle of

---

(276) HANS KÜNG, *L'infallibilità*, pp. 114-118.

Truth and with other beings; it wants to impose dried up concepts, without any content of life, deprived of nuances and outside of all lived hope, to impose them as objective truth and as universal principle of knowledge of the truth.

Christianity, that is, the message of the person and teaching of Christ, has brought, precisely in the midst of the relativity of the philosophy and natural experience of men, criteria and reference points which resolve in harmony of peace, in the understanding, memory and heart, the perpetual movement and oscillation between subject and object, between objectivity and subjectivity.

It is thus that the luminous mystery of Revelation manifests itself, when it is received not only as a concept in the intellect, but as love in the will.

Negation of the Incarnation.

Alteration of the Reality of Christ.

Jesus Christ, from the beginning, even before his Passion, was contested by the scribes and the doctors. He was condemned because he brought, by his Person, the message of the salvation of men, being the Son of God and because He had declared before the highest authority of Israel that He was the Son of the Blessed God. Then he has been contested even within his Church by the «scribes and doctors», throughout all the centuries of the life of Christianity.

It has happened that again in our century, the negation of the divine Reality of Christ and of the Mystery of his Incarnation has penetrated, more or less consciously, in the ambit of the Church. What is particularly evident in the frame of certain theologies in the Church and in all the denominations, is that this negation is the manifest result of a reversal of the hope of which we have already spoken. And it is also evident that this negation and this reversal of hope obligatorily entail the always greater loss of the constitutional order of truthfulness and charity of the language.

It is certainly difficult, for the great number of the faithful, by the simple means of reflection and intellectual exterior information, to discern, in the midst of the multiplication of the continual calling into question of each notion, consideration, meaning, principle and postulate of the teaching Church, the narrow but royal way of internal logic and eternal order of the word. Without these fundamental notions and principles of the teaching Church, there would be no possibility or right to speak in theology, within the Christian world.

For the orientation of the will towards historicist concepts of hope has provoked a revolt in depth against the word of theology, of thought in general and of Christian life, born of the true hope brought by Christ.

The truth of the Incarnation of the Word that the Apostles received from Jesus Christ himself and transmitted in deposit to the Church, deposit which the Church has defended and preserved throughout the centuries of her life, that truth is rejected by some theologians and authors within the Church.

In this book (page 77) we have already shown that Karl Rahner teaches that God and man have the same essence.

Karl Rahner in his theological Encyclopedia "Sacramentum Mundi", in the few pages of his article on the Incarnation, as in the pages of his article on Jesus Christ, not only affirms in several ways that identity of the essence of God and man, but he also destroys, by a large number of propositions learnedly entangled, the whole truth of the doctrine on the Incarnation of Jesus Christ.

If our young man has the patience to disentangle the diverse, often contradictory meanings of Rahner's statements and propositions, he will clearly see a laborious construction which radically changes the whole doctrinal basis and authentic internal meaning of the word and the predicates which have from the beginning constituted − with all the enrichment of the centuries − the teaching of the Church.

a) According to Rahner, three doctrines on the Incarnation should be distinguished: first, a doctrine of the New Testament about Jesus; second, an «ecclesiastic» doctrine; and third, a doctrine of «present day predication». [277]

b) According to Rahner, «it cannot be denied that within the Christology of the New Testament can be found diverse basic conceptions of this Christology, but without, for all that, their cancelling each other, according to whether (gnosologically and ontologically) a line of ascendance or descendance is preferred». [278]

Now there would not only be a doctrine of the New Testament about Jesus, an ecclesiastic doctrine and doctrine of present day predication, but even that which is accepted as doctrine of the New Testament could contain some

---

[277] KARL RAHNER, *Sacramentum mundi,* ed. Morcelliana, Brescia 1975, vol. 4, col. 485-491.

[278] KARL RAHNER, *Sacramentum mundi,* vol. 4, col. 485.

different «basic conceptions». That should suffice to understand the abyss between the Gospel and all these considerations which offer themselves as teaching of the Church of Christ. But there is, as regards the Gospel something more, in the direct context of these propositions of Karl Rahner's statement which says:

«The doctrine of the New Testament about Jesus is beyond the self-testimony of the historic Jesus». [279]

This means that the New Testament would not be a truthful witness of the mystery and teaching of Christ. Such postulates regarding the New Testament and the Person of Christ are the result of the «reinterpretations» and the «demythologizations» of the texts which the Church received from the hands of the Apostles and Evangelists. This simple and clear phrase: «the Church received from the hands of the Apostles and Evangelists her sacred texts», can seem antiquated and non-scientific. But the young man will have already understood that there are two different general notions of Science, and each of them corresponds to a different position, radically different, in view of the creation, in view of man, in view of the history of men and in view of the intelligence and memory of man. Now according to one of these notions, the expression: «the Church received from the hands of the Apostles her sacred texts» corresponds to a profoundly historic and scientific truth.

---

(279)   KARL RAHNER, *Sacramentum mundi*, vol. 4, col. 485.

Thus the young man will certainly wonder:

— What value can a doctrine of the New Testament have, if that Document which is the New Testament alters the witness that Jesus Christ has borne regarding himself?

— If one believes that the New Testament has altered the witness of Christ, and being given that it is impossible to honestly establish the differences between the information brought by Tradition and the written information (altered, according to Rahner) of the New Testament, how can one be an apologist of Christ and refer to that same New Testament?

But for Rahner that young man's question has been surpassed without receiving any real answer, by speculations which he himself calls «Transcendental Christology». For he says clearly in these same pages of his article on Jesus Christ that Pauline and Johannine Christology which, although constraining, is already an interpretation, cannot be the point of departure for a current, systematic theology:

«A current, systematic Christology cannot however take its natural point of departure in that'theological understanding of Jesus Christ. That at base is also valid for the more ancient Christologic assertions of the pre-Pauline Scripture». (280)

---

(280)   KARL RAHNER, *Sacramentum mundi*, vol. 4, col. 194.

According to Karl Rahner one of the points of the doctrine of the New Testament which goes beyond the witness that Christ has borne regarding himself, is precisely *the pre-existence of Christ*, that is the pre-existence of the Word of God before the birth of Jesus of Nazareth:

«The Christology of today, in the announcement and theological reflection, must in some way take up again – and preach!– that story of the 'Ascendance Christology', which already in the frame of the New Testament, passing with an enormous rapidity from the experience of the historic Jesus to the formulae of the descent of the Christology of Paul and John, has been transformed into a doctrine of the incarnation of the pre-existent Son-*Logos*». (281)

From that text this comes forth:

The doctrine on the Incarnation must *therefore* be preached in such a way to reinforce in predication that theology which one wants to call «theology of ascendance»; that is, it must be preached that the Church, in coming to a standstill and conforming to the teaching of Saint Paul and Saint John, transformed headlong the «Ascendance Christology» into the doctrine of the Incarnation of the pre-existent Word-Son. That is, the first duty of predication is to denounce the Christologic errors of Saint Paul and Saint John. Consequently the elevation of

---

(281)   KARL RAHNER, *Sacramentum mundi*, vol. 4, col. 492.

man towards God, the perfection of man, would constitute, as Rahner says, «that which the Church calls incarnation» and the descent of the Logos-Son in the humanity of Mary, would constitute a deformation, which would have to be set aside by the new predication. That is why, when in another place Rahner speaks of union, it must be understood in the sense of «absolute proximity» between man and God, a meaning totally different from that of the Incarnation. And it is thus that Karl Rahner in his article on Jesus Christ, refers to the Biblical part of this same article in order to make his thesis explicit:

> «The Judeo-Hellenistic doctrine on the wisdom anterior to the world would be the one to have led to faith in the pre-existence of Jesus, thus leading to, the *affirmation of the incarnation*». (282)

> «One can reckon that titles of dignity such as 'Messiah', 'Son of Man', 'Lord', maybe even 'the Son', were only taken by the original community to characterize the consciousness, and thus the claim, on Jesus' part, to have been sent, as well as in order to express its faith in him». (283)

By all these considerations, which give the impression of a superhuman effort to skirt the luminous Mystery of the Incarnation in the Virgin Mary of the Word of God, is

---

(282)   KARL RAHNER, *Sacramentum mundi,* vol. 4, col. 173-174.

(283)   KARL RAHNER, *Sacramentum mundi,* vol. 4, col. 171.

explicitly and implicitly stated the theory of a man Jesus, who, in his activity to become «autonomous», goes towards God, who on his part goes to encounter man in order to self-communicate himself. And there would then be a meeting, a «culminating point» of absolute and definitive proximity.

It is that which must be preached, according to Karl Rahner, under the vocable of «Incarnation of Christ». This Jesus is not a prophet like the others. His proximity with the divine is much more perfect, and thus he has become the «absolute bearer of salvation». It is this theory which with much speculative and linguistic hermetism, is presented as being able to be in harmony with the «formulae of classical Christology», and which must be preached as the doctrine of the Church.

In so far as the harmony of these Christologic theories is concerned, of this «Ascendance Christology» with «classical formulae», Rahner does not explain how it can be conceived, but he says that all the same it must be upheld «for many reasons that need not be illustrated here». (284)

Rahner asks precisely that «the Incarnation be preached *in such a way*» that the theory of the «absolute and definitive proximity» appear as the doctrine of the Church for the Incarnation. (285)

---

(284)   KARL RAHNER, *Sacramentum mundi*, vol. 4, col. 191.

(285)   KARL RAHNER, *Sacramentum mundi*, vol. 4, col. 492.

In his theory as a whole, expounded in all his writings, as also in his articles of the "Theological Encyclopedia", the mystery of the Annunciation is ignored and implicitly refuted, that is, the mystery of the Incarnation.(286)

The multitude of the explicit and implicit propositions which touch on the mystery of the Incarnation and which promptly turn away from it, by means of speculations with neither basis nor consequence, the multitude of apersonal expressions, that is of expressions of which the ontological subject cannot be specified, cannot present a doctrine — erroneous perhaps for the Church, but which would allow some consistency between starting point and ultimate end; and they certainly cannot veil the clear negation of the mystery of the Incarnation which they contain.

For Rahner the Incarnation is *in* Jesus; it is not the conception of Jesus Christ. That is said in several ways:

«The fact of the Incarnation in Jesus of Nazareth represents a moment of the concretization of this mystery of the incarnation». (287)

---

(286) In his «Encyclopedia», there is an article on the Revolution, on the French Revolution, on Tourism, on Depth Psychology, on Psycho-Hygiene, on Psychoanalysis, and other articles the names of which out of respect for the Blessed Virgin are not mentioned here, but there is no article on the Annunciation, nor on the Immaculate Conception, two dogmas of the Church.

(287) KARL RAHNER, *Sacramentum mundi*, vol. 4, col. 484.

That is, concretization of the mystery of the Incarnation is comprised of many moments, and the Incarnation in Jesus is one of all those moments. Thus the fact of the Incarnation «in Jesus» would not be the whole Incarnation. The statement of the Incarnation is proposed in the frame of a Christic evolution of humanity and the cosmos, which in any case has never been the teaching of the Church.

The waiting of the creation which groans (Rom. 8:19) does not mean that the Incarnation is an event of the «proximity» of God and man, nor a long-term collective event. The whole creation waits for the redemption. It does not follow the successive moments of an event of an Incarnation which must, in the long run, come to a close.

Rahner, resuming the basis of his theory in a very expressive image, says explicitly:

«When the auto-communication of God and the auto-transcendment (288) of man occur, in the categorial-historic sense, at their absolute and irreversible culminating point, that is, when in the spatio-temporality God 'exists' in an absolute and irreversible manner, and the auto-transcendment of man thus reaches exactly a similar full transference in God, one has what is Christianly called incarnation». (289)

---

(288)   Auto-transcendment: word created by the Italian translator to express the notion of a transcendence which would be accomplished progressively(?).

(289)   KARL RAHNER, *Sacramentum mundi*, vol. I, col. 498.

There are therefore two who are acting, God who auto-communicates Himself, and man, already existent, who auto-transcends himself. When God becomes existent in space-time, not in a relative manner, but in an absolute and irreversible manner, and when at the same time man, in his effort at auto-transcendence reaches a full transference in God, then there is, according to Rahner, the realization of that which one Christianly calls the Incarnation.

It is certain that in Scholastic Theology the study of the man Jesus held a large place. Particularly Saint Thomas Aquinas applied himself scrupulously to all that concerns knowledge, science, the will of man, as well as knowledge, science, the will of God, in Jesus Christ. But here we are far from these questions. For Saint Thomas speaks of the human reality of Jesus Christ as being conceived in the womb of a woman, by the direct intervention of God. That is why Rahner's theory cannot look for support in referring to the fact that the humanity of Jesus Christ held a great place in Scholasticism.

Through Rahner's hermetism, the young man will have understood that Saint Thomas speaks of Jesus conceived by divine intervention; and that Rahner speaks of a Jesus who, conceived naturally and acting by his «desire for autonomy» reaches the «absolute and irreversible proximity» of God, who desires his «auto-communication». It is not therefore a question here of the delicate nuances and images often ineffable through which at times one intimately lives the mystery of the Incarnation, the mystery of a man conceived in the womb of a woman by direct intervention of God.

Rahner's discourses as a whole concern the intellectual and spiritual course of a man conceived naturally, and that cannot be called «incarnation». That theory, whether one wants it or not, is the negation of the Incarnation and the alteration of the reality of Christ.

Anthropology is a term which can have and has several meanings, several points of departure. But all that Rahner says reveals an anthropologic theory which leads directly to a total historization of God and to the identity of the essences of God and man. And that is why Rahner expresses himself thus:

«What man is, constitutes the affirmation of the totality of theology in the absolute». (290)

* * *

Some considerations about the person of Christ evoke certain occult doctrines regarding the Incarnation of the Word of God, particularly those of the Anthroposophists and the Rosicrucians. According to that doctrine, Jesus, the great initiate, successor of the great initiates, accepted that his soul leave his body in the waters of the Jordan, and the

---

(290)   KARL RAHNER, *Sacramentum mundi*, vol. 4, col. 273.

Word of God took his place. The one who emerged from the waters of the river was another person, Jesus Christ. (291)

Professor Hans Küng says repeatedly that Jesus may have become «aware of his vocation during his baptism — and from that moment he felt himself flooded by the Spirit». (292) Certainly Küng says even less than the occultists, because he does not accept any divinity in Jesus Christ, either before or after his baptism. By all his writings, Küng confirms his doctrine about Jesus Christ with much less hermetism than Rahner. According to that doctrine the Incarnation and all that concerns the Annunciation and the Nativity of Christ in the texts of the New Testament are pious legends due to anonymous compilations of the first Christian community. (293) In Küng, the explanation of the person of Christ is more social and psychological than speculative. By the term «Incarnation», he means the life and teaching of Christ:

«In no place in the New Testament is the incarnation of God himself spoken of — If today one wishes nevertheless to speak without making errors about the

---

(291) Cf. RUDOLF STEINER (1861-1925, Founder of the Theosophico-Christian Anthroposophical Society), *De Jésus au Christ,* éd. La Science spirituelle, Paris 1947; and MAX HEINDEL, Cosmologie des Rose-Croix, éd. Paul Leymarie, Paris 1947.

(292) Cf. HANS KÜNG, *Essere cristiani,* ed. Mondadori, Milano 1976, p. 197.

(293) Cf. HANS KÜNG, *Essere cristiani,* pp. 510, 511 and 388.

incarnation of the Son of God, that incarnation will not be able to be reduced to the *punctum mathematicum* or *mysticum* of the conception or the birth of Jesus, but rather it will have to be extended *to the whole of the life and the death of Jesus»*. (294)

And it is thus that he then expresses in his book "Does God exist? ", with large letters, his creed which refutes the mystery of the Annunciation of the Creed of the Church:

«Incarnation of God in Jesus means that: in all Jesus' discourses, in all his predication, in the entirety of his behavior and destiny, the Word and the Will of God took human form: in the whole of his word, his action, his passion and his death, in short in the totality of his person, Jesus announced, manifested, revealed the Word and the Will of God. He in whom word and will, teaching and life, being and acting, perfectly coincide, is corporeally, is in human form Word, Will, Son of God». (295)

And elsewhere he has already explained this creed:

«In the community's tendency to define him above everything else 'the Son', one must see, as it were a reflection, on the face of Christ, of the God proclaimed by him Father. It is easy by this way, to explain the

---

(294)   HANS KÜNG, *Dio esiste,* ed. Mondadori, Milano 1979, p. 763.

(295)   HANS KÜNG, *Dio esiste,* p. 763.

passing to the other title, 'Son of God', coined by tradition». (296)

And Küng says that it is in this sense, and certainly only in this sense, that he «accepts even the Nicene Council of the year 325». (297)

This acceptance on Küng's part «even of the Nicene Council» is conditioned by all his doctrine according to the meaning of which he says he would have accepted it. It is clear that this means that it would be necessary to empty the formulae of the Council of all ontologic meaning and replace it by Küng's historic-sociologic-psychological meaning.

Küng, as many theologians of today, is heir to the intellectual and spiritual attitude of Hegel before the world and before God. He amply bears witness moreover to his gratitude, in declaring that Hegel's thought «stimulated and encouraged him to reflect upon the historicity of God and upon the historicity of Jesus». (298)

But here is the image that Küng gives of Jesus, an image which not only expresses an insolence of bad taste or an unconsidered fantasy; but it expresses the inner outcome of a thoroughly historicist eschatological view:

---

(296)   HANS KÜNG, *Essere Cristiani*, p. 440.

(297)   HANS KÜNG, *Dio esiste*, p. 764.

(298)   HANS KÜNG, *Incarnazione di Dio*, ed. Queriniana, Brescia 1972, p. 604.

«Jesus was not a priest, but an ordinary layman, guide of a lay movement — Neither was he a theologian — Jesus was a peasant and illiterate besides — He could not boast of any theologic culture — He did not present himself as an expert of all possible doctrinal, moral, juridic, legal questions — He was, if you will, a public raconteur, one of those persons whom one still meets today in the great square of Kabul». (299)

There is a little book whose author is unknown and we think, without any theological pretension and which is entitled "No Man Ever Spoke Like This Man". (300) In the pages of this little book, one sees that the word of Christ is revered for its superhuman grandeur, profundity, vitality and its eternal origin.

This little book whose title already constitutes a teaching, transmits a true image of Jesus of Nazareth, of Jesus Christ, of the Son of Man, of the Son of God, the incarnate Word; it shows how and how much Christ's word transmits his vibration of real life and reveals his divine truth to those who, without being either doctors or professors of theology, according to the word of Saint John, receive Him with simplicity and truth.

When one does not receive Him, one pushes Him away with hostility and sometimes with a lack of elementary decency. Even a «raconteur from Kabul» can be perhaps,

(299)   HANS KÜNG, *Essere Cristiani,* pp. 192-193.

(300)   H.L. CHEVRILLON, *Jamais homme n'a parlé comme cet homme,* éd. St Paul, Paris 1975.

more than many learned people, receptive and sensitive to the unique, inimitable grandeur and beauty of the word and the acts of Christ.

* * *

The Incarnation constitutes the most profound basis and at the same time the keystone of the mystery of the Redemption. That is why the Incarnation, by Mary and the Holy Spirit, of the Word of God, constitutes the basic foundation of the whole doctrinal truth which has been set forth and intimately lived in the Church, through all the moral as well as intellectual trials in which the Church has had to and must live her Mystery of Redemption.

Now the Incarnation is not a construction or the projection of human considerations made with love and piety.

— It is not the product of the collective exaltation of a fervent but groping community with regard to the origin of its truth, of its own birth and its own mission.

— It is not the voluntary conclusion of an interpretation of certain texts or certain words orally transmitted; interpretation always readapted to the different cultures.

— It is not the product of an interpretation of the New Testament and of a predication which would have constructed, by its continual adaptation, the history-legend of Christ, the message of Christ and the doctrinal development.

— It is not the product of a predication according to which the New Testament and Tradition would not have had to treat of what Christ was (ontologic Christology), but only of what Christ had done (functional Christology).

— It is not the product of a desperate desire for «liberation» in time, from the shackles and the miseries of Adam's race.

— It is not the poetic mythologization of a beloved and «eternal» Hero.

— It is not the symbolic personification issuing from a feeling of a religious kind which would be immanent in man.

— And it is not the name of a perfection of man which rises up to God through love, combat and sacrifice.

— It is not the product of the imagination or of human astuteness within a group with a social and political aim.

It is the highest revealed truth: the truth of the ontologic salvation of man.

This fundamental truth of the reality of the Incarnation constitutes a general criterion through which all subjects, questions, themes regarding the whole economy of Redemption must be seen and understood. Thus the mystery of the Church, its origin and its constitutional reality are founded on the Incarnation.

The question of the relations of the Church with the world, the question of the natural and the supernatural, the question of the essence and meaning of the sacramental reality, the question of the vocation of man and his mission in history, the question of the rapport of the individual and humanity with history and with eternity, all questions, as much in what concerns the knowledge of God, as in the means and ways of salvation, have a common denominator: the Incarnation of the Word of God by Mary and the Holy Spirit.

If this truth is contested and altered, as indeed it is, at the same time, all the other realities of man, his history and his final ends, are de facto contested and altered. No question can be treated and envisaged independently of the fundamental notion of the Incarnation.

That is why it is impossible to have a radical change in the statement of the Incarnation without the entirety of the doctrinal, spiritual and moral questions, the entirety of Revelation, being altered in the thought, consciousness and will.

To have a fundamental criterion, a principle with which one thinks about universal reality, about the reality of each man, about revealed truths and human learning, does not blur the nuances and particularities of each case that we envisage through this general criterion. But neither does the multitude of nuances and particularities change the uniqueness and universality of the criterion and the principle. If that uniqueness is differentiated in multiplicity, no perception and no judgement can situate an order of knowledge and life in man.

That is why it must never be forgotten that the loftiest speculations about the Holy Trinity, for example, or the meditation on the global phenomenon of the history of men or on the real essence of the notion of sacrament, logically and inevitably depend on the notion of the Incarnation; and especially on our intimate rapport with that notion.

The roots of the mystery of the Church plunge directly and ontologically into the mystery of the Incarnation. It has always been a great illusion to believe that an «investigation» can be followed, to seek a better interpretation and comprehension of the texts, to seek to establish a doctrine regarding grace or the Passion or Death or Resurrection of Christ, independently of the notion of the Incarnation or simply in leaving it — sometimes maliciously — in the shadows.

Men live, love God and their fellow-men without all having the same intellectual knowledge of the mystery of God and of the creation. But that difference in degree of intellectual knowledge does not necessarily prevent men from being in inner harmony with the Truth and the Will of the Creator. But if man consciously endeavors to construct, by his own strength and according to the inclination of his own will, explanations of God's secrets, refuting or altering or willfully ignoring what has been given to him as revealed truth, he de facto departs from all harmony and all possibility of perception of the real.

It is according to this law that humanity has trod to this day, and the Church has been constituted, has received

Revelation, has maintained it, and transmitted it intact through many expectations and hesitations, much suffering and much holy ignorance. For that holy ignorance does not prevent the receiving, living and transmitting in acts of life and in words of life, the truth revealed and received.

* * *

As much as it is humanly permitted to picture the reality of the early days of the Church, the Incarnation of the Word of God has been revealed and also has remained an arcanum. Arcanum does not always mean a secret life and a secret knowledge which must only be revealed to a few initiates. It also means that there are truths that cannot always be transmitted to everyone, not because of a command or a cult for secrecy, but because there are truths which necessitate a degree of inner liberation and a particular spiritual elevation in order to be intellectually realized and then expressed by means of the vocabulary of the external word.

When Saint Paul says that «he heard things which cannot be told, which man may not utter» (301), it does not mean that it concerns a secret confided which he must keep at all cost, but that he heard words which are unutterable in themselves and which it is not given to man to speak. Thus he speaks of a mystery, but not of a secret. Every mystery contains a hidden reality.

_____

(301)   2 Cor. 12 : 4.

But it is not a question of a secret that someone must keep. It concerns the impossibility of communication on the level of the human word. Certain realities can be conceived according to the interior word, without being able to transmit them by an exterior word. The Church has had a limpid existence from the beginning; but in herself she is a mystery, as life is a mystery.

Thus Christ was immediately received but his mystery has been deepened intellectually more or less slowly according to the individuals, at the same time being received totally by the same men. It is one of the data moreover which causes the Church of Christ to be, in spite of her human lacunae, the unique holder of the mysteries of eternal Truth.

It is in the profound life of the Church, through the Blessed Virgin and the Apostles, that Christ deposited the great truths regarding the mystery of his Person and his work as Redeemer. The predication by totally renewed beings has sprung from this eternal deposit of revealed truth and charity as a light and as a strength. And whereas the predication certainly adapted itself to the languages and levels of the peoples, at times undergoing perturbations, the great truths of the sacred deposit were immutably transmitted, and illumined the spirits and were little by little formulated and defined according to the providential necessities within the vast effervescent life of the Church.

Such is the image, altogether too synthetic certainly, but real, of the transmission of the Revelation about God, about the Son of God, about salvation and the eternal mission of man; the image of the doctrinal march. For Christ, as was already said at the beginning of this book (p. 36), did not entrust the transmission of the sacred deposit to the relativity and instability of historic man.

The predication has spread within many diverse peoples. But Revelation, the deposit of Christ through the Blessed Virgin and the Apostles, has been transmitted in the depths of the soul and the life of the Church. It is not predication which has conditioned the transmission of Revelation. It is the presence of the deposit, radiating its original light of immutable divine truth, which has conserved unchanged and at the same time alive and active, in spite of all the external fluctuations and tribulations, and all the temporary, kerygmatic adaptations, the transcendent mystery of the Church.

The Radical Alteration
of Revelation

From the beginning, as we have already said, the divine reality of Christ has been contested. It was inevitable because if the Son of God were accepted without contestation, it would be the sign that the aim of the Incarnation, in that flesh of man in the history which followed Adam, would have been attained before the Incarnation.

The way of revealed truth has unfolded, is unfolding and will unfold in the image of the life of Christ: originating directly from God, hidden, public, contested, calumniated, integral, sacrificing, filled with love, mysterious and limpid, divine and human. It is thus that Truth has appeared at the surface of the Church at large and it has been little by little consigned in the formulae and the definitions of the faith of the Church.

Philosophic and social historicism, inasmuch as a fastening of the consciousness of man on temporary and last ends, ends enclosed in the interminable historic time and movement, has given rise, in the Christian consciousness in the so-called modern times, under a large number of fictitious arguments through rationalist but irrational criteria, to a direct or indirect contestation, hidden or admitted, of the integral reality of the Son of God.

All the large scale critical effervescence of the last centuries, the calling into question of all the foundations of historic information about the reality of Christ, about the reality of the Church, about the reality and understanding of the texts considered as scriptural expression of revealed truths, all the efforts of erroneous and disintegrating analysis of the language of man, have had, consciously or unconsciously, as central target, the Incarnation of the Word of God. But man's faith in this truth is the unique basis of his liberation in eternal life.

It is humanly impossible to enumerate all the manifestations of what has resulted from it. Often men, instead of being enamoured of the truth and seeking it in itself, that is, following the ways opened by Revelation and illumined by Revelation, are captured by the pleasure of research and by the historicist penchant for hope, and they stray in endless meanderings, in the ever new ways which have no outlet.

If one really wanted to enumerate and face one after another all the manifestations of rationalistic and irrational historicism, it would be like wanting to empty the Mediterranean with a teaspoon. The image may seem exaggerated, but it is true. For the possibility of cogitation and argumentation, cut off from an initial order objectively eternal and revealed, is endless. Anything can be said. One can accumulate mountains of considerations about arbitrary and sometimes too fanciful arguments without any real reference, without any proof, without any correspondence to the real aspirations of man.

Often one lets himself be caught, arbitrary argument after arbitrary argument, until he forgets the point of departure and the goal of his research, God's call.

If our young man, on opening a book on ancient philosophy, found written on the first page that Aristotle had not understood well the sense in which Plato used certain terms, and that the author of the book claimed to have understood it better twenty-four centuries later, the young man would think that the author couldn't be serious. He would say to himself:

— Certainly Aristotle, Plato's ex-disciple might not have been in agreement with Plato on many things and many notions. But he knew better than most of his contemporaries the meaning that Plato gave to the terms, independent of the fact that he, Aristotle, was not in agreement with these meanings of Plato's.

If the young man opened a book on the history of medicine and read on the last page of the chapter about Pasteur, that his first and most faithful assistant had not understood well the meaning that Pasteur himself gave to the terms «bacillus», «microbe», «-coccus» and that the author, one hundred years later claimed to have understood it better, the young man would remain struck by that claim, especially since the author, in order to claim that, would have no basis of support, no proof, but only his imagination or at bottom, his own desire to justify his personal ideas.

The same astonishment and the same doubt about the seriousness of the author would result if the young man read in a book on political economy or sociology, that Engels had not well understood the meaning that Marx gave to the terms of his analysis of the economic process in "Das Kapital", and that the author had understood better than Engels the meaning that Marx gave to the terms used.

These examples may seem to be constructions of the mind. But they express, very feebly moreover, the unbelievable consequences of the development of rationalist criticism and of the historicist mentality in general.

It is easy with uncontrollable, terminological fictions, to create a doctrinal and cultural halo, without ever allowing oneself, or allowing others, to reduce the questions to their essential and profound simplicity.

That is why our young man, in his charity, will be very perplexed before a very large number of cases, as for example the following:

1. In the book "The New Hermeneutics" by James M. Robinson and Ernst Fuchs (302), one reads on the first page:

---

(302)   JAMES M. ROBINSON: Professor of Theology and Neo-Testamentary Exegesis at the Southern California School of Theology.
ERNST FUCHS, born in 1903: Professor at the University of Marburg.

«Glossolalia, indeed, did not consist of speaking in foreign tongues as Luke seemed to understand it». (303)

The young man at first would certainly not have understood the implication of that assertion. But to the extent that he realized it, he would be dismayed at the enormity of the sentence. Robinson refers at the same time to Saint Paul and Saint Luke, as regards the fact of «speaking in tongues», and he refers particularly to the First Letter to the Corinthians, where Saint Paul speaks of «the interpretation of tongues» (ἑρμηνεία γλωσσῶν). (304)

Saint Luke, in "The Acts", uses the expressions «to speak in other tongues» (305) and «to speak in tongues». (306) Saint Luke was Saint Paul's companion and collaborator. It is more than normal to think that Saint Luke knew better than many of his contemporaries what Saint Paul meant by certain terms and expressions too synthetic perhaps. But independently of Saint Paul's expression «to speak in tongues», the fact which that

---

(303)   JAMES M. ROBINSON and ERNST FUCHS, *La nuova ermeneutica,* ed. Paideia, Brescia 1975, p. 9.

(304)   1 Cor. 12:10.

(305)   Acts 2:4: «And they were all filled with the Holy Spirit and began to speak in other tongues, as the Spirit gave them utterance».

(306)   Acts 10:46: «For they heard them speaking in tongues and extolling God».
Acts 19:6: «The Holy Spirit came on them and they spoke with tongues and prophesied».

expression signified, had occurred several times after Pentecost. And Saint Luke could not write lightly about an extraordinary fact, since – as he himself says at the beginning of his Gospel – he has written «having followed all things closely from the beginning». (307) On the other hand, it is inconceivable that he had understood the fact of speaking in tongues differently from Saint Paul. To be able to assert that we understand better than Saint Luke what he knew about the events and what Saint Paul meant by the expression «to speak in tongues», shows to what alteration in judgement the long wear and tear of criteria and references by the growing plethora of considerations of the rationalist criticism has led, in the historicist and existential mentality.

2. Professor Rudolf Schnackenburg (308), in a study on the "Christology of the New Testament" writes apropos of the confession of Saint Peter at Caesarea Philippi:

«The historic debut of faith in Christ is precisely the Resurrection of Jesus in the sense that only in taking off from there, can one really speak of faith in Jesus the Christ and Son of God. – One refers especially to Saint Peter's confession at Caesarea Philippi: 'You are the Son of the living God'. The recent investigation on the Gospels has, in any case, taught us not to take such assertions simply in an

---

(307)   Luke 1:1-4.

(308)   RUDOLF SCHNACKENBURG, born in 1914, Professor of Exegesis of the New Testament at the University of Würzburg.

historic sense. — Matthew wanted on this point to introduce his special tradition on the subject of Jesus' promise to construct, on Peter the rock, his community and the confession of faith of this disciple praised by Jesus; he formulated it in a manner which did not truly correspond to the historic situation of that time, but to his full, subsequent faith». (309)

This investigation regarding the Gospels of which Schnackenburg speaks, would have proved that the Apostles did not intend to give an account of the historic facts, but an account of their faith, which «presents the facts of the history of Christ in the light of their Paschal faith». (310) That is, that the Evangelists would have expressed their faith as they had had it and would have modelled it after the Resurrection by reports not historically true. The Apostles and the Evangelists would have illustrated, by imaginary facts and words, what they would have believed after the event.

Schnackenburg, in order to explain what he understands by the expression «investigation regarding the Gospels», refers to "The History of Forms", to "The History of Traditions and Redactions". That means that literary considerations, that is philologic and morphologic con-

---

(309) RUDOLF SCHNACKENBURG, *Mysterium salutis*, vol. 5, pp. 293-294.

(310) RUDOLF SCHNACKENBURG, *Mysterium salutis*, vol. 5, p. 294.

siderations, on the basis of the hypotheses regarding the groups of the Church of the first times, would have modelled what has been received as message and as history of Christ; modelled in such a way that the «written witnesses», the Gospels and the entire New Testament cannot serve as an historic reference for the reality of Christ. For after the Resurrection and after Pentecost, the reality and the message of Christ would have already been too adapted and thus transformed by feelings, thoughts and beliefs, for one to be able to find in the life of the Church, the sacred texts and the apostolic and patristic testimonies, the undamaged truth regarding the Person of Christ and regarding his message.

Before such an assemblage of hypotheses and arbitrary considerations based on these hypotheses, the young man might think he was dreaming. For he would ask himself:

— If Saint Matthew can relate an imaginary fact and imaginary words solely by a pious apostolic tactic, and with as an excuse, the faith that Saint Peter had after Pentecost. who then can guarantee the sacredness and the truthfulness of the Gospels? Doesn't the fact itself of continuing to hold them up as the true book of Christianity automatically constitute a work of disintegration of the Christian faith?

— Doesn't this practice of giving the name of science to that assemblage of interhypotheses, automatically provoke a disintegration of the notion as profound as it is practical, of science? Is it science to attribute suddenly to a person, considered as a «sacred author», tendentious accounts relating non-existent facts, and that, in order to refute, by a long series of such negative hypotheses, the basis of the sacred author's message and of the transcendent nature of the historicity of the Church of Christ, and therefore of the message received and of the Church's teaching?

And Schnackenburg continues in maintaining that the Evangelist Saint Matthew always proceeded in that manner, that is, in relating fictitious facts in order to confirm after the event, the faith such as it has been elaborated by and in the Christian community.

«Another passage confirms this manner of proceeding of the first evangelist (Saint Matthew). At the end of Jesus' walk on the waters he writes regarding the disciples: "Those who were in the boat worshipped him, saying 'Truly you are the Son of God' ". (311) If it were a precise historic narrative, in what would Simon Peter at Caesarea have been superior to his co-disciples? ».(312)

And then afterwards Schnackenburg refers to Saint Mark who relates the fact of that night of Jesus' walk on the waters, speaking only of the disciples' fright and incomprehension, because «they did not understand about the loaves (the multiplication which had preceeded in the narrative) and their hearts were hardened». (313)

---

(311)   Matthew 14:33.
(312)   RUDOLF SCHNACKENBURG, *Mysterium salutis*, vol. 5, p. 295.
(313)   Mark 6 : 52.

Schnackenburg here wants to put Saint Matthew in contradiction with himself and with Saint Mark. If Saint Peter, according to Schnackenburg, had declared at Caesarea that Jesus was the Christ, the Son of God, after the frightened disciples on their boat had said, amazed: «Truly you are the Son of God», Saint Peter would not have said anything exceptional to merit the word of Christ: «Blessed are you Simon Bar-Jona, for flesh and blood has not revealed this to you, but my Father who is in heaven!». (314)

And then, after that «contradiction» of Saint Matthew with himself, there would be, still according to Schnackenburg, a «contradiction» with the narrative of Saint Mark who says nothing about that confession of the Apostles on the boat, when he ends his narrative on the fright of the disciples and their heaviness of heart in view of the miracle of the loaves. And Schnackenburg feels himself completely justified in explaining this type of difference of narratives by a complete reversal of the moral, spiritual and sacral order of the word of the eye-witnesseses.

And moreover, Schnackenburg notes that Saint Mark, when he relates Saint Peter's confession at Caesarea Philippi, writes that Saint Peter answered Jesus: «You are the Christ!». (315) And Schnackenburg concludes that there is a contradiction between Saint Matthew and Saint Mark

---

(314)   Matthew 16:17.
(315)   Mark 8:29.

because in Saint Matthew, Christ confirms Saint Peter's confession, in telling him that it is the eternal Father who has illumined him, whereas in Saint Mark, first Saint Peter says only «You are the Christ», and then the narrative ends without the praise of Peter, but only with the grave order of Christ not to speak to anyone of the mystery of his Reality. (316)

And our young man will certainly have thought: why this reversal? And what if the disciples had received in their hearts all of Jesus' miraculous action and all his word, simple and dense, full of the mystery of his origin and his mission, what if they had received it, realizing little by little what they were engaged in living and at the moment of their fright and astonishment, in spite of the heaviness of their hearts in view of the preceeding miracle of the multiplication of the loaves, they had knelt down and said, or one of them had said, frightened and wonder-struck: «Truly you are the Son of God»?

And what if Jesus, knowing how and how much He was accepted in the Apostles' hearts, who had left all and followed him everywhere, knowing that their faith was more and more expanded, deepened and supernaturalized, knowing that the notion of the «Son of God» recurred in their speech and in their meditation with more or less apprehension and wonder, and what if Jesus had found the propitious moment to clearly ask his disciples the capital

---

(316)   Cf. RUDOLF SCHNACKENBURG, *Mysterium salutis*, vol. 5, p. 294.

question regarding his Person: «Who do the people say that the Son of man is? — But who do you say that I am? » (317) What if?

What if Saint Mark, Saint Peter's disciple, following the councils and desires of this humble one among the humble, who, even at the moment of his crucifixion, showed on what kind of rock Christ had promised to build his Church, what if therefore Saint Mark had soberly recounted Saint Peter's confession, and the order of silence which was to follow Christ's response to Saint Peter and the promise to build the Church on the rock which was Saint Peter?

And what if Saint Matthew had simply given the order of silence after having related the glorious promise of Jesus to Saint Peter, and that instead of there being a contradiction, there is a marvelous harmony of facts and intentions of mind and heart, speaking of the inconceivable mystery and of the inconceivable love of the God-Man?

3. Saint Matthew cites the famous passage of Isaiah (318) to show the fulfillment of the prophecy by the virginal Incarnation of Jesus Christ. He uses the verse from the Septuagint: «Behold a virgin will conceive and bear a son». The young man will surely be dizzy if he follows one after the other all the considerations for and against the translation of the Hebrew word «almah» by «virgin».

---

(317)   Matthew 16:13,15.

(318)   Isaiah 7:14.

For Saint Jerome, according to Migne's "Dictionary of the Bible" (319), «almah» means «virgin» and «betulah», «maiden». The "Universal Dictionary of Sacred Philology" translates «almah» by: «a maiden, good for marriage, consequently a virgin, in the rigorous sense of the word». (320) Father Giuseppe Girotti, in his commentary on the Old Testament, translates the word «almah» by «virgin», and qualifies all contrary translations as the result of a «partial» exegesis which does not correspond to a real scientific study of the text. (321) Angelo Penna, in his commentary on the book of Isaiah, translates «almah» by «virgin» and says that this word «virgin» is «the most discussed point of the translation, which, as always is also partly interpretation». (322)

Dennefeld, in the "Dictionary of Catholic Theology" (323), just as many others, like Josef Schmid, in his commentary of the Gospels of Saint Matthew and Saint Luke (324), translate first the word «almah» by «virgin» and

---

(319)   Migne, *Dictionnaire de la Bible,* Paris 1846, vol. I, col. 511.

(320)   HURÉ, *Dictionnaire universel de philologie sacrée,* éd. Migne, Paris 1846, col. 923.

(321)   GIUSEPPE GIROTTI O.P., *Il vecchio testamento,* ed. L.I.C.E., Torino 1942, vol. VII, p. 211 and ff.

(322)   ANGELO PENNA, *Isaia* in *La Sacra Bibbia* a cura di Mons. Salvatore Garofalo, ed. Marietti, Torino-Roma, p. 97.

(323)   Dictionnaire de théologie catholique, *article «Messie»,* col. 1435.

(324)   JOSEF SCHMID, *L'Evangelo secondo Luca,* ed. Morcelliana, Brescia 1965, p. 65 and fol.

then they find that it is not possible that the prophet Isaiah, addressing himself to all Israel, to all the house of David, has another woman virgin in sight than the one revealed in him by God, the Most Holy Virgin Mary. And especially Josef Schmid writes, among other things:

«As much Matthew (1:18-25; cf. also 1:16) as Luke (1:26-38) clearly and distinctly attest that Joseph was not the true father of Jesus. — Matthew, for his Judeo-Christian readers, expressly supports the fact that he relates, by referring to the prophecy about Emmanuel (Is. 7:14)».

«The attempt by A. Harnack and others to expunge in the important paragraph of Luke 1:26-38, the two decisive verses, 34 and following, and in verse 27, the word «virgin» repeated twice, just as also, in (still Saint Luke) chapter 3:23 the words (concerning Saint Joseph, considered by the people as Jesus' father) «as was supposed», as if they were words added subsequently, Harnack's attempt therefore, is not only completely arbitrary from the point of view of the textual critique, but it is really impossible in view of the context. Because thus the kernel of the entire paragraph would be precisely eliminated». (325)

It is certainly not difficult to realize what it was that brought about a general contestation of that reference of

---

(325)   JOSEF SCHMID, *L'Evangelo secondo Luca*, p. 65.

Saint Matthew's to a verse in Isaiah, and of that translation of the word «almah» by «virgin». That is not difficult, but it remains unbelievable.

In the "Introduction to the Bible" under the direction of Henri Cazelles, it is written that the exegesis of that passage of Isaiah would be less «complex» if, in the study of the text, all «Christian preoccupation» (326) were excluded.

In the "Large Biblical Commentary", it is written that the announcement of the birth of a child, of Emmanuel, could refer to the son of Ahaz, Hezekiah, thus manifesting the continuity of the lineage of David (327), and that Saint Matthew cited the verse of Isaiah, putting the accent on the birth of the child saviour rather than on the word «virgin».(328)

In "Mysterium Salutis" one reads that it is not impossible that Isaiah made use of a myth known at the time, to speak of the «young woman». (329) That «young woman» could have been the goddess Anat, goddess of vegetation, who, as the vegetation dies and grows again

---

(326)   HENRI CAZELLES, *Introduction à la Bible*, éd. Desclée, Paris 1973, vol. 2, p. 385.

(327)   RAYMOND E. BROWN, JOSEPH A. FITZMYER, ROLAND E. MURPHY, *Grande commentario biblico* (translated from the English), ed. Queriniana, Brescia 1973, p. 349.

(328)   *Grande commentario biblico*, p. 905.

(329)   *Mysterium salutis*, vol. 5, p. 153.

each year, likewise, in spite of «her holy marriage» which is celebrated each year, is still a virgin. (330)

According to D. Guthrie and J.A. Motyer, in their "Biblical Commentary", the Septuagint translated the word «almah» by the Greek word $\pi\alpha\rho\theta\acute{e}\nu o\varsigma$ «for reasons which are still not clear». (331)

In Gerhard Kittel's "Large Lexicon of the New Testament", one reads that the etymology of the Greek word $\pi\alpha\rho\theta\acute{e}\nu o\varsigma$ is uncertain. The semantic development could only be deduced from the literary usage. And one reads there this incredible «information»:

«It is evident that the word $\pi\alpha\rho\theta\acute{e}\nu o\varsigma$ indicates in the first place a mature young woman». (332)

But he also cites Plutarch who says regarding the Pythia, that she was a «virgin in her soul». What's more "The Large Dictionary of the Greek Language" cites Aristophanes, Homer, Hesiod, Xenophon, Sophocles, Herodotus, Euripides, by whom the word «$\pi\alpha\rho\theta\acute{e}\nu o\varsigma$» is used to mean «a young woman who knows not a man». (333) That is why Kittel's definition of the Greek word «virgin, $\pi\alpha\rho\theta\acute{e}\nu o\varsigma$», astonishes and leaves one wondering.

---

(330) *Mysterium salutis,* vol. 5, p. 153, note 28.

(331) D. GUTHRIE and J.A. MOTYER, *Commentario biblico,* ed. Voce della Bibbia, Modena 1976, vol. 3, p. 45.

(332) GERHARD KITTEL, *Grande Lessico del Nuovo Testamento,* ed. Paideia, Brescia 1974, vol. IX, col. 752.

(333) HENRY G. LIDDEL and ROBERT SCOTT, *Grand dictionnaire de la langue grecque,* 1948, the word «$\pi\alpha\rho\theta\acute{e}\nu o\varsigma$».

Regarding the passage of Isaiah 7:14, in Kittel we read that the prophet speaks of a very specific woman: either of the wife of the prophet, or of Hezekiah's wife or of an unknown woman in the crowd, or unknown even to Isaiah or of «all the young women of Israel who were then with child». (334)

There are cases which prove how much a certain innner attitude with regard to scriptural and traditional testimonies of the Mystery of Christ, takes away the light and the discernment, sometimes from the most gifted men. Hugo Gressmann (335), friend and contemporary of Gunkel, was of the opinion that Isaiah could only be referring to a tradition which would be a surviving trait of the polytheistic belief in goddess-mothers. For Gressmann, the fact that the prophet does not say «a virgin» but «the virgin» proves that Isaiah is referring to known notions. The prophet must have spoken as if he already knew that virgin. That is why, still according to Gressmann, Isaiah could not have had in mind either his wife or the wife of King Ahaz or another known woman of history who would have been with child at that moment. For — and this is the strangest point of this reasoning — «how could he have said with such assurance that she would give birth to a son rather than a daughter? » (336)

---

(334)   GERHARD KITTEL, *Grande lessico del Nuovo Testamento,* vol. IX, col. 765.

(335)   HUGO GRESSMANN (1877-1927), Professor of Exegesis at the Faculties of Protestant Theology of Kiel and Berlin.

(336)   A. FEUILLET, *Etudes d'exégèse et de théologie biblique. Ancien Testament,* éd. Gabalda, Paris 1975, pp. 231-232.

In a large number of commentaries and articles of theological and biblical dictionaries, the quoting of Isaiah 7:14 by Saint Matthew, Saint matthew's intention in citing this passage of Isaiah, the true meaning of the word «almah» in the Hebrew text, the messianic signification of the verse are contested, put into discussion so that at least a doubt covers the evangelic testimony of Saint Matthew.

Nevertheless there are facts and considerations which bear witness to the absence of all valid argumentation in all of that critique and devaluation. For example, there is a fact which should cause to reflect all those who claimed that the translation in the Septuagint of the word «almah» for the Greek work «παρθένος» was unjustified. This fact is that the famous rabbi Akiba who lived in the second century, thoroughly anti-Christian, understood the word «almah» to mean «virgin». [337]

"The Jerusalem Bible" moreover, which translates in the text the word «almah» by «maiden» specifies its conception in a note:

«The text of the LXX is a precious witness of the ancient Jewish interpretation which will be consecrated by the Gospel». [338]

From where then that manifold and opinionated forced interpretation of the text and the facts? It is not useless

---

[337]   *Dictionnaire de la Bible,* éd. Migne, vol. I, col. 311.

[338]   *Bibbia di Gerusalemme,* ed. Dehoniane, Bologna 1977, p. 1566.

nor far from the truth to recall that the conscious or unconscious aim of the contestation, the critique and the negation is unique: to shake, if not to take away from the consciousness of Christians, the certainty of the truth brought into the world by Christ, and then by his Apostles and his witnesses, regarding the Mystery of His divine reality. To achieve that, before all else, the certitude concerning the Incarnation of the Word of God had to be shaken.

Now it was necessary to shake the testimony of the Gospel and of the Tradition of the Church. That is why Josef Schmid, in his commentary on the Gospels of Saint Matthew and Saint Luke regarding the virginal conception expresses himself thus:

«Matthew makes shipwreck of every attempt to expunge the virginal conception of the virgin, because the whole paragraph 1:18-25 serves only to prove this fact. Its elimination from Luke's work would come about uniquely because of prejudice or because of the negation of the possibility of miracles, and thus also of the virginal conception». [339]

* * *

---

[339]   JOSEF SCHMID, *L'Evangelo secondo Luca*, p. 65.

Historic criticism has been for a long time the general mode of thinking in everything. It is a very strong and very specific manifestation of the historicist mentality. In the philosophic and theological climate of modern times, a vast world of arbitrary postulates has been created, a world in motion, which tends to reverse every certitude, historic as well as theological and spiritual.

This vast universe has developed with a strong élan towards independence. It would be henceforth rash to wish to separate what has been positive for the march of men towards the truth and in the truth, from what has been negative. In all activity, there are both positive and negative elements, and that, because of the imperfection of our state of being in the life of the earth.

What characterizes a true, positive life of truth, is that man, even in his gropings, is stably fastened to a deep love of that truth; which is the guarantee of the final outcome of his march. Certainly on the road to Damascus a direct intervention by God was manifested, an intervention so radical and efficacious that Saint Paul came out of that trial, one could say of light and of grace, a new man, an absolute servant of absolute Truth. But one often forgets that Saint Paul, before knowing the Truth so directly, had passionately loved it, and that Truth presented itself to him and flooded him.

This certainly does not mean that that grace was not truly grace, that it was not a truly free gift, but that this gift, as imperative as it was, was received with love, freely and totally. Saint Paul is one of the major examples of the almost impalpable but thoroughly objective harmony between God's irrevocable decision and man's liberty in his love of the truth.

That love is manifested even when one walks in erroneous paths; and its absence is also manifest, even when one is walking in the paths which, from a strictly conceptual point of view, can be considered just.

It is to the degree of that transcendent love of the truth, before it is recognized by the intellect, that in the study of the past and the present, in the study of currents, doctrines and methods, man can more or less discern what is positive, because based upon eternal truth; and discern what is negative, because based on the autonomous personal will.

Now in the development of the historic criticism of texts, of all the doctrinal methods and considerations which today constitute exegetic activity and hermeneutics in general, there are very positive intellectual and spiritual principles and orientations; positive because within this development and by the new data themselves, man has been able to feel the great truths confirmed in his understanding and his heart, with always more intensity, fullness, and intimity; the great truths revealed by the Incarnation of Christ and by his message transmitted in a lived way, and consigned also by writing, in the Church.

And there have also been deteriorations and orientations of thought such that the criteria based on the revealed truths have been degraded and even rejected. Thus often, on all sides, as much in the consciousness of those who were anchored in the forms emptied of spirit but which remained traditional, as in the consciousness of those who were carried off by the frenzy of an uncontrolled renewal without real attachment to the revealed truth, there has been a more or less radical deterioration of the Person of Christ, of his ontologically redemptive action and his message of redemption for man.

The mass of critical works, the social extension of the new principles and new methods of approach to the truth and of research of the truth, have created almost a new world of being and thinking. In this world, even those who had a right view and a clear and free love of the truth have been led to use the language, to follow methods and to proceed by modes of judgement foreign to the principles which had inspired them when they heard the call of God. Such has been the wearing out of the principles and criteria in the development of the historicist mentality and in the spreading of existential relativism.

Certainly what has been positive is in itself always positive. What is petrified letter remains and will remain dead letter. But that which is falsely alive and is only mundanely «dynamic» spreads like an immense haze which penetrates everywhere and envelops everything. Now the first thing that must be realized is that one cannot pack the haze into sacks; one must come out of it; one must keep his lamp lit, walk prudently in the expectation that the haze dissipate by a great wind of grace, in orienting oneself always towards the heights.

The sinking of man into a hope other than the one Christ gave and that the Apostles transmitted, the speculation with no fundamental and engaging reference to Revelation, that is, to the Incarnation of the eternal Word and to the redemptive action of the God-Man and to his lived and oral message to men, have little by little led the theological thought and spiritual life of a large number of people to a conscious or unconscious internal break with Revelation and the transcendent Mystery of the Church. Men's exterior acts are not here being spoken of; but rather the manifestation of their thought and of their implicit or explicit teaching.

There would be no real and edifying utility in trying to add another itinerary from Saint Augustine up to Luther, and from Luther, passing through Dr. Astruc (340) and the whole forest of modern Protestant and Catholic critics, up to Bultmann and the critics of our times, in order to explain, by new analyses and references, the outcome of a certain historicist criticism, which demonstrates a limitless probabilism and existential relativism, in the theological thought and Christian sensibility.

It would suffice for the young man to fix his gaze on a few cases among the large number which assail him from every side.

---

(340) JEAN ASTRUC (1684-1766), Doctor, Cardiologist of Louis XIV, was the first known to affirm the existence of several sources of the Pentateuch: His work is considered the point of departure of the attacks against the authenticity of the Pentateuch.

1.— We have seen on page 278 that Rahner considers the teaching of Saint Paul and Saint John to have altered the initial «Ascendance Christology», transforming it into the doctrine of the Incarnation of the pre-existent Word-Son.

In the same book, Rahner writes that the Christology of Saint Paul and Saint John is already a «theology», that is, a reflection made after the Resurrection regarding the consciousness that the historic Jesus Christ had of himself, and he adds:

> «A systematic Christology of today cannot however take its natural point of departure in that theological understanding of Jesus Christ; that, at bottom, is true also for the Christologic assertions of the oldest, pre-Pauline Scripture». (341)

Therefore there would be an older serious scriptural documentation, before Saint Paul, which would be the most authentic and which would have been altered by reflections made piously certainly, by Saint John and Saint Paul after the Resurrection, and this Christology of Saint Paul and Saint John must not be the basis for a theology on Christ, therefore for a present day Christology. But even that pre-Pauline supposed authentic Christology must not be taken either by present day Christology as a basis and a point of departure, in order to attain the true reality of Christ and his message.

---

(341)   KARL RAHNER, *Sacramentum mundi,* vol. 4, col. 194.

Before meditating on Rahner's whole doctrinal tableau, it would be good to fix one's gaze on other considerations presented by E.R. Brown, J.A. Fitzmyer, R.E. Murphy, in the "Large Biblical Commentary":

a) — «The ontological interest of the later Church can be seen in the contradiction between Paul's confession of faith 'God in Christ was reconciling the world to himself' (2 Cor. 5:19) and the confession proclaimed at Nicaea of Jesus Christ 'true God from true God, begotten, not made, one in substance with the Father'».(342)

And the "Commentary" continues:

b) — «Paul's confession assures men that God was present with them in Jesus; the Nicene Creed assures men that Jesus was God. One assertion leads, in the last analysis, to the other — but from one to the other there is an evolution of doctrine».(342)

Now, according to the "Commentary" there would be a contradiction between Saint Paul's Christology and the Nicene Council; that is, between Saint Paul's conception according to which Christ would not be God but God would be present in him, and the conception of the Council of Nicaea, according to which Christ was God, begotten and not made, one substance with the Father.

---

(342)   E.R. BROWN, J.A. FITZMYER, A.E. MURPHY, *Grande Commentario biblico*, p. 1836, col. 2.

For Rahner, on the contrary, Saint Paul's conception as well as Saint John's would be in contradiction with the «original»(?) Christology, transformed in the New Testament into the doctrine stated subsequently by the Council of Nicaea, that is, of the pre-existent Son-Logos.

Both of them, Rahner and the "Commentary", despite their differences of opinion regarding Saint Paul's Christology, agree in their view: Christ was not God and therefore the Annunciation is a legend which came from the piety after the Resurrection, following the current which has deviated the truth and finally ended in the Creed of the Nicene Council.

First the young man would seek to find the documents and the witnesses of that pre-Pauline Christology which would have been altered within the frame work of the New Testament, an altering which would have penetrated in the Church, would have been crystallized in the Councils of Nicaea and Chalcedon, would have traversed the centuries and would have reached us. Then he would realize the enormity of the propositions, he would feel deeply distressed, for he would perceive that in all this language and all these reasonings, there is a total absence of basis.

Where can the pre-Pauline and pre-Johannine Christology be found? What does the expression «within the frame of the New Testament» mean? Who has proved that the original predication betrays, transforms, alters, «goes beyond» the auto-consciousness and the auto-revelation of Christ?

What remains of the notion of Church, for men who are supposed to recite the Creed during the Holy Mass every Sunday, when they refute it in multifarious ways, and especially regarding the capital point of the Redemption, the Incarnation of the eternal Word of God?

What good is there in speaking and returning with a continual insistence to the Resurrection? Who would the Resurrected One be in that new Christology of Rahner's and of the "Commentary", for example? It would be the man who, by his development and spiritual ascension would have forged ahead to receive the auto-communication of God who came to him. It would not be the God-Man of the Church's teaching. The Church would not be the continuation of God's redemptive work. It would be nothing but an arena of confrontation, of research, without the immutable doctrinal «ballast» of the Mystery of the Redemption.

But what is for many the most important, is to tear down in the consciousness, in hope and in worship, the Incarnation.

That is why regarding the Mystery of the Blessed Virgin Mother of God a black-out has come. No exaggeration of a popular, simplistic pietism and no mechanical, formalist and purely intellectual reference or invocation to her could ever justify such an obstruction and such an illogicality in view of the true data of the Scripture and Tradition.

This historicist mentality has deteriorated all the terms, for example the term anthropology, which, absolutely innocent and positive, has become a channel of deviation. It isn't for nothing or by habit that the Church carries as major external sign, the Crucifix. The whole Mystery of the Redemption is founded precisely on the fact that the eternal Son of God became also Son of man. So anthropology in the sense of the Incarnation of the Word of God constitutes a basis, one could say a theological place, for all theologic speculation and all comprehension of the texts and the Tradition. But it is not in this sense that the historicist existential hermeneutics uses and proposes anthropological theology or theological anthropology. It is by innumerable linguistic biases that one implants in the consciousness and in the thought, the concept of a theology based on the principle that Christ would be a man raised up to the proximity («absolute nearness») of God. The Son of God would be the man having fully received the divine Word, and already the image is for many, too exalted.

The young man certainly will think that it is necessary to refer to the life of Christ such as the New Testament has handed it down to us, in spite of the alterations which the contesting theology discovers in it; he will reflect on how the doctors treated Christ and he will understand how he is still treated today. How else can these hypotheses put forth by «theologians» be explained?

The eye witnesses would have «interpreted» the reality and the message of Christ, as Saint Matthew, by «holy tactics» let us say, and two thousand years later, by the magic key of historic criticism and «the history of forms», one would be in a position to discover the intentions of Saint Matthew or Saint Luke or Saint Mark and also of Saint Paul and Saint John, and also what words would have been authentic historically, and what words would have been used for reasons of predication. And when one says «words of predication», that always means for this exegetic vein, an altering of the original message.

For according to a certain branch of criticism, one could never preach without altering; altering every reality by additions of personal faith and piety or by the desire to impress in the consciousness this or that personal meaning of the initial message.

All the key words would be added later and after the fact. The key facts of the evangelic narrative would be entirely invented in order to show the abstract teachings or personal meanings coming forth from faith or from apologetic polemics. Some have frequently set themselves up as experts of literary styles and genres and would claim themselves capable of unearthing all the psychological and intellectual mechanisms of all the personages who have been the great witnesses and the great Apostles of Christ.

All the words, such as the words of the Last Supper, all the confessions, all the major facts such as the Annunciation, are judged, either as belated additions, or as writings with pious intentions but which would impair the original reality. From the historic criticism has come forth a branch we can call special, of formal contestation of every assertion or fact of Revelation, of the message and history of Christ and the Church which contains, implicitly or explicitly, the message of the hope of eternal life; hope which transcends all the temporal hopes of history.

2.– There are hermeneutic postulates which contain the annihilation of the notion of truth, the notion of logic, the notion of the word and the notion of the true evolution in the history of men. There are postulates which draw man towards a state of thinking and feeling which can be called a state of perpetual existential instability. For man, in his love of eternal Truth, develops and broadens indefinitely, in proportion to the augmentation of his inner stability. This stability is a stability of knowledge and of criterion which causes him to be in an increasingly great harmony with the revealed truths and also with the intimate order of the cosmos.

The postulates of which we are speaking here, contain the destruction of all stability of criteria and all responsibility regarding the knowledge of the truth revealed by God, and of all knowledge granted, always by God, through the natural order of things.

The historicist existential mentality has created, through the activity and the problems of hermeneutics, a penchant of the will and also an intellectual penchant for instability and incertitude, which at times dominates and is very nearly transformed into a sort of fixed intellectual complacency: to have no stable method, reference or knowledge, consequently no immutable criterion of revealed truth.

In the "Dictionary of Biblical Theology", one reads this conclusion to the article on Jesus Christ by Xavier Léon-Dufour:

«The presentations of the mystery of Jesus of Nazareth become Lord and Christ cannot be reduced to a unique system. — After the New Testament, hermeneutics follows its movement; it comes to the point, for example, of speaking of the «consciousness» of Jesus, of «nature» and of person, without claiming to stabilize forever the interpretation; today still, it must be practiced in the diverse cultures where faith in Jesus Christ is expressed».(343)

This postulate says first of all that the understanding of the meaning of the expression «consciousness» of Jesus must always be uncertain and one must always expect a new interpretation. Now, interpretation does not mean expression, illustration of a concept or of an idea. If the interpretation must be modified, that means that the first one would no longer be valid; and then, according to this postulate, this hermeneutics must be practiced in diverse milieus in which the author says faith in Jesus Christ is expressed. But what must hermeneutics do, within these diverse cultures? Why would the interpretation depend on the culture of the milieu? To use the linguistic means and local data to have understanding between people is neither

---

(343)   XAVIER LEON-DUFOUR, S.J. (born in 1912), *Dizionario di Teologia biblica*, ed. Marietti, Torino 1971, col. 464-465.

a problem of hermeneutics nor of new interpretation. It is the same interpretation which must be transmitted everywhere using diverse means and forms, according to the necessity.

The postulate, such as it is formulated, cannot mean anything other than this: hermeneutics must give always new interpretations according to the cultures. That is: it is as if the interpretation were the instrument which must play the local music. It is not the effort of putting within reach of everyone the great immutable Truth, for in that case the interpretation would be immutable, in spite of the more or less relative expressions. It would be a question only of finding the linguistic means, parallelisms and examples, in order to transmit that same and unique interpretation within different cultures.

A more complete interpretation of the Truth of Christ would mean that something would be completed which would illustrate the stability of knowledge. But to say that «one must never claim to fix the interpretation», is to delude oneself and thus play upon words.

But the question is much more serious than one may think at the beginning, because in the name of perpetual interpretation, the stable reference of Revelation and the universality of a basic comprehension is abolished. Hermeneutics, according to that tendency, becomes «a problematic of the understanding». It would no longer be a question of interpreting realities, for according to these postulates there would no longer be any stable reality to interpret. It would therefore be only a question of a perpetual adaptation to situations and cultural data in motion.

Thus the abusive use of a sound and simple word is explained, which has become the key word of all contestation of the revealed certitudes and of the certitudes therefore truly theologic: kerygma, κήρυγμα.

The kerygma is opposed as the anti-matter to the stable, humanly formulated truth, dogma. Thus explains Father Piet Smulders regarding the doctrine of Jesus Christ formulated in the dogmas of the Councils of Nicaea, Ephesus, Chalcedon and Constantinople III:

«Not only do the Roman Catholics and the Oriental Orthodox Churches accept these definitions, but so do the major part of the Churches of the Reform. 'One person in two natures' — thus is continually professed according to a summary synthesis of the doctrine of the Council of Chalcedon: likewise in the instruction of the faithful every day. However in no point does the problem and the scandal of the distance between kerygma and dogma so painfully torment us as precisely in this point».(344)

Now according to Father Smulders and many others certainly, there would be a «scandalous» distance between kerygma and dogma. But these very trenchant assertions

---

(344)   PIET SMULDERS S.J. (born in 1912, Professor of Dogmatics and Church History at the Catholic College of Amsterdam), *Mysterium salutis*, vol. 5, p. 493.

cause many new questions to arise in our young man, in his touching search for the truth.

Kerygma, which means proclamation and by extension, predication, here would be the content of the faith, or let us say, the doctrinal content or simply the doctrine proclaimed by the Apostles immediately after Pentecost. Where then would this proclaimed doctrine, this kerygma be found consigned wholly without omission and without addition?

For it would have been necessary to have found consigned such as it is, this proclamation, such as it is, this apostolic kerygma, in order to confront it with the Christologic dogma of the Councils. The only witnesses that we have of the doctrine consigned to the Apostles by Christ are the New Testament and the oral Tradition and the life of the Church.

Therefore, first one would have to admit that the New Testament is not an apostolic proclamation, that it contains serious impairments of the doctrine concerning the identity of Christ proclaimed by the Apostles, and that this Christologic doctrine of the New Testament, as we said earlier regarding Rahner's writings, would have led to the solemn formulation of that Christologic alteration as dogmas of faith of the Church.

It is what Smulders also asserts, following his assertion regarding the scandal of the opposition between kerygma and dogma. He specially says that he doubts that «the

Christology of Ascendance still had value in the post-Apostolic Church», the Christology according to which man born naturally would have been raised up to the «meeting» with God. And he asks himself at the same time if that «good» Christology of Ascendance of the Apostles would not have taken, in the time of the post-apostolic predication, an underdeveloped «form which was later surpassed by the reasonings of Paul and John».(345) That means that in every case it is the doctrine of ascendance which would have been that of the Apostles of the first period, because, according to these theories, there would be the Apostles of the second period, Saint Paul and Saint John, who would have altered the Christology of the Apostles of the first period.

Then the young man would say to himself:

— If Saint Paul and Saint John already contain the post-apostolic predication, which would have abandoned the «Christology of Ascendance», shouldn't one conclude that there was a scission, a deviation among the Apostles; and then that the Apostles' proclamation would be lost as such; and thirdly wouldn't one have to conclude that the Church since the New Testament, is not only making her way through internal and external perturbations, but on a false doctrinal trail regarding a fundamental question which concerns its own foundations, that is, the identity of its founder?

---

(345)   PIET SMULDERS, *Mysterium salutis*, vol. 5, p. 496.

Smulders concludes his study by observing that after the Third Council of Constantinople (680-681), there has been no development in Christology. There has been a calm for centuries which «can mean that the ancient councils had fixed a frame for Christologic thought, in which without great pains, deviations could be avoided and errors suppressed».(346)

But Smulders, immediately after that statement about the long doctrinal tranquillity in the Church on this point, emits a thought which, if it corresponded to the truth, would express a terrible reality, because the Church would be only an age-old mystification. He says:

«This calm (age-old Christologic calm in the Church) also has something which creates anxieties. Would it (this calm) have been possible if predication and theological thought had truly inserted the mystery of the God-man in the heart of the faith? » (346)

Why would this calm be worrysome? Only if this calm expressed a torpor of the Christian people, theologians, preachers, pastors included, would it be worrysome; or if it expressed an age-old compromise of the theologians and preachers, who while not having faith in the meaning of the Incarnation, would have preached the dogma of Nicaea just the same; or if the predication, not having put in the center of the doctrine preached the «Mystery of the God-man», caused the people to live without Christologic anxiety.

---

(346)   PIET SMULDERS, *Mysterium salutis*, vol. 5, p. 595.

Otherwise why would the calm be disturbing? Only if it expressed a long, false situation, a deep wound of long duration in the Church, could it cause anxiety in the «awakened ones» of a later time.

Smulders asks a question which contains an answer both apropos of the calm and apropos of Christology in general. According to Smulders the calm in the Church would not have been possible if the theologians and the preachers had taught a doctrine contrary to that of the councils; there would not have been a calm if predication and theology had been opposed to the solemn doctrine of the Magisterium. And what's more, there would have been this contrast if the true doctrine regarding the «Mystery of the God-man» had been placed in the center of the predication regarding the faith, «in the heart of the faith». The calm therefore, during the long centuries since the Third Council of Constantinople up until the current «awakening» of recent times, would be due to the fact that all the world would have been subject to the same error, to the «false» doctrine of the Incarnation.

That is why these questions themselves asked by Smulders, in any case mean two things: first, that during this long period, the Church would have in fact lived the dogma of the Incarnation, be it by a Monophysitism, be it by a Nestorianism, because — according to what comes forth — the dogma of the Incarnation would be at base inconceivable and unlivable. And secondly, that the «Mystery of the God-man would not have been truly inserted» as basis of the doctrine of the faith preached, and it would be this fact, this absence, as much in the dogma as in the predication by the Church of the «true» doctrine regarding Christ, which would have preserved the calm. This true doctrine of the Mystery of the God-man, suffocated by the Magisterium, theologians and predicators for long centuries, would be therefore the doctrine of ascendance and not the doctrine of the dogma of the Incarnation.

And Smulders in conclusion, probably in order to explain the awakening, goes on thus:

«The Hellenistic world and the Byzantine world of the beginnings, where the Christologic dogma attained its form, have disappeared for centuries now; their conceptions, their concepts, their categories and mental schemes have become foreign to humanity».(347)

* * *

The young man, bewildered before all the assertions of these theologians, will have thus noted all that he has grasped:

a) That according to the historic criticism and the theology based on it, the Church, from the time of Saint Paul, has been living in a capital error: the mystery of the Annunciation and therefore of the Incarnation of the Word of God.

---

(347)   PIET SMULDERS, *Mysterium salutis,* vol. 5, p. 595.

b) That all the faith defined on the basis of the mystery of the Annunciation, from Nicaea until 1950, that is, until the proclamation of the dogma of the Assumption, would have been founded, would have spread and would have been lived, in an erroneous belief: the Christology of the Incarnation.

c) That a preservation of the terms of the faith on the part of the Church was currently being preached as possible, while giving those terms, little by little, a new content, an absolutely contrary Christology; that is: calling Incarnation the doctrine of the ascendance of a man towards a culminating point where the meeting with a God «descending», to communicate Himself would occur; calling Christology the theology of the ascendance of man; calling the Son of God the perfected man, the man «perfectly humanized» according to Küng ([348]); calling God's Church the association of men under the inspiration of the perfectly humanized man. And so on, regarding every notion and every experience and every revelation.

d) That there would be no sufficiently objective document which would have transmitted to the Church, at the time of Saint Paul and Saint John, the fundamental bases of the reality and the message of Christ, and this, because already a predication from Saint Peter's time would have been altered by the predication also from Saint Peter's time, since the writings of Saint Paul and Saint John would be carrying the consequences of that alteration.

---

[348]   HANS KÜNG, *Incarnazione in Dio*, p. 604.

e) That we would not have the integral testimony of any eye-witness, since Saint Matthew, who was among the Twelve, would have related facts and words not corresponding to reality.

f) That the Fathers of the first centuries, as Saint Irenaeus for example (349), would not have had a true knowledge of the language of the Septuagint nor certainly of Hebrew, since all of them would have seen and read in Isaiah 7:14 the announcement of the Annunciation. Saint Irenaeus specifically, would have been greatly wrong in declaring so firmly and so clearly:

«It was therefore God who became man and the Lord in person saved us, he who gave us the sign of the Virgin (Isaiah 7:14). That is why the interpretation of some who dare translate the Scripture thus is not true: 'Behold a maiden shall conceive and bear a son'. — The apostles, in fact, who are prior to them, are in agreement with the version of which we speak, that is, the Septuagint, and our version is in agreement with the apostles'. Peter and John, Matthew and Paul, and still others and their disciples announced all the things prophesied, in the way contained in the version of the ancients (the Seventy)». (350)

---

(349) SMULDERS criticizes Saint Ireneaus because he condemned the «Christology of ascendance» of the Ebionites, (*Mysterium salutis,* vol. 5, p. 498).

(350) SAINT IRENAEUS, *Contro le eresie,* book III, 21, 1-21,3.

g) That the idea of the pre-existence of the eternal entity (Word of God) in Saint Paul and Saint John and in the Epistle to the Hebrews would not come from Christ. First, because all the words of Christ regarding his pre-existence would be the result of a belated theological cogitation and were not really spoken by Christ, and that moreover it would be without importance to know whether Christ pronounced any Christologic title. (351)

h) That a current Christology could never be based on the theology of Saint Paul and Saint John, nor even — as Rahner clearly says — on the Christology previous to Saint Paul (of which, moreover, we have no document whatsoever except arbitrary interpretations that could be made today regarding the passages of the texts of Saint Paul himself and of Saint John himself and the Acts of the Apostles and of all the New Testament itself in general).

i) That these considerations are not isolated in some writings of one or two or three or four or five people. It is the tenor of the writings of a large number of authors, professors, teachers and even of pastors, at times even going beyond all boundary and all limit of doctrine, history and logic, with more or less clarity in expression or concepts. It is a question of a disintegration not only Christologic but necessarily ecclesiologic. If Christ is man and only man, the Church is only human. The identity of Christ is the basis of all true theology for Christianity.

---

(351)   Cf. *Mysterium salutis*, pp. 298 and 313.

All that long error of the Church regarding the identity of Christ, the true proclamation of the doctrine, and regarding the reality of the Church herself «would be particularly put in evidence» by the appearance, at the beginning of our century, of the flower of criticism presented by the works of Dibelius, Bultmann, Schmidt, Bertram. (352) It is the theory of the «method of the history of forms» (Formgeschichtliche Method). It is the time of the great myth: of the myth of demythologization.

* * *

The theory of «the history of forms» that is, the theory which wants first of all to place the archetypes of literary forms as categories to which it would be necessary to reduce all the writings of the New Testament, on the basis of the most mechanical of historic criticisms, is an invention which, independently of the role which it has played within the Church and Christianity in general, does not in itself correspond to a law or a general experience of the human sciences. Nor does it correspond to what man can seriously conceive as notions and principles of Science in general.

---

(352)   MARTIN DIBELIUS (1883-1947), RUDOLF BULTMANN, KARL LUDWIG SCHMIDT and GEORG BERTRAM, by publications between 1919 and 1922, in Germany, each one on his own presented the «method of the history forms».

Everything contains some truth, or rather corresponds in some way, however relative, to a reality. Apropos of the «method of the history of forms», one can say without fear of error that it is the case of applying that martyr's apophthegm:

O you men, in the name of my slight obscurities, you want to stifle my great truth, and in the name of your little lights, you want to cover your great darkness.

Criticism by the «method of the history of forms» is a false way of returning to the past and of «reconstitution of history» as much in what concerns the facts and texts with which it occupies itself, as in what concerns the real experience of men apropos of information, of transmission of things seen and heard.

Above all it is a great illusion from the point of view of the objective knowledge of the past. The great error is the pursuit of a mirage: «to pierce time and seize the past with an absolute objectivity». It is the death of the objectivity conceded to man by the Creator. That is true for the whole field of life, of experience and of human learning.

Criticism on the basis of the literary forms of the New Testament has not shed any more light on certain differences between texts and certain not easily explicable «voids» in the New Testament, than that which the first Fathers and all the Doctors of the Church had noticed, known and deeply lived.

The only difference is the intellectual and spiritual climate in which one began to explain at all cost, by arbitrary references and parallelisms, the obscure points and the differences between styles, forms, words, order of relation of the facts. And that, with the still deeper illusion of believing that the «present day critic» can be in himself more objective than the authors of the New Testament, more objective than the pastors of the Church of the early times, who received and transmitted, by oral means and by life, the global message of the Person and teaching of Christ. This illusion has become possible even with very sincere persons, because of the historization of the mentality, and consequently of the criteria.

The young man could ask a fervent disciple and master of the historic criticism of the «method of the history of forms»:

— By what criteria can one be assured of the absolute objectivity of one of the manifold histories of the French Revolution or of the Risorgimento, considering the «omissions», the «additions» and the relations common to all history books?

— How can one be assured of the objectivity of the exposés regarding much more recent facts, such as the history of the Russian Revolution of October 1917 and what followed? According to what criteria can the book of objective truth be found?

— What is the criterion for finding the objective truth of still more recent facts, as for example the history of

Vatican Council II? What is the criterion which, in order to perceive the true «Consiliary Fact», allows me to choose between the spirit of the texts of Karl Rahner and the spirit of the texts of Urs von Balthasar?

He could lengthen the list of his questions indefinetely, without ever receiving an adequate response from the critic-disciple of the «Formgeschichtliche Method».

This is not the place to enlarge upon the great question of the objectivity of knowledge and information. But hardly has one come out of this «incantation» of parallelisms, of the a priori precisions of one source or two sources, when one becomes aware of the suffocation of the great truth in the name of the slight obscurities and the «voids», with no immediate practical explication. The young man will also understand that to follow the manifold paths already open and opened every day by all kinds of exegetical cogitation, is to lose the royal way of study, of the comparison of the texts with the deep life of man, and thus lose the true visage and message of Christ; that is, to lose the true History.

And he will realize thus, the true basis and the true aspect of the problem of knowledge of the historic truth. He will realize how and why the Church, in spite of the contradictions, seemingly insoluble for the average mind, and in spite of the at times distressing narrowness of certain of her sons, has been able to grasp, inasmuch as a whole Body, and with the best intellects of humanity, the historic reality and the historic mystery of Christ, by means of the historic reality and the historic mystery of the New Testament and Tradition.

And he will realize that the Church has been able to grasp that profound reality in the midst of perpetual crises of all peoples and also within herself, from the beginning. Now the young man will grasp the criteria and the method of true scientific thought and consciousness. And he will then understand many simple, profound and great things:

— He will understand that none of our present day learned critics could be a more objective and truthful witness than Saint Matthew, Saint Luke, Saint Mark, Saint John, Saint Paul, nor a more objective relator and continuator of the apostolic message, than the apostolic Fathers, receiving and continuing the Tradition which comes from Christ's own being and word.

— He will understand how simple it is not to make an artificial distinction between the New Testament-historic document and the New Testament-religious document. For it is exactly the luminous character of the apostolic testimony, direct and indirect, to be highly religious because deeply historic, and highly historic because deeply religious.

— He will understand that the objectivity of the facts which concern man and God is never neutral, because the truth is never neutral. It is always of God. And without God, no reality of the relations of man and God can be grasped and transmitted objectively.

— He will understand that the reference to the anonymous «primitive community» regarding the witness and
message of the highest meaning for the redemption of man
lying in his temporal relativity, is meaningless. It is to force
the logical order of things, to disfigure the most elementary
reality of the relations of the spirit and the word, so much
the more as it concerns a unique being, Christ.

— He will understand that it is unhealthy to cut up and
readjust the texts and to try to find different sources at
any cost, provided the source is not the one whom Christ
sent as an Apostle and the one to whom the Apostle
transmitted the great experience of having totally and
ontologically accepted Christ.

— He will understand that it is not the differences of
accounts which can invalidate the sacred historicity and
veracity of the New Testament. For in all these cases he
will remember Saint Peter's words apropos of the writings
of Saint Paul:

«So also our beloved brother Paul wrote to you —
there are some things in them (in his letters) hard to
understand, which the ignorant and unstable twist to
their own destruction, as they do the other scrip-
tures». (353)

— He will understand that it is deeply saddening to see
how far one can go once the testimony of the pre-existence
of the divinity of Christ is annulled; as for example the

---

(353)   2 Peter 3 :15-16.

invention of Bultmann regarding the Prologue of Saint John's Gospel, characterizing it as a «gnostic hymn originating in the circles of the Baptist» ([354]); or as Schnackenburg does, who accepts all solutions providing the author is not Saint John. And the young man will learn how one can reach the point of claiming, as Schnackenburg, for example, that Saint John's Prologue is «a hymn sung by the community» that the evangelist received and adapted to his Gospel. ([355])

— He will understand that the spiritual and intellectual climate which creates this opinionated negation of every important assertion and any miraculous fact of the Gospel, as Bultmann often does, a heavy climate full of doubts and suspicions, is an immediate proof that the spirit and the method of criticism, analysis and explication, do not come from God.

— He will understand that what the Church calls Tradition, as a source and way of true information regarding the reality of Christ and the message of Christ, is an historic reality, not an invention.

— And he will have understood that no method, such as «the history of forms» or that of «the history of

---

(354)   RUDOLF BULTMANN, quoted by RUDOLF SCHNACKEN-BURG, *Commentario teologico del Nuovo Testamento — Il Vangelo di Giovanni, I Parte*, ed. Paideia, Brescia 1973, p. 287.

(355)   Cf. RUDOLF SCHNACKENBURG, *Commentario teologico del Nuovo Testamento — Il Vangelo di Giovanni, I Parte*, p. 289.

traditions» and «the history of redactions» will be able to either confirm or invalidate a testimony. He will understand why the most perfect proof of a true testimony cannot come from the exterior, but from the testimonies themselves. When the proof is immanent in the testimony, no comparison or confrontation can alter its transcendent veracity. It is the truth immanent in the testimony which judges the means and the instruments of research. It is not the means and the instruments of research which judge the transcendence of the testimony.

The Pluralist Disaggregation

The long historization of the fundamental criteria and of hope, historic criticism and all its ramifications such as the «method of the history of forms», have led to the blossoming of a multitude of propositions, postulates, analyses with theological claims and even with the claim of fundamental renewal of the doctrinal bases of Christianity. This discourse which calls everything into question is endless. If one begins to follow argument after argument, consideration after consideration, assertion after assertion and contestation after contestation, one is drawn into the forest, on semblances of paths traced by mysterious hands, but paths which are illusory, and when one realizes it, he is lost in the depths of the jungle, without being able to rejoin the departure point, except by superior help.

Thus it happened and still happens, because of the multitude of apparently particularist tendencies under differing vocables. However the whole arc of these tendencies is only the expression of three forms overlapping one another, under which is manifested the unique orientation of a great part of modern theology. The arc of these multiple and apparently particularist tendencies is the expression of historic consciousness, of modern hermeneutics and of the existential reference.

It is thus that the Christian world has seen these theological denominations (356) come to birth, with no connection to either Revelation or true life:

- Secularization Theology
- Anthropological Theology
- Theology of Liberation
- Theology of Hope
- Political Theology
- Theology of Earthly Realities
- Theology of Revolution
- Theology of Progress and Development
- Work Theology
- Theology of Orthopraxy
- Theology of Culture
- Theology of Predication
- Lay Theology
- Theology of the Future
- Theology from Below or Ascendant
- Theology of Representation
- Death-of-God Theology

The problematics which these postulates, propositions and considerations present are already outside of the field

---

(356)   Several of these appellations, as well as several other vocables which are used in profusion now, can have a really positive meaning: But very often, almost always now, the utilization of the vocables and appellations has as point of departure and as orientation a mentality and a will which are manifestly naturalist and anti-supernatural.

and the perennial norms of theology. For, as we already said at the beginning and showed on several occasions throughout this book (page 12), the whole problem of pure objectivity consists in perceiving the fundamental references brought by Revelation and sacred logic.

If there is no fundamental, perceptible and definable reference, brought into the intellect and human experience by Revelation, and if there is not a logic which expresses an eternal order of the Creation in man, and which is therein sacred, all problem of objectivity is annulled, and all effort of knowledge is vain. Theology is therefore the science of Revelation received, and we have no other Revelation than Revelation received.

The first constatation that the young man will have made after his first contact with all these «theologies», is that they express, implicitly or explicitly, an ever-growing tendency of transcendental pluralism, that is, of a pluralism which overturns every distinction and every limit set by stable criteria; and it is so, in what concerns the point of departure of these tendencies, in what concerns the orientation pre-established by the will, and in what concerns terms, language and interior word.

It is not a question of a pluralism of expressions or of means of expression, pluralism of images, parallelisms. It is a question of a total pluralism, as if each man could be a point of departure, and his thought and will could be absolutely autonomous.

From many writings, as Karl Rahner's for example, emanates a doctrinal pluralism such as does not henceforth allow any objective basis for a Christian theology founded on Revelation received. The nuances, all that remains indefinite or indefinable, all that remains unknown, all the elevations and free creations of man cannot justify in any way a pluralism which annihilates all notion of universal truth from the point of view of method and from the point of view of essence; pluralism which annihilates the foundations of the understanding, in so far as relationship of the individual with God, and relationship of the individual with other individuals who form human society.

Nothing, no signification or consideration can annihilate the notion and the fact of the Revelation. Nevertheless, that is the result, in the consciousness of many, of total pluralism. And Karl Rahner, always trying to present as reconcilable, things which are fundamentally irreconcilable, expresses himself thus:

«The theology of the future will be marked by a notable and henceforth insurmountable pluralism of theologies, despite the unique profession of the unique church». (357)

Pluralism has ceased to be only a concept of distinction and of «coexistence»; it has ceased to be an expression of the incertitude of several significations about a same

---

(357)   KARL RAHNER, *Sacramentum mundi,* vol. 8, col. 345.

subject. It has become a way of thinking and sensibility: to live without stable reference, without quest or possibility of discernment, with no intimate exigency of harmony, which causes one to endeavor — the motives of that effort matter little — to endeavor to equilibrate the yes and the no regarding everything. One gets to the point of putting forth propositions whose simultaneous application is impossible and unreal.

And so Karl Rahner, in the same study writes the following affirmations which, despite the best of intentions and the broadest and most tolerant intellectual openness are impossible to co-ordinate:

«— The theology of the future must be a demythologizing theology.

— It must be said in all frankness that the traditional statements of faith are inadequate, to a large extent at least, in so far as concerns what is necessary *before everything else:* the proclamation of the faith.

— Of course they remain — precisely for theology — a point of departure and a norm. But if theology wishes to be at the service of the proclamation, the traditional formulations of the faith *cannot represent the arrival point* of theological reflection».

After these declarations Rahner says in the same text:

«— The traditional formulations of the faith, the antecedent declarations of the ecclesiastic magisterium which have the value of definitions, in the future will continue to be not only the point of departure and the norm of the theology of the proclamation, but also their arrival point».

And then still in the same text:

«— A 'demythologizing theology' well understood must realize that propositions such as: 'there are three persons in God' —'God sent his son into the world' —'We are saved by the blood of Jesus Christ' are purely and simply incomprehensible for modern man, if they remain, in the ancient style of theology and of the proclamation, the point of departure and the arrival point of the Christian statement. They make the same impression as the pure mythology in a religion of times past.

— Theology has always 'demythologized', but only today has it become a duty which must be carried out with full consciousness in a pluralistic form». (358)

Pluralism is a grave event, because it expresses, as we have just said, anything but a holy modesty before the immensity of things unknown. It is the formal negation of Revelation, of all content of a moral and spiritual order which is signified in the natural order of the creation. It is the negation of the internal order of the word of man. Such is the transcendental pluralism to which a large part of present day theologies testify.

---

(358)   KARL RAHNER, *Le vie future della teologia* in *Bilancio della teologia del XX secolo,* vol. 3, pp. 577-579.

Pluralism is a universal calamity which takes away the discernment between sign and fact from man's intellectual, spiritual and moral climate, and the word evolves with no common or even individual guiding thread. Pluralism as a doctrine means total detachment from God the creator, consequently from true love.

The plurality of the forms of the creation, the plurality of the movements, manifest for the free spirit the unity and stability of the internal order of the created. Pluralism dissolves in the consciousness the unique link of the manifold forms. It is the destruction of the multiplicity of the forms of life, by the absence of a stable departure point of truth, and particularly for the time of the Church, of revealed truth. Pluralism expresses the obstruction of the internal revolt against every superior principle, being and truth.

Pluralism, in the field of theological activity, even without a conscious intention, ends up in the reversal of every principle and every organism of life. It distorts, above all, the profound notion at once human and superhuman, of the Church.

It will be sufficient for the young man to glance at certain writings, which now fill the bookstores and libraries, in order to realize the inadequation and contradiction which characterize all the manifestations of doctrinal pluralism. He will ask himself with deep sorrow: who is speaking in this text? A man who is seeking the truth of God, or a man who wants to destroy in the consciousness all that men have received from God as revealed truth, and received through the natural order of things? Of what Church is he speaking? Of what salvation does he speak? Of what love does he speak? In the name of what Church does that man speak?

Karl Rahner, in his "New Essays", speaks of the Church, the theology and the Magisterium of the Church, and says that there is a great «difference between the true content of the faith in the sense of the profession of faith and the theology which expresses it and interprets it», and he specifies:

«Today pluralism of theology cannot be adequately surmounted. That is why one must perhaps take into account that in the future the magisterium will only be able to issue very few doctrinal declarations. The unity of theology that must be presupposed in this aim, (the issuing of doctrinal declarations) no longer exists». (359)

Now in order to realize what the outcome is of the pluralist thought and sensibility in present day theology, it suffices to know that it is claimed, that in order to save the «content of the faith», it is necessary to preach Christianity without beginning with Jesus Christ:

1. «If the basic course on faith were concentrated in a restricted manner on Jesus Christ, seeing in him the

---

(359) KARL RAHNER, *Il pluralismo teologico e l'unità della professione di fede nella Chiesa*, in *Nuovi Saggi IV*, ed. Paoline, Roma 1973, p. 34.

key and the solution to all the existential problems and the total justification of the faith, it would offer us a conception which is too simple. It is not true that it suffices to preach Jesus Christ and that in this way one has resolved all the problems. Jesus Christ is a problem also today». (360)

2. «We possess different sources of experience and knowledge whose plurality must be developed and communicated. There exists a knowledge of God which is not communicated in an adequate manner through the encounter with Jesus Christ». (361)

3. «It is neither necessary nor objectively justified to begin this basic course simply with the doctrine concerning Jesus Christ, although in the Conciliary decree 'Optatam Totius' the basic course is presented as 'introduction to the mystery of Christ' (Introductio in Mysterium Christi)». (362)

All these appellations of the diverse theologies which have just been enumerated above, and by which one wants to indicate a basis or a particular new orientation of theology, correspond to the same general tendency and to the same unique orientation. All these particularities can be multiplied ad infinitum without giving a more perfect

---

(360) KARL RAHNER, *Corso fondamentale sulla fede,* ed. Paoline, Roma 1977, p. 31.

(361) KARL RAHNER, *Corso fondamentale sulla fede,* pp. 31-32.

(362) KARL RAHNER, *Corso fondamentale sulla fede,* p. 32.

knowledge of man and of God, without opening a positive way of meditation and study. For all are descended from the idea and the will of secularization. All are led and lead towards the mirage of historicist solutions of the problems of man.

The great principle of death, which from their origin has dominated all these tendencies, is the principle of secularization: the world contains the forces of the full realization of men, and it is also the milieu of it, in which the goal of man's life must be reached; all distinction, therefore, between sacred and profane, between Church and world, should be abolished.

That is why pluralism is a unilateral pluralism, a pluralism of secularization. For by its fundamental principle, pluralism is the negation of a basic common reference which would guarantee the harmony of life to the plurality of the forms of expression.

Now there is a vertiginous activity in the midst of this unilateral plurality of secularization, in which all these theologies apply themselves, consciously or unconsciously, to disfigure the Person and message of Christ and the notion, the essence and the mission of the Church. All the foundations and all the theological notions, all the terms of spiritual activity within society are transformed and utilized with another content.

A «theology of hope» infuses in souls another content than that of the hope brought by Christ. Man would have to hope from then on in the «salvation» through the intermediary of the community, making its way towards the ideal future society. Hope, therefore, would have to be revolutionary in all senses. Thus for example, Father Schillebeeckx thoroughly misrepresenting the thought of Vatican Council II, writes:

«Lastly, the Council states that the salvific will of God is present in the political and socio-economic developments of humanity. − To give the Christian faith a valid legitimation for every epoch proves impossible. − Even without theology, the revolution can doubtlessly count on Christians. − In Christ it is possible to say Amen to every mundane reality and to consider it as worship, since, after the apparition of Christ, the fullness of God inhabits the earth». (363)

Schillebeecks refers, particularly for that last statement regarding the fullness of God which inhabits the earth, to the Letter to the Colossians,(364) where Saint Paul speaks of the fullness of God. But Schillebeeckx avoids saying in his book, of what plenitude Saint Paul speaks and to whom the Apostle is referring. For Saint Paul is speaking of the fullness of God dwelling in Christ and uniquely in Christ. And the continuation of the text explains by what means there can be reconciliation between the world and God:

«For in him all the fullness of God was pleased to dwell, and through him to reconcile to himself all

---

(363)   E. SCHILLEBEECKX, *Dio, il futuro dell'uomo,* ed. Paoline, Roma 1970, pp. 132, 205, 219, 112.

(364)   Col. 1 : 19-20.

things, whether on earth or in heaven, making peace by the blood of his cross».

Now Saint Paul speaks of the fullness which dwells in Christ, and then he speaks of the reconciling to God of all things, which can only be done by the blood of the Cross. Therefore one can neither refer to the Council nor to Saint Paul in order to «say Amen to all mundane reality and consider it as worship».

What rapport have these statements with the Gospel, with the Council, with the Church? Only an unconditional pluralism which is at the same time unilateral can give the illusion that all these thoughts , all these cogitations are theology, on the basis of an individual who is called Christ, Jesus of Nazareth.

And it is in that spirit of absolute pluralism in connection with secularization that Rahner mutilates the notion of the Church and rejects its mystery:

«The Church is not, absolutely does not want to be, the integral director of human and moral reality in the world; she is not all the human and all the moral, but an element of this all; and this all is already pluralist by its nature». (365)

There is not one single reality of the mystery of the Church which is not a target for the spirit and the desire of secularization. When Schillebeeckx, for example, regarding

(365) KARL RAHNER, *Riflessioni teologiche sulla secolarizzazione*, in *Nuovi Saggi III*, ed. Paoline, Roma 1969, p. 731.

the Holy Eucharist writes that the Sacrament is the changing of signification given by man, immediately a concept of trans-signification spreads, and then Schillebeeckx feels he is in a position to formulate these statements which are fundamentally naturalist, humanist, foreign to all the realities and to all the theology of the Church:

«Man lives naturally by continual trans-signification. He humanizes the world. — Transubstantiation is irrevocably a creation of human signification». (366)

Secularization, the normal outcome of the historicist mentality, engenders and justifies all sorts of formulae and intellectual and moral attitudes. It becomes inevitable, for example, that one build a whole language and statements on the vocable of a «liberation theology». (367) It becomes inevitable that the liberation of man, brought and preached by Christ, transform itself in an action for the revendication of social and personal order.

It becomes inevitable that one elaborate, in the pluralist liberty, a whole language of «theology of hope», and that one dare to solemnly teach, in the name of Christ, contrary to every true interpretation of the Gospel:

---

(366) E. SCHILLEBEECKX, *La presenza eucaristica*, ed. Paoline, Roma 1969, pp. 142 and 145.

(367) Among the principal promoters of this tendency, there is Gustave Gutiérrez (cf. note 94) and Johann-Baptist Metz, (born in 1928), disciple of Rahner, Professor of Theology at the University of Münster.

«That hope indeed, to speak as Ludwig Feuerbach, puts 'in the place of the beyond which in heaven holds sway over our tomb, the beyond which goes beyond it (our tomb) on this earth: the historic future, the future of humanity'. It discovers in the Resurrection of Christ not the eternity of heaven, but the future of this earth itself». (368)

We have already said it, the change of the content of hope is at the base of the historicist and existentialist mentality. It is also the horizon of the mirage.

The existential thought and language which characterize the manifestations of the whole historicist process of theologic, philosophic and even literary thought, in themselves express in all cases, a refusal to refer ontologically, spontaneously to immutable references, references of life immutable. This refusal is not without a far-off origin and not without serious consequences, for man's spirit and peace of mind before the Truth.

The young man, in this regard, will be very instructed in remembering with charity, with great charity, how Husserl's discerning assistant, the profound and holy soul, Edith Stein, defined the philosophical thought and attitude of Martin Heidegger: it is «the philosophy of bad conscience». (369)

---

(368)   JÜRGEN MOLTMANN, *Teologia della speranza,* ed. Queriniana, Brescia 1970, p. 14.

(369)   TERESIA RENATA DE SPIRITU SANCTO, *Edith Stein,* Morcelliana, Brescia 1952, p. 143.

But in all cases there is one thing which escapes the promotors of pluralist secularization. This phenomenon is condemned to perish come what may, be it with the world, be it alone. For the infinity of forms of the visible universe and of spiritual forms of man's conception and creation contains — when these forms remain in harmony with their original sacred order of creation,— contains the principle of basic reference to the unity of eternal Truth. And it is in order that that multitude of forms of man's life and creation find again the fullness of harmony with eternal Truth, that the eternal Word was incarnated for the resacralization of everything. And that is why the Church, issued from the love of Christ, has been implanted in the disharmonious relativity of the world.

GETHSEMANE

GETHSEMANE

Gethsemane, the door of the sanctuary by which History finds again its true visage and its true order in the understanding and consciousness of the liberated man. It is the sanctuary where, in solitude, the supreme offering has been spiritually accomplished, so that man each time unique, and the whole race of men can find again the eternal order of their creation, and thus have the possibility of entering by grace, into the joy of direct contemplation of the Creator.

It is only in Gethsemane's enclosure that theology can be divested of all vain, intellectual dilection, of all dead letter and of all scheme of congealed thought, of all dryness of heart, of all illusion of autonomy and all torpor of feverish naturalist activity. It is only there that the understanding and the will are liberated by the truth according to the word of Christ ([370]), because it is there that the Redeemer lived in his human intimacy, with all his divine love, the Cross of the history of men.

([370]) *John* 8 : 32.

And it is in the secret of the agony of Jesus of Nazareth that one can glimpse the meaning of man in the mystery of the history of men.

In the mystery of Gethsemane the two greatest, most poignant and sweetest mysteries are unveiled: the Incarnation of God in perfect man in Mary, and the engendering of holy Church in the relativity of temporal man.

There have been many Saints among the people of Israel, many Prophets. There have been many souls who suffered for their people and who knew how to love God to the point of total sacrifice. There have been many strong and great souls who, by God's grace, penetrated the secrets of nature, more than the men of science of the future generations.

But the man of the nocturnal agony on the Mount of Olives was the Being of another economy; he corresponded to another necessity, another expectation of the creation. And it is because of that, that this agony not only concerns every man, but is ontologically linked to every man. Man is not linked to the agony of Christ only by imagination and compassion towards someone who suffers unjustly. Man is linked to it because he has been the subject of the solitary offering in the garden of Gethsemane, which was not a moral act, but an action of being.

The «Fiat» of the Virgin Mary had as immediate consequence, an event in the nature of the human being, an event ontologically new. The words by which Christ abandons himself totally to the will of the Father constitute the second «Fiat» of the economy of man's salvation. The «Fiat» of Gethsemane was the consequence in a new period, of the first «Fiat» of the human being Mary. The second «Fiat», pronounced and accomplished by the Being begotten by God in human nature, had as outcome the union of God with the existences of all men, that is, with the existence of all beings constituting the History of men.

What could be the finality of all the suffering of the Cross accepted in advance? Such an offering is not conceivable without conceiving, however feebly, the reason of that offering. And then the essence of the mysterious agony of Christ appears in all its luminous simplicity.

«My Father, if it be possible, let this cup pass from me; nevertheless, not as I will, but as thou wilt». (371) When Jesus spoke this «if it be possible», was he asking to be liberated from the burden of the salvation of souls? When his spirit had uttered that appeal, had he suddenly preferred, be it only for a moment, to disengage himself from his mission and then to live, grow old and one day pass away, according to the lot of every man?

Those are some of the thoughts which fade away like empty fabrications of man's pride, they fade away when our understanding and our heart penetrate humbly and

---

(371) *Matthew* 26:39.

with abandon into the enclosure of Gethsemane. There the categories according to which we perceive and judge grow dim, or are transformed, taking on another tenor and another fullness. And it is thus that the understanding as well as the heart, in a harmony of peace, receive the mystery of the Being who prayed, prostrate on the ground, for the salvation of men. For the cry of «if it be possible» did not mean lassitude and that Christ preferred that another take on the salvation of men. Christ did not pray only for himself; he prayed in the name of all men, to whom he had linked himself by his offering: «as thou wilt».

Christ, unique Person of divine essence, lived interiorly as Redeemer of men in his human fullness, the suffering, by inconceivable love, before the wickedness and sin which engendered his Passion and his Death.

Then the soul, with all its potential of intelligence and love, penetrates into the mystery of the Incarnation and the agony of Gesthsemane and understands that the Redemption of man was not the work of a new teaching, nor the example of a great perfection unknown until then. Man understands that his redemption was not a moral renewal; it was first of all an act touching on the principle of the being of man, touching on the regeneration of the law of the generation of man.

If a man had not been begotten by the Word of the Creator, the Redemption of man would still be an expectation of moral renewal. That teaching and that example had been accomplished by the Prophets and Saints of Israel who would have been able to accomplish them always. But the initial act of the new generation, by the direct intervention of God, would not have been accomplished; and the divine ontologic intervention in Adam's race would not have been accomplished.

Now the Being who was praying prostrate on the ground in the garden of Gethsemane was exactly this ontologic penetration of God into Adam's race. God called forth a being by his own Word thus become man, having taken the «form» of man in the natural human organism.

Man, despite all his investigations and inquiries, cannot penetrate by his own means, the secret of the difference of level of peoples, both in the past and in the present. Rarely does one suceed in distinguishing from afar in the depth of the present, the true initial image of man and of humanity, because we have lost the freshness and continual joyous wonder of the active and ever-new contemplation of the infinite Reality of God the Creator.

That loss prevents us from perceiving at every moment the grace and the continous miracle of the existence of everything and it prevents us from perceiving the «simple natural» of the works which go beyond our own experience, the great miraculous works of our Creator God.

Man can never touch, by his investigations and his inventions of curiosity, the beginning of things and beings.

That is why we have difficulty in conceiving the mysterious act of love and harmony which was accomplished with the first «Fiat» of the Virgin Mary.

Nevertheless, it is that act which permitted the Being who was praying, his face covered with a sweat of blood, to unite himself ontologically to the existence of each man, in the anarchic and sorrowful disorder of History.. And it is this union which gives man the possibility of becoming a new being and to know that a second will is rising up in him, which is in struggle with the first will of his nature in disorder; the disorder of sin.

It is this particular union which was accomplished by the «Fiat» of Gethsemane: «Not as I will, but as thou wilt». For it is this union which was the subject of the prayer of the agony and of the «Fiat»; and it was the cause of the Cross which must follow.

The agony of Gethsemane, in its ontologic mystery, would not have been possible if the Being of the agony had not been the Being of the Incarnation. The agony of Christ expresses suffering in the spirit and the heart, thus in the whole human nature; suffering which belongs to that unique Fiat of unutterable love: to unite with the existence of all human beings who constitute History.

The only Person who has always had objective knowledge of everything is He who was conceived at Nazareth, and He who was conceived at Nazareth is God.

Only He who at Gethsemane, linked himself to the existence of every man, having accepted by love to suffer in his unique being, the suffering of all the centuries, knows with absolute objectivity that which we call History. It is He who, following his universal inner suffering at Gethsemane, suffered the physical and moral pain of the martyrdom and death on the Cross; He who, man and God for eternity, resolved in his being, for all men, the mystery of iniquity, by his Resurrection.

Man desires objectivity, as he desires eternal life. Only the Master of eternal life can give objectivity to man. Man cannot advance in objective knowledge except by increasingly uniting himself to the Master of History, who, for him, spoke the «Fiat» of Gethsemane.

When man receives this truth, all the laws, norms and categories of human reason are regenerated and are freed more and more from the shackles of dead works and dead words. To the degree that man subjects God and God's works to his often very subtle but impetuous desire for autonomy, the true laws of human reason grow dim and the categories petrify.

Only the absolutely free subject can be absolutely objective. That is why man can only obtain objectivity in his vision of beings and things to the degree that he intimately receives with love the Revelation of the absolute Subject. The objectivity of man's learning, that is, the degree of true knowledge depends on his ontologically spiritual union with the One who possesses all the objective reality, because He is Himself the eternal Truth incarnate for eternity.

This fundamental truth excludes from the march of man towards knowledge any pluralist theory. Man is not in the forest at night without knowing where to go, nor is he «a succession of moments». He is a being gifted with memory, which places him both in time and outside of time. For by the gift of memory he goes beyond time and the «succession of moments»; growing richer indefinitely and developing himself continually throughout existence, man remains immutable as being and as potential of infinite enrichment and broadening. Christ follows the whole march of humanity and He is the same yesterday and today and in eternity.

Putting aside Revelation in order to cogitate on God and the world, basing ourselves, by a subtle desire for autonomy, uniquely on our own means of investigation, we lose all possibility of objectivity and we enter the «existential night». For it is a deep night for the spirit, when man, all man's faculties of understanding and action are fixed on the passing «moments», on the «being-here» or the «being-there». This existential gaze, that is, the fact of seeing everything without referring continually to our most profound reality, above all language-games of external words, eliminates in our approach our own reality of consciousness and memory. And it is impossible to get one's bearings and to be truthful, because the denial of the Master of objectivity is the ontologic denial of the truth.

The relativity of passing moments cannot affect the being who knows and who loves. But when he allows himself to be caught by relativity, he enters the whirlwind of the existential discourse, which is why man does not have a true image of his existence nor of the notion of existence. The discourse can be indefinite; the endless making of vocabularies and expressions; it is the sad game of a false philosophy which refuses to submit in everything to the Master of History, who is Truth incarnate, who is the eternal order of all the multiple of the universe and of History.

When, in our spirit and in our heart, the mystery of Gethsemane and its rapport with the «Fiat» of the Annunciation is unveiled, a whole language becomes antiquated, for one perceives that History cannot give up any secret either regarding the laws which govern it or regarding the final ends of man. It cannot because, of itself it has neither knowledge nor consciousness. The only thing that it can teach is that the Master of History pronounced the «Fiat» of suffering and union with the existence of all men, in order to deliver each man, each time unique, from death, and to have him enter another reality, of eternal life.

To refer each time to History, in order to avoid referring to the Master of History, is to want to speak to polyphony without addressing oneself either to he who composed the music or to those who sing it. Only the Creator of the laws and ends can know the reality of the final ends of everything, the Creator and those to whom He reveals it and who receive his Revelation with humility and love.

Each man cannot be redeemed as a society. It is the Redemption of each person which can create an ensemble of redeemed persons. It is by love for each person of Israel, for each Israelite, that Simeon had the joy of receiving the Redeemer in his arms. He had received the divine message, according to which he must see the Redeemer before dying. And when he saw Him, he had joy for the redemption, not for an abstract entity, but for all who would be redeemed, and not because of a desire for a strong and flourishing state in history; therefore he said:

«Nunc dimittis servum tuum, Domine».

He was joyful for the Light of all men which Christ was, and for the Glory of Israel. That Glory was Christ, who called every Israelite to salvation. For Israel was not an idea; it was an ensemble, of which every member was called to redemption.

The young man, the dear young man will be able to find, in the mystery of the «Fiat» of Gethsemane, the way of knowledge, of the mystery of man in History, a hidden way, but full of light. And he will see illumined before him the enigma of the Church, and he will know a deep joy, the joy which Christ said no one can take away.

And he will have great certainties about natural and supernatural realities. And he will have great peace, the peace of truth, which only Christ gives. He will understand with his whole being that the mystery of the Incarnation of the inconceivable God, in our poor, weak flesh, contains the whole secret of the origin of man, of the sorrow of the earth and of the true final ends.

He will understand that the Master of objectivity alone, by our receiving of his divine and at the same time human identity, can instruct us regarding the meaning of time and eternity and about the vanity of believing that the notion of eternity and hope in eternity can be changed by inviting men, in the name of God, to «discover time».

He will understand why Christ refused to be the arbiter of the dividing of the fields of two brothers, and why, in all his teaching He presents before the eyes of men of all conditions, the same way for entering eternal life.

He will understand in the deepest intimity of his being that everything which evolves, before evolving and after, is, and that all that changes, all enrichment or impoverishment, neither destroys nor alters that reality of the being who is enriched or impoverished. And in man's impalpable and a-spacial reality of being, there is an immensity: consciousness and memory. Whoever denies this immensity denies himself and enters the anarchic existential impasse, where he cannot truly meet the Master of all objectivity. It is an insane race behind the mirage of «the

being-there» or «the being-here», the mirage of being able
to establish a language and found a science of man on what
is moving, not on what is, what remembers and has
consciousness of being, and is drawn to adore; and to be drawn
means that one moves, and adoration means a stability
which embraces and harmonizes all that moves and all
movement.

He will understand that to understand History outside
of the «Fiat» of the incarnate Word, the God-Man at
Gethsemane, is a vain fiction, which can give the
opportunity of creating nothing less than myths of
philosophy of history, or even of theology of history. One
cannot seize, by force of information and parallelisms, the
secret of life of the ensemble of men. All the experiences of
all the human and natural sciences, all the prophecies about
the future of peoples and about the future of the Church,
concern, consciously or not, the life within a century at
most, of that man who has an immortal soul.

He will understand that the Church, by its origin and
its intimate essence, from the beginning, has had and will
have until the end of the world, the fervent concern of the
good of all men. This good entails everything which
sweetens the heart and maintains physical life until the end,
when man leaves history for eternity.

He will understand that it is a vain or perverse fiction
to oppose the identity and mission of the Church to the
real, natural and social good of men; it is an empty fiction

to alter her mission and to adapt it to the temporal perspectives which are always temporary.

He will understand that the future of humanity can be the liberation of man in his century only in so far as that man will have thought and worked so that the innumerable men who will people time in flight, are able to depart from History at the end of their lives, towards eternal light.

He will understand that it is an empty fiction, unconscious or perverse, to oppose in the consciousness of the baptized, person and group, human being and community, soul called to eternal life and humanity. The "Apocalypse", speaking and prophesying apropos of the future of the Church and humanity, speaks of the faith and salvation of each man. The new Jerusalem which comes down from Heaven, can only mean — in every interpretation of the image — an ordered ensemble, where each human being adores and enjoys the immense mystery of the Lord. «Come, Lord Jesus». Yes, come, so that all men may enter, if possible, the eternal life of your Kingdom.

He will understand that all the known or unknown betrayals of few or many members of the Church, the pettiness of soul, the narrowness of spirit, the cruelty and all infidelity that the Church may have had and lived within herself, are only the correspondence to the sweat of blood at Gethsemane and to the wounds and blood of the Cross. That is why one must think of the holy Being of the

God-man. One can neither change nor abandon the Lord because of his wounds.

He will understand that the Church, despite her wounds, carries not only in her word, but in her heart, Truth and Life, because her heart is that of Christ.

He will understand that the whole creation, all that is, is a sign of an immutable reality, and man can indefinitely read and recognize that immutability. Man can, within every situation, calm or explosive as in our days, learn to read this language which is the created. He can, because his own word, despite all its relativity, has its origin, as man himself, in the eternal word of God.

He will then understand why, in the race of men, there is a privileged being. It is the being who spoke the first «Fiat» in the history of salvation, Mary; and he will understand why it is not a question of a literature composed by a pious sentimentality, when the Church calls the Virgin Mary, Mother of God.

He will understand that no urgency, no personal or general danger, no hostility towards the incarnate Word and the Mother of the incarnate Word, must alter, in the mind and heart, the real basis of holy theology and unique historic finality: that is, the Incarnation of the Word, of Christ Jesus in the Blessed Virgin Mary.

He will understand that the only way to serve the truth is to bring to birth or rebirth in men true hope, brought by the Person and the Word of Christ.

And he will remember that the Lord said, according to the Gospel of Saint John: «In the world you will have tribulation, but be of good cheer, I have overcome the world»; and in the "Apocalypse": «Be faithful unto death and I will give you the crown of life».